GREAT LAKES NATURE GUIDE

James S. McCormac

Krista Kagume

Lone Pine Publishing Int

© 2009 by Lone Pine Publishing International Inc.
First printed in 2009   10 9 8 7 6 5 4 3 2 1
Printed in China

The Distributor: Lone Pine Publishing
1808 B Street NW, Suite 140
Auburn, WA, USA 98001

Website: www.lonepinepublishing.com

Publisher's Cataloging-In-Publication Data
(Prepared by The Donohue Group, Inc.)

McCormac, James S., 1962-
   Great Lakes nature guide / James S. McCormac, Krista Kagume.

   p. : ill., map ; cm.

   Includes bibliographical references and index.
   ISBN-13: 978-976-8200-51-8
   ISBN-10: 976-8200-51-0

1. Natural history--Great Lakes (North America)--Guidebooks. 2. Natural areas--Great Lakes (North America)--Guidebooks. 3. Great Lakes (North America)--Guidebooks. I. Kagume, Krista. II. Title.

QH104.5.G7 M3 2009
508.77

Illustrations: Please see p. 4 for a complete list of credits. That page constitutes an extension of this copyright page.

Disclaimer: This guide is not intended to be a "how-to" reference guide for food or medicinal use of plants. We do not recommend experimentation by readers, and we caution that a number of woody plants, including some used traditionally as medicines, are poisonous and harmful.

PC: 16

TABLE OF CONTENTS

ILLUSTRATION CREDITS

DEDICATION

To my parents, John & Martha McCormac, who have always encouraged my interest in nature.

ACKNOWLEDGMENTS

The labors involved in creating this book represent but a year in a lifetime of exploration, much of it within the Great Lakes region. Along the way I've met many wonderful guides and mentors. I would be remiss not to extend my gratitude to Jim Bissell, Guy Denny, John Pogacnik, Tony Reznicek, Larry Richardson, Larry Rosche, Ronald Stuckey and Ed Voss. Special thanks to Mike Penskar for information on Michigan sites and Sharon Stiteler for tips on Minnesota locales. Finally, special thanks and appreciation to my patient and tolerant editors at Lone Pine, Krista Kagume and Gary Whyte, who are a true pleasure to work with.

MAMMALS

Elk
p. 42

White-tailed Deer
p. 42

Moose
p. 43

Canada Lynx
p. 43

Bobcat
p. 44

Coyote
p. 44

Gray Wolf
p. 45

Red Fox
p. 45

Gray Fox
p. 46

Black Bear
p. 46

Northern Raccoon
p. 47

American Marten
p. 47

Fisher
p. 48

Ermine
p. 48

Long-tailed Weasel
p. 49

Least Weasel
p. 49

American Mink
p. 49

American Badger
p. 50

Striped Skunk
p. 50

Northern River Otter
p. 51

Eastern Cottontail
p. 51

Snowshoe Hare
p. 52

White-tailed Jackrabbit
p. 52

Eastern Chipmunk
p. 53

Least Chipmunk
p. 53

Woodchuck
p. 53

Franklin's Ground Squirrel
p. 54

Thirteen-lined Ground Squirrel
p. 54

Eastern Gray Squirrel
p. 54

Eastern Fox Squirrel
p. 55

Red Squirrel
p. 55

Northern Flying Squirrel
p. 55

Southern Flying Squirrel
p. 56

Plains Pocket Gopher
p. 56

Beaver
p. 57

Eastern Heather Vole
p. 57

Meadow Vole
p. 58

North American Deer Mouse
p. 58

Prairie Vole
p. 58

Southern Red-backed Vole
p. 59

White-footed Deer Mouse
p. 59

Common Muskrat
p. 59

Southern Bog Lemming
p. 60

Brown Rat
p. 60

House Mouse
p. 60

Meadow Jumping Mouse
p. 61

North American Porcupine
p. 61

Big Brown Bat
p. 61

MAMMALS

Eastern Pipistrelle
p. 62

Eastern Red Bat
p. 62

Eastern Small-footed Myotis
p. 62

Hoary Bat
p. 63

Indiana Bat
p. 63

Evening Bat
p. 63

Little Brown Myotis
p. 64

Northern Myotis
p. 64

Silver-haired Bat
p. 64

Virginia Opossum
p. 65

Arctic Shrew
p. 65

Cinereus Shrew
p. 65

Least Shrew
p. 66

Northern Short-tailed
Shrew, p. 66

Pygmy Shrew
p. 66

Water Shrew
p. 67

Eastern Mole
p. 67

Star-nosed Mole
p. 67

Snow Goose
p. 70

Canada Goose
p. 70

BIRDS

Tundra Swan
p. 71

Wood Duck
p. 71

Mallard
p. 72

Blue-winged Teal
p. 72

Canvasback
p. 73

Ring-necked Duck
p. 73

Common Goldeneye
p. 74

Common Merganser
p. 74

Wild Turkey
p. 74

Common Loon
p. 75

Pied-billed Grebe
p. 75

Double-crested Cormorant
p. 75

Great Blue Heron
p. 76

Great Egret
p. 76

Green Heron
p. 77

Turkey Vulture
p. 77

Osprey
p. 78

Bald Eagle
p. 78

Northern Harrier
p. 79

Cooper's Hawk
p. 79

Red-tailed Hawk
p. 79

American Kestrel
p. 80

Sora
p. 80

American Coot
p. 80

Killdeer
p. 81

Spotted Sandpiper
p. 81

Greater Yellowlegs
p. 81

Pectoral Sandpaper
p. 82

9

BIRDS

American Woodcock
p. 82

Bonaparte's Gull
p. 82

Ring-billed Gull
p. 83

Herring Gull
p. 83

Caspian Tern
p. 83

Common Tern
p. 84

Rock Pigeon
p. 84

Mourning Dove
p. 84

Yellow-billed Cuckoo
p. 85

Eastern Screech-Owl
p. 85

Great Horned Owl
p. 85

Barred Owl
p. 86

Common Nighthawk
p. 86

Whip-poor-will
p. 86

Chimney Swift
p. 87

Ruby-throated Hummingbird
p. 87

Belted Kingfisher
p. 87

Red-headed Woodpecker
p. 88

Red-bellied Woodpecker
p. 88

Downy Woodpecker
p. 88

Northern Flicker
p. 89

Pileated Woodpecker
p. 89

Eastern Wood-Pewee
p. 89

Eastern Phoebe
p. 90

Great Crested Flycatcher
p. 90

Eastern Kingbird
p. 90

Red-eyed Vireo
p. 91

Blue Jay
p. 91

American Crow
p. 91

Horned Lark
p. 92

Purple Martin
p. 92

Tree Swallow
p. 92

Barn Swallow
p. 93

Black-capped Chickadee
p. 93

Tufted Titmouse
p. 93

Red-breasted Nuthatch
p. 94

White-breasted Nuthatch
p. 94

Carolina Wren
p. 94

House Wren
p. 95

Golden-crowned Kinglet
p. 95

Blue-gray Gnatcatcher
p. 95

Eastern Bluebird
p. 96

Wood Thrush
p. 96

American Robin
p. 96

Gray Catbird
p. 97

Northern Mockingbird
p. 97

Brown Thrasher
p. 97

European Starling
p. 98

11

Cedar Waxwing
p. 98

Yellow Warbler
p. 98

Magnolia Warbler
p. 99

Yellow-rumped Warbler
p. 99

American Redstart
p. 99

Ovenbird
p. 100

Common Yellowthroat
p. 100

Scarlet Tanager
p. 100

Eastern Towhee
p. 101

American Tree Sparrow
p. 101

Song Sparrow
p. 101

White-throated Sparrow
p. 102

Dark-eyed Junco
p. 102

Northern Cardinal
p. 102

Rose-breasted Grosbeak
p. 103

Indigo Bunting
p. 103

Bobolink
p. 103

Red-winged Blackbird
p. 104

Eastern Meadowlark
p. 104

Commmon Grackle
p. 104

Brown-headed Cowbird
p. 105

Baltimore Oriole
p. 105

Purple Finch
p. 105

House Finch
p. 106

AMPHIBIANS & REPTILES

American Goldfinch
p. 106

House Sparrow
p. 106

Mudpuppy
p. 108

Red-spotted Newt
p. 109

Blue-spotted Salamander
p. 109

Smallmouth Salamander
p. 110

Spotted Salamander
p. 110

Eastern Tiger Salamander
p. 110

Northern Two-lined
Salamander, p. 111

Four-toed Salamander
p. 111

Redback Salamander
p. 111

Northern Dusky
Salamander, p. 112

American Toad
p. 112

Fowler's Toad
p. 112

Gray Treefrog
p. 113

Blanchard's Cricket Frog
p. 113

Northern Spring Peeper
p. 113

Western Chorus Frog
p. 114

Wood Frog
p. 114

Northern Leopard Frog
p. 114

Pickerel Frog
p. 115

Green Frog
p. 115

Mink Frog
p. 115

American Bullfrog
p. 116

AMPHIBIANS & REPTILES

Common Snapping Turtle
p. 116

Common Musk Turtle
p. 116

Painted Turtle
p. 117

Northern Map Turtle
p. 117

Blanding's Turtle
p. 117

Spotted Turtle
p. 118

Wood Turtle
p. 118

Spiny Softshell Turtle
p. 118

Eastern Box Turtle
p. 119

Five-lined Skink
p. 119

Eastern Garter Snake
p. 119

Northern Ribbon Snake
p. 120

Northern Water Snake
p. 120

Queen Snake
p. 120

Northern Brown Snake
p. 121

Smooth Green Snake
p. 121

Northern Ringneck Snake
p. 121

Eastern Hognose Snake
p. 122

Eastern Milk Snake
p. 122

Eastern Fox Snake
p. 122

Black Rat Snake
p. 123

Eastern Racer
p. 123

Eastern Massasauga
p. 123

Sea Lamprey
p. 126

Lake Sturgeon
p. 126

American Eel
p. 126

Gizzard Shad
p. 127

Chinook Salmon
p. 127

Rainbow Trout
p. 127

Brown Trout
p. 128

Brook Trout
p. 128

Lake Trout
p. 128

Lake Whitefish
p. 129

Rainbow Smelt
p. 129

Northern Pike
p. 129

Common Carp
p. 130

Emerald Shiner
p. 130

White Sucker
p. 130

Channel Catfish
p. 131

Stonecat
p. 131

Banded Killifish
p. 131

Burbot
p. 132

FISH

Brook Stickleback
p. 132

White Bass
p. 132

Pumpkinseed
p. 133

Smallmouth Bass
p. 133

Yellow Perch
p. 133

Walleye
p. 134

Rainbow Darter
p. 134

Logperch
p. 134

Freshwater Drum
p. 135

Round Goby
p. 135

Mottled Sculpin
p. 135

Zebra Mussel
p. 137

INVERTEBRATES

Virile Crayfish
p. 137

Common Green Darner
p. 137

Chinese Mantis
p. 138

Walkingstick
p. 138

Carolina Grasshopper
p. 138

Common Katydid
p. 139

Common Water Strider
p. 139

Large Milkweed Bug
p. 139

INVERTEBRATES

Dog-day Cicada
p. 140

Firefly
p. 140

Multicoloured Asian Ladybug
p. 140

Eastern Tiger Swallowtail
p. 141

Cabbage White
p. 141

Monarch
p. 141

Luna Moth
p. 142

Carpenter Ant
p. 142

Eastern Yellowjacket
p. 142

Yellow Bumble Bee
p. 143

Zebra Jumping Spider
p. 143

Dark Fishing Spider
p. 143

TREES

Banded Garden Spider
p. 144

Harvestman
p. 144

Balsam Fir
p. 148

White Spruce
p. 148

Black Spruce
p. 149

Eastern Hemlock
p. 149

Tamarack
p. 150

Eastern White Pine
p. 150

Jack Pine
p. 151

Arborvitae
p. 151

Eastern Red Cedar
p. 152

Tulip Tree
p. 152

Pawpaw
p. 153

TREES

Sassafras
p. 153

Sycamore
p. 154

Witch-hazel
p. 154

American Elm
p. 155

Hackberry
p. 155

Osage-orange
p. 156

Black Walnut
p. 156

Shagbark Hickory
p. 157

American Beech
p. 157v

White Oak
p. 158

Red Oak
p. 158

Black Oak
p. 159

Yellow Birch
p. 159

Paper Birch
p. 160

American Basswood
p. 160

Quaking Aspen
p. 161

Eastern Cottonwood
p. 161

Black Willow
p. 162

Black Cherry
p. 162

American Plum
p. 163

Showy Mountain-ash
p. 163

Cockspur Hawthorn
p. 164

Downy Serviceberry
p. 164

Redbud
p. 165

TREES

Black Locust
p. 165

Eastern Wahoo
p. 166

Sugar Maple
p. 166

Silver Maple
p. 167

Red Maple
p. 167

Box-elder
p. 168

Tree-of-heaven
p. 168

White Ash
p. 169

SHRUBS & VINES

Green Ash
p. 169

Spicebush
p. 172

Pussy Willow
p. 172

Labrador-tea
p. 172

Bog Laurel
p. 173

Leatherleaf
p. 173

Highbush Blueberry
p. 173

Large Cranberry
p. 174

Wild Black Currant
p. 174

Steeplebush
p. 174

Ninebark
p. 175

Shrubby Cinquefoil
p. 175

Black Raspberry
p. 175

Multiflora Rose
p. 176

Swamp Rose
p. 176

Black Chokeberry
p. 176

19

Autumn-olive
p. 177

Bunchberry
p. 177

Red-osier Dogwood
p. 177

Dwarf Mistletoe
p. 178

Winterberry
p. 178

Glossy Buckthorn
p. 178

Bladdernut
p. 179

Staghorn Sumac
p. 179

Poison Sumac
p. 179

Prickly-ash
p. 180

Buttonbush
p. 180

Twinflower
p. 180

Northern Arrowhead
p. 181

Common Elderberry
p. 181

Wild Cucumber
p. 181

Hog-peanut
p. 182

Bittersweet
p. 182

Virginia Creeper
p. 182

Riverbank Grape
p. 183

Poison Ivy
p. 183

Hedge Bindweed
p. 183

Michigan Lily
p. 186

Large-flowered Trillium
p. 186

Yellow Trout-lily
p. 186

| False Solomon's-seal p. 187 | Downy Solomon's-seal p. 187 | Southern Blue Flag p. 187 | Showy Lady's-slipper p. 188 |

| Wild Ginger p. 188 | American Lotus p. 188 | Marsh-marigold p. 189 | Hepatica p. 189 |

| Hispid Buttercup p. 189 | Wild Columbine p. 190 | Mayapple p. 190 | Bloodroot p. 190 |

| Dutchman's Breeches p. 191 | Wood Nettle p. 191 | Pokeweed p. 191 | Prickly-pear p. 192 |

| Spring-beauty p. 192 | Water Smartweed p. 192 | Swamp Rose-mallow p. 193 | Pitcher-plant p. 193 |

| Sundew p. 193 | Canada Violet p. 194 | Common Blue Violet p. 194 | Cut-leaved Toothwort p. 194 |

Dame's-rocket
p. 195

Garlic Mustard
p. 195

Indian-pipe
p. 195

Fringed Loosestrife
p. 196

Grass-of-parnassus
p. 196

Common Strawberry
p. 196

Common Agrimony
p. 197

Wild Lupine
p. 197

Crown Vetch
p. 197

Red Clover
p. 198

Panicled Tick-trefoil
p. 198

Eurasian Water-milfoil
p. 198

Purple Loosestrife
p. 199

Fireweed
p. 199

Common Evening-primrose
p. 199

Enchanter's-nightshade
p. 200

Flowering Spurge
p. 200

Wild Geranium
p. 200

Spotted Touch-me-not
p. 201

Ginseng
p. 201

Clustered Snakeroot
p. 201

Smooth Sweet-cicely
p. 202

Queen Anne's Lace
p. 202

Poison-hemlock
p. 202

Wild Parsnip
p. 203

Angelica
p. 203

Fringed Gentian
p. 203

Indian-hemp
p. 204

Common Milkweed
p. 204

Bittersweet Nightshade
p. 204

Blue Phlox
p. 205

Virginia Bluebells
p. 205

Blue Vervain
p. 205

Heal-all
p. 206

Wild Bergamot
p. 206

Common Monkeyflower
p. 206

Common Mullein
p. 207

Foxglove Beardtongue
p. 207

Wood-betony
p. 207

Water-willow
p. 208

Common Bladderwort
p. 208

Tall Bellflower
p. 208

Cardinal-flower
p. 209

Bluets
p. 209

Partridgeberry
p. 209

Cleavers
p. 210

Common Teasel
p. 210

Green-headed Coneflower
p. 210

Sneezeweed
p. 211

Nodding Beggar's-ticks
p. 211

FORBS, FERNS & GRASSES

Giant Ragweed
p. 211

Common Yarrow
p. 212

Oxeye Sunflower
p. 212

Lake Huron Tansy
p. 212

Golden Ragwort
p. 213

Canada Goldenrod
p. 213

Awl Aster
p. 213

New England Aster
p. 214

Common Boneset
p. 214

Common Burdock
p. 214

Canada Thistle
p. 215

Common Dandelion
p. 215

Chicory
p. 215

Broad-leaved Arrowhead
p. 216

Eel-grass
p. 216

Long-leaved Pondweed
p. 216

Skunk-cabbage
p. 217

Jack-in-the-pulpit
p. 217

Lesser Duckweed
p. 217

Beach Grass
p. 218

Common Reed
p. 218

Broad-leaved Cattail
p. 218

Pickerelweed
p. 219

Bracken Fern
p. 219

Cinnamon Fern
p. 219

The Great Lakes ecosystem is one of the world's most important natural resources. The five major lakes are among the largest lakes on the planet, and collectively hold 20% of the freshwater on planet Earth. They are much more than water, though.

Aquatic ecosystems are amazingly diverse and productive; Lake Erie, for instance, supports a walleye and yellow perch fishery that is unrivalled anywhere. Scores of migratory birds stream through the Great Lakes system, and many of these species breed in the North American Arctic and winter in South America. Thus, these feathered wanderers link our Great Lakes to the global bio-economy, and make plain that how we protect our habitats has ramifications far beyond our borders.

Thousands of native plant species paint the Great Lakes' habitats in showy palettes of every hue; included are some very rare and local species to excite botanists. The diverse plant communities, in turn, provide the vegetative bedrock that supports myriad insect species, which then provide fodder for higher animals.

Scenery along the Great Lakes is always interesting, often awesome, and never disappointing. Whether an undisturbed coastal beach, a craggy island, or a lushly vegetated, bird-choked marsh, a Great Lakes visit will always be memorable.

This guide provides an overview to the incredible diversity of the Great Lakes region, but it is just a beginning. Our book would have to be many feet thick to cover the thousands of animals and plants that occur along the lakes. We hope it helps you to discover the rich natural history of lakes Erie, Huron, Michigan, Ontario, and Superior, and the eight states that border them.

The Great Lakes System

The largest system of freshwater lakes in the world, the five Great Lakes collectively hold water in such abundance that their contents could flood the lower 48 states to a depth of over nine feet. Lake Superior is the largest, and could hold the water of 25 Lake Eries, the smallest Great Lake by volume.

Each lake has a unique flavor, and varies somewhat in its physical features and surrounding habitats. Jointly, they cover a staggering amount of real estate: 94,710 square miles! That's an area nearly the size of New York and Ohio, two of the Great Lakes states. About 35,000 islands dot the Great Lakes, with the largest being Manitoulin Island in Lake Huron, which sprawls over 1068 square miles. Manitoulin is the world's largest island in a freshwater lake, and it in turn holds the largest freshwater lake on an island. The smallest Great Lake islands are little more than exposed rocks that one could toss a stone across, such as Lake Erie's Starve Island.

Eight states buffer the lakes, and Michigan has the most expansive shorelines by far, bordering four lakes. The Wolverine State has an impressive 3288 miles of shoreline, a distance equivalent to driving from Lansing to the border of Peru. Illinois and Indiana have the smallest amount of lakefront. The total shoreline distance of all five Great Lakes is an incredible 10,900 miles: about the distance from Cleveland, Ohio to Sydney, Australia!

The Lakes

The five Great Lakes should be thought of as a linked ecosystem, easily the largest such system in the world. A glance at a map of North America bears this out: the lakes are the most obvious feature. Superior is the northern and westernmost lake, sits 609 feet above sea level, and flows into Lake Huron via the St. Marys River. Huron is at 577 feet and joins Lake Michigan via the Straits of Mackinac. Michigan is also at 577 feet, and geologically and hydrologically is part of Huron, although it is distinct geographically. Huron-Michigan empty into Erie, dropping only six feet in the process but taking a convoluted course to get there. Water flows from Huron into the St. Clair River, then into Lake St. Clair, where it exits via the Detroit River into Lake Erie. Erie, at an elevation of 571 feet, flows into Lake Ontario via the Niagara River, dropping over majestic Niagara Falls enroute. The elevational drop from Erie to Ontario is 325 feet, by far the greatest descent in the Great Lakes system. From the 246-foot elevation of the easternmost lake—Lake Ontario—water passes out through the St. Lawrence River, which flows through the Province of Quebec and ultimately into the Atlantic Ocean.

Great Lakes Physical Characteristics

		Superior	Michigan	Huron	Erie	Ontario
Rank (world's largest lakes)*	By surface area	2nd	5th	4th	12th	14th
Area	sq. mi.	31820	22400	23010	9940	7540
Volume	cu. mi.	2900	1180	849	116	393
Altitude	ft. above sea level	609	577	577	571	246
Average depth	ft.	483	279	195	62	283
Greatest depth	ft.	1332	923	770	210	808
Bordered by		MN, WI, MI, ON	WI, MI, IL, IN	MI, ON	MI, OH, PA, NY, ON	NY, ON
Outlet		St. Marys River	Straits of Mackinac	St. Clair River	Niagara River & Welland Canal	St. Lawrence River

*ranking of the world's lakes may vary, depending on a number of factors.

Interesting Facts about the Great Lakes

- largest group of freshwater lakes on Earth
- contain 20% of the Earth's fresh water, 95% of the U.S. supply
- watershed (area where all rivers and streams drain into the lakes) covers 295,000 square miles
- 35,000 islands in the Great Lakes, half of which are in Georgian Bay, part of Lake Huron in Ontario

Lake Superior

- largest freshwater lake in the world (Caspian Sea is larger but salty)
- storms can be brutal; waves can exceed 30 feet in height during hard blows
- As with all the Great Lakes, numerous ships have gone down in Superior, the most storied being the SS Edmund Fitzgerald, which sank on November 10, 1975. All 29 crewmembers perished.
- It's a good thing a dam doesn't hold Superior back. If such a dam were to break, all of North and South America would be covered with a foot of water!

Lake Michigan
- only Great Lake completely bordered by the United States
- Michigan and Huron are at the same elevation and are considered a single lake hydrologically (Lake Michigan-Huron)

Lake Huron
- closely linked to Lake Michigan by the Straits of Mackinac; both lakes are at 577 feet above sea level
- has the world's largest island in a freshwater lake in the world (Manitoulin Island in Ontario)

Lake Erie
- shallowest of the Great Lakes
- smallest of the Great Lakes by volume

Lake Ontario
- smallest Great Lake by surface area
- easternmost of the Great Lakes
- average depth is second only to Superior among the Great Lakes

Habitats

The Great Lakes region harbors biodiversity on a grand scale, and a nature enthusiast could spend a lifetime exploring its varied habitats. The diversity of flora and fauna is fantastic. Several thousand native plant species occur in the Great Lakes region, and form the habitats that support the rich animal life of the area. About 225 bird species breed here, and another 175 species pass through in migration or have occurred at least rarely. Rich fisheries support a commercial fishing industry and draw thousands of sport fishermen to the lakes. In total, about 135 species of fishes are found in the Great Lakes drainage, ranging from massive lake sturgeon to minute sand darters. Insects? Who knows how many species but there are many thousands. Some can't be missed, such as the cloudlike swarms of mayflies that emerge in spring. Others, like beach-dwelling tiger beetles, are intriguing but easily overlooked, yet all have their place in Great Lakes ecology.

While many animals and plants, like the ones featured in this guide, are easily observed, others are far rarer. There are several globally significant habitats along the Great Lakes, and they are home to equally significant animals and plants. Examples of federally endangered or threatened species include the Kirtland's warbler of Michigan's jack pine barrens; the lakeside daisy of Ohio's Marblehead Peninsula limestone pavements; and the Hine's emerald dragonfly in fens of Wisconsin's Door Peninsula.

Forests are the most prominent habitats within the Great Lakes drainage. Forest types vary depending on soils and mean annual temperature. Cooler regions support dense coniferous woodlands: pines, firs and spruce, often mixed with deciduous species like maple, American beech and oak. Steep-sided sandstone gorges, especially in the eastern regions, can be dominated by Eastern hemlock. These are boreal forest associations that predominate to the north of the Great Lakes.

Warmer regions are cloaked by classic eastern deciduous forest associations: tulip tree, maple, ash and beech on moister, low-lying sites, and oak and hickory in the best-drained areas. Waterlogged soils support swamps of American elm, green ash, cottonwood and other trees that favor wet feet.

Shallow shoreline regions are often buffered by mixed-emergent marshes, fantastic cradles of biodiversity. Some of the most spectacular marshlands in the midwestern United States occur along the Great Lakes, such as those that border western Lake Erie. Marshes are composed of herbaceous vegetation—cattails, arrowheads and the like—as opposed to swamps, which are forested wetlands dominated by woody shrubs and trees. Great Lakes marshes support tremendous numbers of birds, both nesters and migrants, and a variety of other animal life. They are also noteworthy for spectacular botanical diversity.

Scattered throughout and becoming more frequent in northern reaches of the Great Lakes are bogs and fens. These wetlands are botanical treasure troves, filled with odd and often rare plants. Bogs tend to be dormant in regards to water movement, acidic, and dominated by Sphagnum moss and plants in the heath family. Fens are fed by artesian springs, have an alkaline substrate and are dominated by sedges and other plants specialized for the harsh growing conditions of a fen.

Expansive prairies once blanketed parts of the Great Lakes drainage, becoming increasingly prevalent westward. Free of overshadowing trees, these incredibly rich habitats were filled with a colorful tapestry of flowering plants, many of which are unique to the prairie. Head-high stands of prairie grass—big bluestem, prairie cord grass, and Indian grass—could conceal a buffalo. The fertile prairie soil also grows lush crops, and today corn, soybeans and wheat flourish in most former prairies. Tragically, perhaps 98% of Great Lakes-region prairies have been destroyed and few good examples, such as Wisconsin's Chiwaukee Prairie, remain.

Hundreds of miles of pristine sand beaches once fronted the Great Lakes. They still do, but many have been degraded by excessive recreational usage. The least disturbed examples harbor distinctive plant communities characterized by native grasses, and unusual forbs such as beach pea, sea rocket and seaside spurge. Many animals that depend on beach habitats are now rare, with the federally endangered piping plover, an impossibly cute and charismatic shorebird, being perhaps the best example.

Craggy, wave-washed sheets of barren limestone pavement known as alvars occur locally, primarily in Michigan, New York and Ohio. These alvars are superficially desolate, but on close inspection are found to be loaded with an intriguing, often elfin flora. Any nature enthusiast should pay a visit to a site like North Shore Alvar State Nature Preserve on Kelleys Island in Ohio.

Challenges

Conserving the Great Lakes region and protecting its globally significant biodiversity is fraught with challenges. Hundreds of rivers and streams feed the lakes, carrying unwanted pollutants. Human development and other activities of people have obliter-ated or degraded many habitats. Invasive non-native species such as zebra mussels and purple loosestrife have taken hold and reduced native biodi-versity. In spite of these adversities, the Great Lakes remain a bastion of diversity and are arguably the most significant natural resource of North America's interior. We hope that this guide helps to intro-duce more people to the wonders of the lakes, and creates more sup-porters of our amazing Great Lakes.

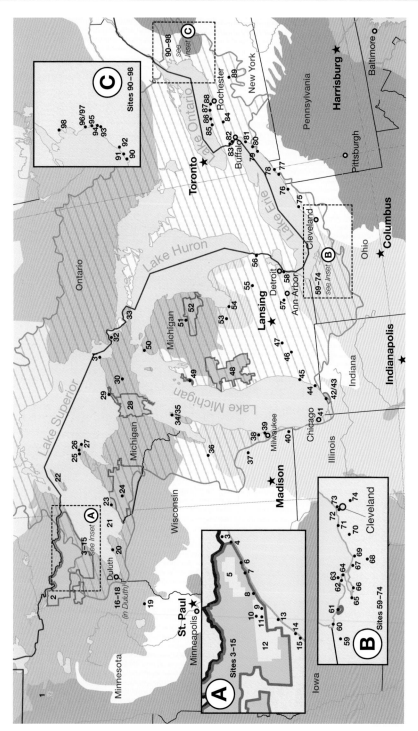

LEVEL I–II ECOLOGICAL REGIONS

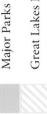

5.0 Northern Forests

5.1 Softwood Shield

5.2 Mixed Wood Shield

5.3 Atlantic Highlands

8.0 Eastern Temperate Forests

8.1 Mixed Wood Plains

8.2 Central USA Plains

8.3 Southern USA Plains

8.4 Ozark, Ouachita-Applachian Forest

9.0 Great Plains

9.2 Temperate Prairies

Major Parks

Great Lakes Drainage Basin

LIST OF TOP GREAT LAKES WILDLIFE WATCHING SITES

Sites in **bold** are described on p. 35-38.

MINNESOTA

1. **Agassiz National Wildlife Refuge**
2. Superior National Forest
3. Grand Portage
4. Judge C.R. Magney
5. Pat Boyle State Forest
6. Grand Marais
7. Cascade River
8. Temperance River
9. George Crosby Manitou
10. **Upper Manitou Forest Preserve**
11. Wolf Ridge Environmental Learning Center
12. Finland State Forest
13. Tettegouche State Park
14. Split Rock Lighthouse
15. Gooseberry Falls
16. Duluth
17. Great Lakes Aquarium
18. **St. Louis River Estuary**
19. Audubon Center of the North Woods

WISCONSIN

20. Bark Bay Slough
21. **Apostle Islands National Lakeshore**
34. **Door Peninsula**
35. Moonlight Bay Bedroc Beach
36. Tellock's Hill Woods
37. **Horicon National Wildlife Refuge**
38. Cedarburg Bog
39. Schlitz Audubon Nature Center
40. **Chiwaukee Prairie**

SELECTED GREAT LAKES WILDLIFE WATCHING SITES

From Buffalo to Erie to Cleveland, west to Detroit, Chicago, Green Bay and Duluth, the Great Lakes offer a wealth of fabulous wildlife-watching locales. Indeed, nearly anywhere you go there is apt to be some spot that supports interesting animals and plants. Short of producing a phonebook-sized guide, there just isn't space to mention them all, so we've provided brief descriptions of some of the sites here and have listed these, along with a more substantial group, on page 33 and on the accompanying map. These sites will provide a wonderful introduction to the natural history of the Great Lakes region.

MINNESOTA

Agassiz National Wildlife Refuge (1)
The 61,500-acre refuge, considered an Important Bird Area by the National Audubon Society, supports a dizzying array of species, especially during migratory periods. Diverse wetland flora also make for interesting botanizing.

Upper Manitou Forest Preserve (10)
Another Nature Conservancy site, this preserve protects about 2200 acres and includes fabulous examples of old-growth maple, birch, fir and spruce. Some of the gargantuan trees are over 300 years old. Manitou offers a trip back to what the Great Lake's primeval northern forests once looked like.

St. Louis River Estuary (18)
The estuary encompasses some 12,000 acres at the point where Lake Superior's largest tributary, the St. Louis River, meets the lake. The Nature Conservancy owns property along the estuary, and works actively to protect the rest of the area. Wetlands and old-growth forests create a wilderness landscape full of fascinating flora and fauna.

WISCONSIN

Apostle Islands National Lakeshore (21)
Over 69,000 acres are included in this National Park, along with 22 islands in Lake Superior. Spectacular beauty combines with rich flora and fauna characteristic of the upper Great Lakes.

Door Peninsula (34)
Named for the Door Strait, this tongue of land juts into Lake Michigan.

Sparsely populated, outstanding natural habitats can be found on the peninsula, including diverse wetlands known as fens. Some of these support the endangered Hine's emerald dragonfly.

Horicon National Wildlife Refuge (37)

A massive 32,000-acre complex of wetlands, in part also owned by the Wisconsin Department of Natural Resources, Horicon lays claim to harboring the largest freshwater cattail marsh in North America. Birding can be mind-boggling, especially during waterfowl migration.

Chiwaukee Prairie (40)

This 400-plus acre prairie is considered the best remaining wet prairie in Wisconsin, and is one of the best in the entire Great Lakes region. A must-see for prairie enthusiasts, Chiwaukee is a portal into our prairie past. Jointly managed by the Wisconsin Department of Natural Resources, The Nature Conservancy and University of Wisconsin-Parkside.

MICHIGAN

Isle Royale National Park (22)

Located on the 206-square mile island of Isle Royale, this park is accessible only by boat or plane. It offers visitors a true wilderness experience—adventurers might see or hear gray wolf, moose and a wealth of other natural history.

Pictured Rocks National Lakeshore (29)

Some of the most spectacular Great Lakes scenery can be found in this National Park, which straddles over 40 miles of Lake Superior shoreline. The park is named for the 200-foot high, multi-hued sandstone cliffs that tower over the lake.

Seney National Wildlife Refuge (30)

Located on Michigan's Upper Peninsula, this 95,212-acre refuge is noted for its sprawling wetlands that support unusual breeding birds such as yellow rail. Bear, moose, otters and wolves can also be found.

Sleeping Bear Dunes National Lakeshore (49)

Stretching along 35 miles of Lake Michigan's shoreline, this National Park Service site is famous for its towering sand dunes. The tallest jut 400 feet above the lake, and are one of the natural wonders of the Great Lakes.

ILLINOIS

Indian Boundary Prairies (41)

A 300-plus acre prairie complex owned by The Nature Conservancy, Indian Boundary is noteworthy for preserving some of the best remaining prairie in the Great Lakes region. Over 250 species of plants have been documented, including major rarities such as prairie white fringed orchid.

INDIANA

Indiana Dunes National Lakeshore National Park (42)
This park covers over 15,000 acres and includes exceptional examples of dunes, beaches, marshes and savannas. Flora and fauna are among the most diverse of any site along the Great Lakes.

OHIO

Oak Openings Preserve (59)
The 3600-acre preserve is owned by the Metroparks of the Toledo Area, and supports outstanding examples of some of the most interesting habitat in the Great Lakes region. Sandy dunes and wet sedge meadows harbor a globally significant array of rare animals and plants.

Magee Marsh State Wildlife Area (61)
This 2000-acre lakefront marsh is one of North America's legendary birding locales, and over 300 species have been recorded. It is adjacent to the 9000-acre Ottawa National Wildlife Refuge. A birder's paradise.

Kelleys Island (63)
This 2900-acre island—with its outstanding alvar, marsh, beach and rocky cliffs—supports perhaps the least-disturbed examples of habitats of any Lake Erie island. Nearly one-third of the island is protected by the Ohio Department of Natural Resources or Cleveland Museum of Natural History.

Headlands Dunes State Nature Preserve (75)
Although Headlands covers only 25 acres, it offers a glimpse into the history of Lake Erie's pre-settlement beaches. The preserve protects the finest remaining example of a natural beach-dune community along Ohio's Lake Erie shoreline.

PENNSYLVANIA

Presque Isle State Park (78)
A 3200-acre sandy peninsula jutting into Lake Erie, Presque Isle attracts scores of migrant birds, and supports a wealth of plant diversity. Its outstanding and varied habitats support Pennsylvania's largest concentration of rare flora and fauna.

NEW YORK

Niagara Falls (83)

Niagara Falls is perhaps the world's most famous waterfalls, and a must-see for anyone visiting the eastern Great Lakes region. The largest set of falls is the Horseshoe Falls, which are on the Canadian side of the border. The Horseshoe Falls are about one-half mile wide and drop 173 feet at the highest point. At peak flow, over 200,000 cubic feet of water per second course over Niagara Falls.

Iroquois National Wildlife Refuge (84)

This expansive 10,828-acre federal refuge contains a diversity of habitats, including large marshes. It offers incredible birding, and a good introduction to a variety of Great Lakes habitats.

Montezuma National Wildlife Refuge (89)

Over 7,000 acres of wetlands and other habitats comprise this wildlife-rich area, which is a must-see for visitors to the Lake Ontario region. Nearly 250 species of birds have been found, and waterfowl are abundant during migration. The Montezuma Audubon Center is on the area.

El Dorado Beach Preserve (97)

Another Nature Conservancy site, this 360-acre beach and dune ecosystem supports large numbers of migrant shorebirds, among other biodiversity.

Chaumont Barrens Preserve (98)

This 2,100-acre site, owned by The Nature Conservancy, features excellent examples of alvar habitat, excellent animal diversity and a number of rare plants.

ANIMALS

A nimals include mammals, birds, reptiles, amphibians, fish and invertebrates, all of which belong to the Kingdom Animalia. They obtain energy by ingesting food that they hunt or gather. Mammals and birds are endothermic, meaning that body temperature is internally regulated and will stay nearly constant despite the surrounding environmental temperature, unless that temperature is extreme and persistent. Reptiles, amphibians, fish and invertebrates are ectothermic, meaning that they do not have the ability to generate their own internal body temperature and tend to be the same temperature as their surroundings. Animals reproduce sexually, and they have a limited growth that is reached at sexual maturity. They also have diverse and complicated behaviors displayed in courtship, defense, parenting, playing, fighting, eating, hunting, in their social hierarchy, and in how they deal with environmental stresses such as weather, change of season or availability of food and water.

MAMMALS

Mammals are the group to which human beings belong. The general characteristics of a mammal include being endothermic, bearing live young (with the exception of the platypus and echidnas), nursing their young and having hair or fur on their bodies. In general, all mammals larger than rodents are sexually dimorphic, meaning that the male and the female are different in appearance by size or other diagnostics such as antlers. Males are usually larger than females. Different groups of mammals include herbivores, carnivores, omnivores or insectivores. People often associate large mammals with wilderness, making these animals prominent symbols in native legends and stirring emotional connections with people in modern times.

Hoofed Mammals
pp. 42–43

Cats
pp. 43–44

Dogs
pp. 44–46

Bears
p. 46

Raccoons
p. 47

Weasels
pp. 47–50

Skunks
p. 50

Otters
p. 51

Hares
pp. 51-52

Squirrels
pp. 53–56

Beavers
p. 57

Mice & Kin
pp. 57–61

Porcupines
p. 61

Bats
pp. 61–64

Opossum
p. 65

Shrews
pp. 65–67

Moles
p. 67

Elk

Cervus elaphus ssp. *nelsoni*

Length: 6–8¾ ft
Shoulder height: 5½–7 ft
Weight: 400–1100 lb

The impressive bugle of elk once resounded throughout much of North America, but advancing civilization pushed these social animals west; the last native eastern elk disappeared from Michigan in 1875. Seven elk originating from western stock were reintroduced to the Wolverine, MI, area in 1918, and the population is healthier than ever. • During the autumn mating season, rival males use their majestic antlers to win and protect a harem of females. An especially vigorous bull might command over 50 females. After the rut, bull elk can gain as much as a pound of weight per day, helping them survive winter. **Where found:** grasslands, open forests; reintroduced in Michigan.

White-tailed Deer

Odocoileus virginianus

Length: 4½–7 ft
Shoulder height: 28–45 in
Weight: 125–300 lbs

White-tailed deer had nearly vanished from many areas around here by the early 1900s; they are now easily our most abundant hoofed mammal. • When startled, they bound away flashing their conspicuous white tail. • Feeding does (females) hide their speckled, scentless fawns in dense vegetation to protect them from predators. • Bucks (males) re-grow their racks, or antlers, each year, and can develop massive racks with age. • No North American wild animal has the economic impact of this species. White-tailed deer hunting generates millions of dollars annually in the Great Lakes region alone. • State mammal of IL, MI, OH, PA. **Where found:** nearly everywhere but the densest forests; common throughout.

Moose

Alces alces

Length: 8–10 ft
Shoulder height: 5–6½ ft
Weight: 500–1200 lbs

Moose are the world's largest deer. Immortalized by the cartoon character "Bullwinkle," these impressive beasts have long legs that help them navigate bogs and deep snow. Speedsters, they can hit 35 mph at full trot. Amazingly, they can also swim continuously for several hours, dive to depths of 20 ft and remain submerged for up to a minute. • Saplings with the tops snapped off and other damaged plants are signs that a moose stopped by for lunch. Voracious eaters, an individual might consume 16,000 lbs of vegetation annually. **Where found:** coniferous forests, young poplar stands, willows; northern MN, WI.

Canada Lynx

Lynx canadensis

Length: 30–39 in
Shoulder height: 18–24 in
Weight: 15–40 lbs

Spotting the elegant but elusive Canada Lynx makes for a gold-letter day. • Ranging through thick, coniferous forests, these small cats are well-equipped hunting machines. Bristle-tipped ears detect the slightest sounds, large paws function as snowshoes and swimming paddles, and dense pelage protects them against bitter cold. Excellent climbers, they often crouch in trees, ready to pounce on passing prey. • Lynx populations fluctuate every 7 to 10 years with snowshoe hare numbers. When hares are plentiful, more lynx kittens survive and reproduce; when there are fewer hares, more kittens starve and the population declines. **Where found:** coniferous forests in northern MI, MN, WI; becoming more common northward.

Bobcat

Lynx rufus

Length: 30–48 in
Shoulder height: 18–24 in
Weight: 15–30 lbs

The bobcat is a nocturnal hunter with the widest distribution of any native cat in North America, from southern Canada to central Mexico. Bobcats are not well adapted to deep snow and are replaced with the Canada lynx in their northern range. All bobcats have dark streaks or spots, but their coat varies from yellowish to rusty brown or gray, depending on habitat and season. Similar-looking lynx have longer ear tufts and longer, black-tipped tails. • Bobcats occupy a variety of habitats and can occur in developed areas. Speedsters, they can hit 30 mph for short bursts. **Where found:** uncommon in forests throughout most of the region.

Coyote

Canis latrans

Length: 3¼–5 ft
Height: 24 in
Weight: 22–50 lbs

Far more common than most people realize, coyotes are secretive and largely nocturnal— yet they can live in densely urban cities such as Chicago. This dog-like mammal has greatly expanded its range owing to large-scale and beneficial habitat changes. Also, widespread eradication of predators such as gray wolves has helped their numbers to boom. • Few sounds of the night are as interesting as a pack of coyotes "singing"; their spirited yips, barks and howls carry long distances. • The coyote has a smaller, thinner muzzle than the wolf, and its tail drags behind its legs when it runs. **Where found:** open woodlands, agricultural lands, near urban areas; common throughout.

Gray Wolf

Canis lupus

Length: 5–6½ ft
Height: 24–39 in
Weight: 55–175 lbs

The large size, and fierce predatory and pack-forming habits of gray wolves caused people to fear them, and in the 19th and 20th centuries these symbols of the wilderness were eradicated from vast areas of their former range. Their spine-tingling, haunting howls should inspire an appreciation of our natural areas and respect for creatures that require expansive wild lands. Fortunately, recovery programs have helped gray wolf populations rebound; there are now an estimated 3500 in the Great Lakes region. • Wolf packs cooperate within a strong social structure dominated by a dominant male and female. **Where found:** forests, streamside woodlands; northern MI, MN, WI marks southern limit of range. **Also known as:** timber wolf.

Red Fox

Vulpes vulpes

Length: 3–3½ ft
Height: 3 ft
Weight: 8–22 lbs

Most red foxes are a rusty reddish-brown, but rare variations include blackish forms and even a silvery type. These small animals look like dogs but often act like cats: they stalk mice and other small prey, and make energetic pounces to capture victims. • Dens are typically in old woodchuck burrows or similar holes. Unlike gray foxes, this species ranges into open landscapes, even suburbia. Tracks are often the best sign foxes are present: their small oval prints form nearly a straight line. **Where found:** open habitats with brushy shelter, riparian areas, edge habitats; common throughout.

Gray Fox

Urocyon cinereoargenteus

Length: 27–42 in
Height: 3 ft
Weight: 7–15 lbs

This forest-dwelling, secretive and mostly nocturnal canine is the only wild dog to regularly climb trees. Some gray foxes even make dens in cavities high in trees—but they are usually just trying to escape danger or hunt prey. We see them mostly at dawn along sparsely travelled forest roads. All foxes are omnivorous, but grays have an especially varied diet, including small mammals, birds, bird eggs, large insects, blackberries and other fruits, and they will even graze on leaves and grasses. • The gray fox's fur is shorter and denser than the red fox's. **Where found:** open forests, shrublands, rocky areas; northern MI, MN, WI marks northern limit of range.

Black Bear

Ursus americanus

Length: 5–6 ft
Height: 3–5 ft
Weight: 90–600 lbs

Don't be fooled by the clumsy, lumbering gait of black bears—they can hit 30 mph for short bursts. They are also excellent swimmers and can climb trees like a squirrel. • Black bears exploit whatever food source is at hand, and up to three-quarters of their diet may be vegetable matter. • The black bear is one of few North American mammals that truly hibernates. After packing on the fat, they retire to a sheltered den for the winter. Vegetable matter in their pre-hibernation diet forms an anal plug, preventing expulsion during their long slumber. **Where found:** forests, open, marshy woodlands; uncommon in north but increasing in some areas.

Northern Raccoon

Procyon lotor

Length: 25–40 in
Weight: 11–31 lbs

Black-masked bandits, raccoons are far more abundant—in nearly every habitat, including suburbia, wet woods and near streams—than most of us realize. They present a hunch-backed appearance and run with a comical mincing gait. While not a true hibernator, they become sluggish and may hole up during inclement winter weather. Agile climbers, they are often seen high in trees or peeking from arboreal cavities. • Raccoons wet their food before eating, a behaviour that allows them to feel for and discard inedible matter. **Where found:** wooded areas near water; abundant throughout.

American Marten

Martes americana

Length: 22–26 in
Weight: 1–2½ lbs

Much smaller than its fisher and mink kin, the American marten often uses woodpecker cavities for dens. Preferred habitat is coniferous forests, although martens also range into mixed hardwood forests. Active during daylight hours, this weasel is more likely to be seen than other similar species. It feeds mainly on small rodents, but also eats fish, snakes, small birds or eggs, carrion and sometimes berries. • The American marten's soft, luxurious fur was highly prized; trapping combined with habitat loss has contributed to its decline. **Where found:** mature coniferous forests throughout upper Great Lakes region.

Fisher

Martes pennanti

Length: 32–44 in
Weight: 4–12 lbs

Like all weasels, these reclusive but aggressive, capable predators rarely eat fish, although they can swim adeptly. Typical prey includes snowshoe hares and other small mammals. If you see remnants of a killed porcupine, a fisher is nearby. They adeptly flip the prickly beasts to get to the soft unprotected belly. • Fishers have ankle bones that allow them to rotate their feet and climb down trees headfirst. They prefer intact wilderness and disappear once human development begins, although they may be becoming habituated to us in some areas. **Where found:** dense coniferous and mixed forests; uncommon to very rare throughout but populations may be recovering in MI and NY.

Ermine

Mustela erminea

Length: 10–13 in
Weight: 1½–3½ oz

If ermines were the size of black bears we'd all be in trouble. These small, voracious predators tend to kill anything they encounter and can take down. Although nocturnal, they sometimes hunt by day. A typical glimpse is of a small eel-like weasel bounding along a downed tree trunk. • Mice and voles form the bulk of their diet. • Their coat becomes white in winter, but the tail is black-tipped all year. **Where found:** dense, mixed and coniferous forests to shrublands, lakeshores, riparian areas, meadows; common and widespread throughout. **Also known as:** short-tailed weasel, stoat.

Long-tailed Weasel

Mustela frenata

Length: 12–18 in
Weight: 3–14 oz

Like other true weasels (mustelids), these capable hunters will kill more than they can consume, sometimes caching prey to be eaten later. They can bring down species twice their size, although normal fare consists of small rodents, birds, insects, reptiles, amphibians and occasionally fruits and berries. • Long-tailed weasels turn white in winter, but the tail tip remains black. They have strange-looking, low-slung tubular bodies, stubby legs and long, switch-like tails. It's too bad they are so difficult to observe in the wild. **Where found:** open, grassy meadows, brushland, woodlots, forest edges, fencerows; uncommon throughout.

Least Weasel

Mustela nivalis

Length: 6–9 in
Weight: 1–2½ oz

Woe to the hiding vole when one of these miniscule barbarians charges into its burrow. Least weasels—the smallest North American weasel species—eat up to their weight in food each day to fuel their incredibly fast metabolisms. These tiny, nocturnal carnivores are rarely seen, but when you move a hay bale or piece of wood, you might glimpse one dashing from its hiding place. Compared with the larger weasels, this species has a much shorter tail with no black tip. **Where found:** open fields, forest edges, rock piles, abandoned buildings; probably common throughout but rarely observed.

American Mink

Mustela vison

Length: 19–28 in
Weight: 1–3 lbs

Many a coat has been made from the coveted fur of these silky mammals, and excessive trapping caused localized declines. Now, most coat fur comes from ranch-raised animals. • Few animals move with the graceful, fluid movements of the mink; it resembles a furry ribbon undulating along the shoreline. Rarely found far from water, the mink has webbed feet, making it an excellent swimmer and diver, and it often finds its food underwater. Its thick, dark brown to blackish, oily fur insulates its body from extremely cold waters. • Mink travel along established hunting routes, sometimes resting in a muskrat lodge after eating the original inhabitant. **Where found:** along shorelines; common throughout.

American Badger

Taxidea taxus

Length: 2–3 ft
Weight: 11–24 lbs

These burly, burrowing beasts are mammalian augers, drilling into the earth more efficiently than a diamond-tipped drill bit. A badger at full whirl quickly disappears from sight and sends a continuous plume of sediment skyward. Badgers have even been seen digging through asphalt. Equipped with huge claws, strong forelimbs and powerful jaws, badgers pursue subterranean dwellers such as gophers, snakes and mice. • Badger holes are essential in providing den sites, shelters and hibernacula for many creatures, from coyotes to black-widow spiders. • State mammal of Wisconsin. **Where found:** low-elevation fields, meadows, grasslands, fencelines, ditches; uncommon, becoming rarer eastward.

Striped Skunk

Mephitis mephitis

Length: 22–30 in
Weight: 4–9 lbs

Equipped with a noxious spray that can be aimed up to 20 feet, the striped skunk gives both humans and animals alike an overpowering reason to avoid it. But come spring, when the mother skunk emerges with her fluffy, 2-toned babies trotting behind her, you may find yourself enjoying her company—from a distance. Skunk families typically den in hollow logs or rock piles in summer then switch to old woodchuck or badger burrows for winter. **Where found:** moist urban and rural habitats including hardwood groves and agricultural areas; abundant throughout.

Northern River Otter

Lontra canadensis

Length: 35–55 in
Weight: 11–24 lbs

These massive members of the weasel family, whether zoo captives or less easily observed wild ones, entertain us with their curious expressions, effortless swimming and playful antics. Their fully webbed feet, long, streamlined bodies and muscular tails make them swift swimmers with incredible fishing ability. • River otters are highly social animals, usually travelling in small groups. Good clues to their presence are "slides": troughs on the shores of water bodies or in snow created by tobogganing otters. **Where found:** near lakes, ponds, streams; uncommon throughout but rapidly increasing in some areas.

Eastern Cottontail

Sylvilagus floridanus

Length: 16–18 in
Weight: 1¾–3½ lbs

Cottontails can have seven litters annually, each of up to 9 young, and they reproduce at a very young age. One pair and all of their offspring could produce up to 350,000 rabbits over a span of 5 years. But predators enjoy eating them as much as humans do, and few survive their first year. • This species is our smallest rabbit and is the most abundant and widespread eastern rabbit. Cottontails' amusing courtship displays involve males and females facing off and making fantastic vertical leaps, often hop-scotching over one another. **Where found:** variety of habitats near shrubby cover; throughout all but the northernmost of the region.

51

Snowshoe Hare

Lepus americanus

Length: 15–21 in
Weight: 2–3⅓ lbs

Snowshoe hares are completely adapted for life in snowy conditions. Large, snowshoe-like feet enable them to traverse powdery snow without sinking. Primarily nocturnal, they blend perfectly with their surroundings regardless of the season. They are grayish, reddish or blackish brown in summer, and white in winter. • If detected, they explode into a running zigzag pattern in their flight for cover, reaching speeds of up to 30 mph on hard-packed snow trails. **Where found:** brushy or forested areas; common in northern MN, MI and WI; recent reintroductions have been attempted in NE Ohio.

White-tailed Jackrabbit

Lepus townsendii

Length: 19–28 in
Weight: 6–9 lbs

This monster weighs up to 4 times as much as the eastern cottontail and is capable of 45-mph sprints to outrun potential predators. Before taking flight, it sits motionless with ears laid flat over its back. • Unlike rabbits, which give birth to altricial young and hide from danger, hares give birth to precocial young capable of running nearly from birth. Recent clearing of forests has created new habitat for this species, which has probably expanded in our region. • Its buffy to brownish-gray pelage turns white in winter. Its undersides, hind feet and tail remain white and the long ears remain black-tipped all year. **Where found:** grasslands, shrublands, sagebrush; MN and WI.

Eastern Chipmunk

Tamias striatus

Length: 9–12 in
Weight: 2–5 oz

Eastern chipmunks ravage landscaping and
undermine porch foundations with their dig-
ging. However, few mammals are more important to the ecology of forests. They
are inveterate seed gatherers, and in addition to hoarding food in their burrows,
often "lose" acorns and other fruit, helping to distribute plants. • Although chipmunks more or less hibernate from fall until spring, they wake every few weeks to
feed, even coming above ground in mild weather. Simple burrows have a main and
a hidden entrance, a food storage chamber and a sleeping den; complex burrows
have multiple passages and chambers. **Where found:** urban habitats, forest edges,
open deciduous woodlands and hardwood stands; common throughout.

Least Chipmunk

Tamias minimus

Length: 7–8 in
Weight: 1–2½ oz

The smaller of two chipmunk
species in our range, this cute,
curious rodent has the widest distribution of the
22 North American species of chipmunks. • Least chipmunks' habitats range from
sagebrush deserts to alpine tundra. They are identified by the gray nape and belly and
by the 5 brown-edged dorsal stripes with 2 extending onto the head. The tail may be
pale orange, yellow or brown underneath but is longer and bushier than the eastern
chipmunk's. **Where found:** campgrounds, coniferous forests, pastures, rocky out-
croppings; common in northern WI, MI, MN and in Ontario.

Woodchuck

Marmota monax

Length: 18–26 in
Weight: 5–12 lbs

A common roadside sight, these ubiquitous, burly
beasts have thick, powerful bodies and claws.
They can dig burrows that might extend for
50 ft. It is a surprise to see woodchucks
10 or 20 ft up a tree—they're squirrels,
after all. More typically, they graze
along forest edges and clearings, using
their sharp incisors to rapidly cut plants, bark and berries. • Woodchucks are true
hibernators and spend much of the year tucked away underground. Groundhog Day
(February 2) celebrates their emergence. **Where found:** meadows, pastures, open
woodlands; common throughout. **Also known as:** groundhog.

53

Franklin's Ground Squirrel

Spermophilus franklinii

Length: 10–12 in
Weight: 12–34 oz

This vocal beast is sometimes heard before it is seen. When alarmed, Franklin's ground squirrels ("gophers") issue whistles and utter frequent, bird-like trills throughout the spring mating season. Vying for mates during courtship, males fight intensely, bumping heads and biting the rumps of rivals, often removing patches of fur in the process. • Their burrows are hidden in dense grass of open prairies and fields. They may spend up to 90% of their lives underground. **Where found:** prairies, meadows, bushy areas; northwest IN, IL, MI, WI.

Thirteen-lined Ground Squirrel

Spermophilus tridecemlineatus

Length: 7–12 in
Weight: 3⅞–9½ oz

The University of Minnesota Golden Gophers football team was named after this striking little creature, the "prairie dog" of the western Great Lakes region. Highly social, these squirrels live in colonies and construct complex underground labyrinths to retreat to when threatened. • From October to March, they retire into their burrows, singly or communally, spending winter curled up into tight balls. During hibernation, their respiration decreases from 100 to 200 breaths per minute to 1 breath every 5 minutes. **Where found:** prairies, abandoned fields, mowed lawns, agricultural areas; locally common in western Great Lakes region. **Also known as:** striped gopher.

Eastern Gray Squirrel

Sciurus carolinensis

Length: 15–20 in
Weight: 14–25 oz

Originally found in large, mature forests, gray squirrels have adapted to suburbia. Their large roundish nests are made primarily of leaves, and are often quite conspicuous in trees, although their winter den sites and birthing locales are in tree cavities. • Gray squirrels can locate their nut caches several months later, even if buried under snow. About 10 to 20% of hidden nuts are forgotten; many will grow into trees. • In some areas, melanistic or black forms predominate. Occasional albinos turn up, and these white squirrels become local celebrities. **Where found:** mature deciduous or mixed forests with nut-bearing trees; common to abundant throughout. **Also known as:** black squirrel.

54

Eastern Fox Squirrel

Sciurus niger

Length: 18–27 in
Weight: 1–2½ lbs

These beautiful, robust squirrels have
richer orange and yellowish overtones than
gray squirrels, and are up to twice as bulky.
They wave their bushy, fox-like tails about
when excited. They bring food to favorite spots; such sites are littered with nutshells.
• Fox squirrels spend more time on the ground than gray squirrels, and are sometimes seen far from trees. A fox squirrel may have a home range of 50 acres; a gray
squirrel's usually does not exceed 5 acres. **Where found:** mature deciduous or
mixed forests with nut-bearing trees; abundant throughout, absent from southwest
WI. **Also known as:** fox squirrel, cat squirrel.

Red Squirrel

Tamiasciurus hudsonicus

Length: 11–14 in
Weight: 5–9 oz

This pugnacious squirrel often drives larger squirrels
and birds from bird feeders, and sometimes takes bird
eggs and nestlings. It can eat highly poisonous *Amanita*
mushrooms, and will bite into sugar maple bark to feed on sap.
Large middens of discarded pinecone scales are evidence of its
buried food bounty. • The red squirrel may chatter, stomp its feet,
flick its tail and scold you with a piercing cry. • During the short spring courtship,
squirrels engage in incredibly acrobatic chases. **Where found:** coniferous and
mixed forests; common throughout. **Also known as:** pine squirrel, chickaree.

Northern Flying Squirrel

Glaucomys sabrinus

Length: 10–14 in
Weight: 2½–6 oz

Long flaps of skin stretched between the fore and
hind limbs and a broad, flattened tail allow this
nocturnal flying squirrel to glide swiftly from tree to
tree. After landing, the squirrel hustles around to the
opposite side of the trunk, in case a predator such as an
eastern screech-owl (*Megascops asio*) has followed. • Flying squirrels play an
important role in forest ecology because they dig up and eat truffles, the fruiting
bodies of beneficial fungi that grow underground. Through its stool, the squirrel
helps the fungus and the forest plants. **Where found:** primarily old-growth coniferous and mixed forests; found in MN, WI, MI.

Southern Flying Squirrel

Glaucomys volans

Length: 8–10 in
Weight: 1½–3 oz

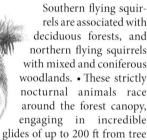

Southern flying squirrels are associated with deciduous forests, and northern flying squirrels with mixed and coniferous woodlands. • These strictly nocturnal animals race around the forest canopy, engaging in incredible glides of up to 200 ft from tree to tree. Loose flaps of skin become stiff when their legs are outstretched; these flaps serve as sails. Their flattened, beaver-like tails serve as aerial rudders. • These squirrels eat the nuts and seeds of oak, beech and maple trees, as well as bird eggs and insects. • During winter, up to 50 squirrels may huddle together for warmth in a tree cavity. **Where found:** deciduous woodlands; common throughout, except northern MN and northwestern WI.

Plains Pocket Gopher

Geomys bursarius

Length: 10–11 in
Weight: 6½ oz

Supremely adapted for underground living, this gopher has naked feet equipped with long front claws for digging; furred lips extending over long incisor teeth to prevent dirt from entering its mouth while eating and digging; and fur-lined cheek pouches for temporary storage of roots, tubers and green plants. It occasionally surfaces at night to find lush herbaceous plants, leaving dirt mounds on the ground. • A pocket gopher's incisor teeth grow as much as 0.04 inches per day. If unchecked by constant gnawing, in a year the lower incisors could grow 14 inches! **Where found:** mountain meadows, fields, shrublands, grasslands, open pine forests; western MN and WI, west and central IL, northwest IN.

Beaver

Castor canadensis

Length: 3–4 ft
Weight: 35–66 lbs

This jumbo rodent—North America's largest—influences its environment more than any other mammal. Its complex dams are engineered marvels that create ponds and wetlands occupied by a diversity of flora and fauna. • Very secretive, this industrious beast is more often detected by the loud warning slap of tail on water, rather than visual sightings. The conical, gnawed stubs of tree trunks are a sure sign that beavers are present. • Beavers were nearly exterminated in many areas at one time, trapped indiscriminately for their valuable pelts. They have made an amazing comeback and are once again common. • State mammal of New York. **Where found:** lakes, ponds, marshes, slow-flowing rivers and streams at most elevations; common throughout.

Eastern Heather Vole

Phenacomys ungava

Length: 4¾–6 in
Weight: 1 oz

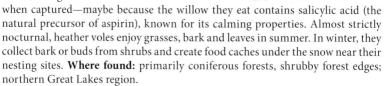

Secretive and seldom seen, eastern heather voles leave evidence of their presence with gnaw marks at the base of willows or birches. They are reputed to have a gentle demeanor when captured—maybe because the willow they eat contains salicylic acid (the natural precursor of aspirin), known for its calming properties. Almost strictly nocturnal, heather voles enjoy grasses, bark and leaves in summer. In winter, they collect bark or buds from shrubs and create food caches under the snow near their nesting sites. **Where found:** primarily coniferous forests, shrubby forest edges; northern Great Lakes region.

Meadow Vole

Microtus pennsylvanicus

Length: 6–8 in
Weight: ¾–2 oz

Little furry sausages with legs, meadow voles are important food for raptors, especially in winter. Their populations have cyclical highs and lows, and in boom years impressive numbers of hawks and short-eared owls will congregate in good vole fields. Primarily active at night, this common vole can be seen during the day as well, especially when populations are high. • Meadow voles rank high among the world's most prolific breeders. If unchecked by predators, they would practically rule the earth. **Where found:** open woodlands, meadows, fields, fencelines, marshes; common throughout.

North American Deer Mouse

Peromyscus maniculatus

Length: 2–2¾ in
Weight: ¾–1 oz

Deer mice range across more of North America than any other native mouse. They are maddeningly variable in appearance and are easily confused with other species in the genus. • Deer mice are seed eaters, but their diet includes insects, fungi, berries and even bird eggs. Active all winter, their food caches help them survive bad weather, but predation means that less than 5% live for a complete year. • Unlike most mammals, the male deer mouse often helps the female raise their young. **Where found:** most dry habitats; abundant throughout.

Prairie Vole

Microtus ochrogaster

Length: 4–6 in
Weight: 1½ oz

Like lemmings and many other small mammals, prairie vole populations peak every 3 or 4 years. As with meadow voles, this species forms runways—distinct tunnel-like paths through the grass. Research suggests that birds of prey can see the glow of vole urine owing to chemicals that reflect in the ultra-violet range. Thus, raptors can quickly locate vole outbreaks. Prairie voles feed mainly on grasses, roots, seeds, fruit and occasionally insects or fungi. Large amounts of food are cached in underground burrows. **Where found:** grassland areas; OH, southwest MI, WI, MN.

Southern Red-backed Vole

Clethrionomys gapperi

Length: 5–7 in
Weight: ½–1½ oz

Active day and night in spruce-fir forests and bogs,
this abundant vole is easily recognized by its
reddish-brown back on an otherwise grayish
body. As with other voles, the southern red-backed vole does not hibernate during
winter; instead, it tunnels through the subnivean layer—along the ground, under the
snow—in search of seeds, nuts and leaves. • Populations of these prolific voles vary
according to predators and food supplies. They are probably the primary prey of the
northern saw-whet owl. **Where found:** mixed and coniferous forests, bogs, riparian
areas; common in northern Great Lakes region, becoming scarcer southward.

White-footed Deer Mouse

Peromyscus leucopus

Length: 6–8 in
Weight: ½–1 oz

This abundant mouse reaches the northern limits
of its range in the upper Great Lakes region. It often
occupies cavities in trees, stumps and logs, old buildings and
bluebird nest boxes, where it builds a dense nest of plant matter. These little critters
are strong swimmers, and they often brave the water to colonize islands. They
primarily eat nuts, berries, seeds, vegetation and insects, but will also raid your
pantry. • Similar to the North American deer mouse, the white-footed is pale to dark
reddish brown above, white below and has protruding ears and a bicolored tail.
Where found: various habitats including woodlands, riparian areas, shrubby areas,
some farmlands; common throughout. **Formerly known as:** white-footed mouse.

Common Muskrat

Ondatra zibethicus

Length: 6–24 in
Weight: 1½–3½ lbs

More comfortable in water than on land, the
muskrat has a laterally compressed tail that
allows it to swim like a fish. Its occurrence in
wetlands is easily detected by the presence of
cone-shaped lodges made from cattails and other vegetation. • Muskrats play an
important role in marsh management by thinning out dense stands of cattails.
They also vex marsh managers by digging burrows in dikes. In general, muskrats
are quite valuable in wetland ecosystems, creating diversified habitats that benefit
many other species. **Where found:** lakes, marshes, ponds, rivers, reservoirs, dug-
outs, canals; common and widespread throughout.

59

Southern Bog Lemming

Synaptomys cooperi

Length: 5–6 in
Weight: ¾–1¾ oz

These little mammals look rather like voles but have larger rounded heads. They rarely occupy their namesake habitat, living primarily in extensive systems of subsurface tunnels. Neatly clipped piles of grass along paths, and their curious green scat indicate this animal's presence. • They feed mainly on sedges, grasses and clovers. Like most voles and lemmings, populations can vary from year to year, and in boom years especially, they are a major prey item for predators. **Where found:** open forests, grassy meadows, shrub or sedge areas; uncommon to locally abundant throughout.

Brown Rat

Rattus norvegicus

Length: 12–18 in
Weight: 7–17 oz

These introduced rats thrive around people and inhabitations. Native to Europe and Asia—but not Norway—the brown rat came to North America stowed away on early ships. • Brown rats can carry parasites and diseases transferable to wildlife, humans and pets, but captive-bred rats have given psychologists many insights into human learning and behavior. • Wild brown rats are brown to reddish brown, often grizzled, with gray tones and gray undersides. **Where found:** urban areas, farmyards, garbage dumps; common throughout. **Also known as:** Norway rat, common rat, sewer rat, water rat.

House Mouse

Mus musculus

Length: 6–8 in
Weight: ½–1 oz

Chances are, if you have a mouse in your house, it is a house mouse. They have been fraternizing with humans for several thousand years. Like the brown rat, they stowed away on ships from Europe, quickly spreading across North America with settlers. • House mice are gregarious and social, even grooming one another. They are destructive in dwellings, however, shredding insulation for nests, leaving droppings and raiding pantries. **Where found:** usually associated with human settlements, including houses, garages, farms, garbage dumps, granaries; common throughout.

Meadow Jumping Mouse

Zapus hudsonius

Length: 7¾–8¼ in
Weight: ½–1 oz

Like tiny kangaroos, jumping mice can bound up to 3 ft
when startled. They have large hind feet and powerful rear
legs, and their long tail helps balance them as they jump. • Mostly
found in damp meadows, they can be identified by their distinctive mode of loco-
motion. • The meadow jumping mouse is brown, with a dark dorsal stripe, yellowish
sides and a white belly. • Meadow jumping mice hibernate for 6 to 7 months in underground burrows, one of the longest periods of any North American mammal. Their
metabolism slows and they survive on stored fat deposits. **Where found:** fields; also
forest edges, marshes, stream banks; common in suitable habitat throughout.

North American Porcupine

Erethizon dorsatum

Length: 24–45 in
Weight: 8–40 lbs

Contrary to popular myth, porcupines cannot throw
their 30,000 or so quills, but with a lightning-fast flick of
the tail they'll impale some of their spikes into persistent attackers. • Slow but excellent climbers, porcupines
clamber about trees, feeding on their sugary cambium
layer. Sure-footed, but not infallible, about one-third of
museum specimen skeletons examined in one study
had old fractures, presumably from arboreal mishaps. • Porcupines crave salt and
will gnaw on rubber tires, wooden axe handles, toilet seats and even hiking boots!
Where found: coniferous and mixed forests up to the subalpine; northern reaches only.

Big Brown Bat

Eptesicus fuscus

Length: 3¾–4¾ in
Forearm length: 1¾–2¼ in
Weight: ½–1 oz

This bat's ultrasonic echolocation (20,000 to 110,000 Hz) can
detect flying beetles and moths up to 16 ft away. It flies above
water or around streetlights searching for prey, which it scoops
up with its wing and tail membranes. • Few animals rest as much as bats, and they
can live for many decades owing to the low stresses on their physiological systems.
After 2 or 3 hours on the wing each evening, they perch with their body functions
slowed down for the rest of the day. **Where found:** common in and around artificial
structures, occasionally roosting in hollow trees and rock crevices; hibernates in
caves, mines and old buildings; abundant throughout.

Eastern Pipistrelle

Pipistrellus subflavus

Length: 3–3½ in
Forearm length: 1¼ in
Weight: ¼ oz

These bats are the smallest bats in our region—smaller than tiny songbirds—and may be recognized in flight at dusk by their Lilliputian size. Pipistrelles often hibernate communally, and their moisture-covered fur glistens like jewels. • Like other bats, eastern pipistrelles are very clean, spending up to 30 minutes each night grooming themselves like cats. **Where found:** usually in woodlands near water; roosts and hibernates in caves, abandoned mines, crevices, old buildings; locally common in summer; winter habitat poorly known; found throughout except in much of MI and extreme northwest.

Eastern Red Bat

Lasiurus borealis

Length: 3–5 in
Forearm length: 1½–1¾ in
Weight: ¼–½ oz

This distinctive species roosts in tree foliage 4 to 10 ft above the ground. Sometimes what looks like a reddish-brown hanging leaf cluster suddenly turns into a red bat! • Red bats have long, slender wings and can reach 40 mph. These fast fliers are highly migratory, and animals in the northern parts of the range migrate to the south for the winter. • Red bats feed on insects attracted to the illumination of a streetlight. Look for their yellowish-orange to red fur; the male's fur is brighter red. **Where found:** roosts on unobstructed branches that allow it to drop into flight; throughout in warmer months.

Eastern Small-footed Myotis

Myotis leibii

Length: 3 in
Forearm length: 1¼ in
Weight: ⅕ oz

This uncommon species prefers heavily wooded areas, and like many bats, often hunts over water. As with many bats, we know very little about this species. Mammalogists call most members of this genus "Myotis" (literally "mouse-eared," a more descriptive term than "bat"). **Where found:** always near water; roosts under bridges, rock ledges, building eaves; individuals hibernate in crevices and groups hibernate in caves or abandoned mines; occurs sparingly in eastern Great Lakes region.

Hoary Bat

Lasiurus cinereus

Length: 4¼–6 in
Forearm length: 1¾–2¼ in
Weight: ¾–1¼ oz

Hoary bats are the most widely distributed—and arguably the most beautiful—bat in North America,. Their large size and frosty-silver fur render them quite distinctive. They roost in trees, and wrap their wings around themselves for protection against the elements. They often roost in orchards, but they are insectivores and do no damage to fruit crops. Identify them at night by their size and slow wing beats over open terrain. **Where found:** roosts on the branches of coniferous and deciduous trees, occasionally in tree cavities; migrates south for the winter; common and widespread throughout.

Indiana Bat

Myotis sodalis

Length: 3–3½ in
Forearm length: 1½ in
Weight: ¼ oz

It's unlikely you'll see this secretive creature, yet it's probably the most famous bat in eastern North America. It is listed as federally endangered in the U.S. and much effort has gone into locating populations. They are nearly identical to the little brown myotis and must be separated by minute details such as foot structure. **Where found:** forages over water at night; during summer roosts under exfoliating bark of trees such as shagbark hickory and older white oak; forms communal roosts during hibernation in caves, abandoned mines; occurs sparingly in southern Great Lakes region.

Evening Bat

Nycticeius humeralis

Length: 3½ in
Forearm length: 1¼–1½ in
Weight: ⅖–½ oz

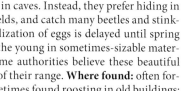

Evening bats have not been found roosting in caves. Instead, they prefer hiding in tree cavities or buildings. They feed over fields, and catch many beetles and stinkbugs. • Mating occurs in the fall, but fertilization of eggs is delayed until spring when females migrate northward to birth the young in sometimes-sizable maternity colonies. Males remain behind. • Some authorities believe these beautiful bats are declining in the northern reaches of their range. **Where found:** often forages over cornfields, other open areas; sometimes found roosting in old buildings; rare in southern Great Lakes region.

Little Brown Myotis

Myotis lucifugus

Length: 3–4 in
Forearm length: 1¼–1½ in
Weight: ¼ oz

Each spring these bats form maternal roosting colonies that can number thousands of individuals—one colony had nearly 7000 bats. Virtually helpless at birth, the single off-spring clings to its mother's chest until it is strong enough to remain at the roost site. • A single little brown bat can consume 900 insects per hour. This species is probably the most common bat in the region and is the most likely to be seen at dusk. **Where found:** roosts in buildings, barns, caves, crevices, hollow trees, under tree bark; hibernates in buildings, caves, old mines; common and widespread throughout.

Northern Myotis

Myotis septentrionalis

Length: 3–4 in
Forearm length: 1¼–1½ in
Weight: ⅐–⅓ oz

With Spock-like ears, the northern long-eared myotis presents an outrageous visage—if you are lucky enough to admire one close up. • Most bats forage by catching insects while in flight, pursuing them with incredible aerial acrobatics. Instead, the northern myotis picks its insect victim from the foliage of trees, then hangs from a branch to consume it. **Where found:** in coniferous and deciduous forests, often close to water; roosts in tree cavities, under peeling bark or in rock crevices; hibernates in caves, abandoned mines; widespread, locally common throughout.

Silver-haired Bat

Lasionycteris noctivagans

Length: 3¾–4¼ in
Forearm length: 1½–1¾ in
Weight: ¼–½ oz

Silver-haired bats are most likely to be found roosting under a loose piece of bark. Sometimes they occur in small, loosely associated groups. They mate in the fall, but actual fertilization doesn't occur until spring. This odd strategy ensures that plenty of food will be available when their young are born. To conserve energy on cold days, they can lower their body temperature and metabolism—a state known as "torpor." • This bat's black flight membrane can span 11 in. **Where found:** roosts in cavities and crevices of old-growth trees; migrates south for the winter; common throughout.

Virginia Opossum

Didelphis virginiana

Length: 27–34 in
Weight: 2–3½ lbs

A maternal pouch, opposable "thumbs" and a scaly, prehensile tail characterize the opossum. The only marsupial north of Mexico has more teeth—50—than any of our other mammals. Honeybee-sized babies are born out of the pouch and must find their way into its folds immediately after birth. • Opossums are famous for feigning death or "playing possum" when attacked. Because they scavenge on road kill, they too often become victims. • Opossums do not hibernate, and they commonly lose parts of their bare ears and tails to frostbite. **Where found:** agricultural lands; common in MI, IN, southwestern IL and east; range may expand northward in mild winters.

Arctic Shrew

Sorex arcticus

Length: 4 in
Weight: ³⁄₁₀ oz

Like the arctic fox and snowshoe hare, tiny arctic shrews also change color with the seasons. Their long, dense winter coat is a vibrant black, with brown sides and a silvery white belly. Their summer coat thins out, becoming an easily recognizable tri-colored pattern of chocolate-brown back, gray sides and lighter gray underparts. The tail is cinnamon colored all year. **Where found:** wet meadows, damp woods, bogs, thickets; found in MN, WI, MI's Upper Peninsula and Ontario.

Cinereus Shrew

Sorex cinereus

Length: 3–4 in
Weight: ¼ oz

This mammal is one of our most abundant—but good luck seeing one live. Mostly nocturnal and prone to scurrying about in dense cover, this voracious shrew consumes its body weight or more in food daily. To balance high late winter mortality rates and year-round predation, females may have 2 to 3 litters per year, giving birth to as many as 8 blind, toothless and naked young. • This shrew has a light brown, velvety coat and a dark nose patch. **Where found:** forests, occasionally tall-grass plains; common throughout. **Also known as:** masked shrew.

Least Shrew

Cryptotis parva

Length: 3 in
Weight: ⅕ oz

This shrew is nearly our smallest mammal—about 109,000 of them would match the weight of a big bull moose! • Shrews have an incredibly high metabolic rate, with heart rates often reaching 1200 beats per minute. Most of the heat energy they produce is quickly lost, so they must eat their own body weight in food each day to maintain their internal body temperature. • This shrew has a brown-gray back, lighter undersides and a relatively short tail. **Where found:** deciduous woodlands, wooded ravines, moist, grassy areas; common in southern Great Lakes region.

Northern Short-tailed Shrew

Blarina brevicauda

Length: 4–5 in
Weight: ½–1 oz

Shrews in this genus have glands that produce mild toxins. It is thought that the toxins paralyze prey—even immobilizing prey much larger than these shrews—and help keep the cached victim as fresh as possible. Voracious predators, these shrews often consume over half their body weight in food daily. • This large shrew is one of the most common of North American mammals, and it is easily identified by its size, gray pelage and short tail. **Where found:** variety of habitats including forests, fields, marshes; common throughout.

Pygmy Shrew

Sorex hoyi

Length: 3½ in
Weight: ⅒ oz

This beast may be the smallest mammal in North America, but if it were the size of a fox we'd probably all be dead. So rapid is the pygmy shrew's metabolism that it routinely eats 3 times its body weight in a day, taking down and consuming any prey that can be overpowered. • These pennyweight shrews stand up on their hind legs, curiously like bears. • Because of their size and secretive habits, they are seldom observed, at least well enough to identify. **Where found:** various habitats, from forests to open fields, sphagnum bogs; throughout, becoming scarcer southward.

Water Shrew

Sorex palustris

Length: 5–6 in
Weight: ¼–¾ oz

The water shrew has large feet fitted with stiff, bristly hairs that allow it to run across the water's surface for a surprising distance. Thick, insulating body fur traps air bubbles between the hairs and allows it to hunt aquatic invertebrates in cold ponds and streams. Robust for a shrew, it catches small fish and tadpoles that other shrews cannot. • The coat is dark, velvety brown to black with whitish-gray undersides and a distinctive, bicolored tail. **Where found:** fast-flowing streams; also lakes, ponds, marshes with vegetated shorelines; widespread but rarely seen in MI, WI, MN and north.

Eastern Mole

Scalopus aquaticus

Length: 4–8 in
Weight: 2–5 oz

Capture this extraordinary digger, and its legs move the entire time it's being held. Drop it to the soil, and with a flurry of all four paddle-like feet, it sends a up plume of dirt and disappears underground in seconds. Its near-surface feeding tunnels create raised ridges that are the bane of gardeners. It prefers sandy or moist loamy soils—not too wet or too dry—and avoids heavy clay or gravely soils. • Eastern moles are almost black in the northern part of their range and silver to gold in the south. **Where found:** woodlands, meadows, golf courses; common in southern MN, southern WI, MI and southeast.

Star-nosed Mole

Condylura cristata

Length: 5–8 in
Weight: 1–3 oz

Looking like it collided headfirst with a tiny sea anemone, the star-nosed mole looks bizarre, to say the least. The anemone-like appendages ringing its snout are actually an extremely sensitive ring of 22 "feelers." Each fleshy appendage can be collapsed or extended individually. The appendages move continuously in all directions, serving as effective detectors of prey. • The unmistakable star-nosed mole is black, with a long tail and a distinctive nose. **Where found:** prefers wet areas such as marshes, low fields, humid woodlands; common throughout.

BIRDS

Birds are the most diverse class of vertebrates. All birds are feathered but not all fly. Traits common to all birds are that they are two-legged, warm-blooded and lay hard-shelled eggs. Some migrate south in the colder winter months and return north in spring. For this reason, the Great Lakes region has a different diversity of birds in summer than in winter. Spring brings scores of colorful migrant songbirds, and the Great Lakes is one of the best areas in North America to observe migration. Even more migratory birds pass through in fall, their numbers bolstered by young of the year, but many are in duller plumage than spring, and they are largely silent. Many migrating birds fly as far south as Central and South America. These neotropical migrants are of concern to biologists and conservationists because of habitat degradation and loss, pesticide use and other factors that threaten the survival of many species. Education and increasing appreciation for wildlife may encourage solutions to these problems.

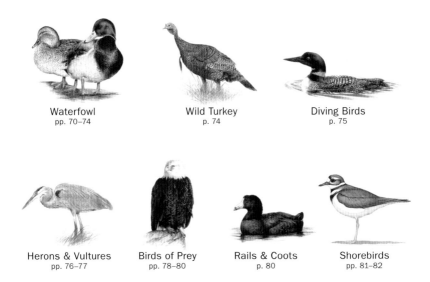

Waterfowl
pp. 70–74

Wild Turkey
p. 74

Diving Birds
p. 75

Herons & Vultures
pp. 76–77

Birds of Prey
pp. 78–80

Rails & Coots
p. 80

Shorebirds
pp. 81–82

Gulls & Terns
pp. 82–84

**Pigeons, Doves
& Cuckoos**
pp. 84–85

Owls
pp. 85–86

**Nightjars, Swifts
& Hummingbirds**
pp. 86–87

Woodpeckers
pp. 88–89

Flycatchers
pp. 89–90

Shrikes & Vireos
p. 91

Jays & Crows
p. 91

Larks & Swallows
pp. 92–93

**Chickadees, Titmice
Wrens & Nuthatches**
pp. 93–95

**Kinglets
& Thrushes**
pp. 95–96

**Mimics, Starlings
& Waxwings**
pp. 97–98

**Wood-warblers
& Tanagers**
pp. 98–100

**Sparrows, Grosbeaks
& Buntings**
pp. 101–103

**Blackbirds
& Allies**
pp. 103–105

**Finch-like
Birds**
pp. 105–106

**Old World
Sparrows**
p. 106

Snow Goose

Chen caerulescens

Length: 30–33 in
Wingspan: 4½–5 ft

Noisy flocks of snow geese fly in wavy, disorganized lines, and individuals give a loud, nasal *houk-houk* in flight, higher pitched and more constant than Canada geese. Snow geese breed in the Arctic, some traveling as far as northeastern Siberia and crossing the Bering Strait twice a year. These common geese have all-white bodies and black wing tips. An equally common color morph, the "blue goose" has a dark body and white head, and was considered a distinct species until 1983. **Where found:** croplands, fields, marshes; uncommon to abundant migrant throughout; more common westward.

Canada Goose

Branta canadensis

Length: 3–4 ft
Wingspan: up to 6 ft

Few avian spectacles rival that of immense flocks of migratory Canada geese. The collective honking of airborne groups can be heard for a mile or more. • This species varies throughout its range, and in 2004 was split into 2 species. The large subspecies are Canada geese, and the smaller, mallard-sized birds are cackling geese. The latter is scarcer in our region. In large part because of "successful" introduction programs by various agencies, Canada geese are now widespread and abundant year-round. They are probably the most instantly recognizable species of waterfowl in North America. **Where found:** lakeshores, riverbanks, ponds, farmlands, city parks; abundant year-round throughout, but seasonal resident only in northern MI, MN.

Tundra Swan

Cygnus columbianus

Length: 4½ ft
Wingspan: 6½ ft

Hundreds of jumbo tundra swans sometimes congregate during migratory peaks in March and November. Most of the swans that pass through the Great Lakes head to the Chesapeake Bay area to winter. Other than the very rare trumpeter swan (*C. buccinator*) this species is the largest native bird in our region—adults can weigh 16 lbs. It would take about 2075 ruby-throated hummingbirds to equal the weight of a tundra swan, illustrating the dramatic diversity of the bird world. **Where found:** lakes, marshes and other wetlands, agricultural fields and flooded pastures; common migrant spring and fall throughout.

Wood Duck

Aix sponsa

Length: 15–20 in
Wingspan: 30 in

In the early 20th century, many ornithologists predicted the extinction of this beautiful duck. Sound hunting regulations and improvement in habitat, in part owing to the recovery of the beaver, aided this species' remarkable comeback. • The wood duck is the best known of the 6 species of North American ducks that nest in cavities. Thousands of nest boxes placed across its breeding range have greatly increased its populations. • Shortly after hatching, ducklings jump out of their nest cavity, often falling 20-plus feet to bounce harmlessly like ping-pong balls on landing. Female woodies often return to the same nest site year after year, especially after successfully raising a brood. **Where found:** swamps, ponds, marshes, rivers and lakeshores with wooded edges; common summer resident throughout.

71

Mallard

Anas platyrhynchos

Length: 20–28 in
Wingspan: 3 ft

The male mallard, with its shiny green head, chestnut brown breast and stereotypical quack, is one of the best-known ducks. • Mallards are extremely adaptable and become semitame fixtures on suburban ponds. They are most common during migration and winter, and migrants from the north are far wilder than their urban brethren. • Mallards freely hybridize with American black ducks, and the result is the most commonly encountered wild duck hybrid. They also freely interbreed with domestic ducks. Despite being the most heavily hunted waterfowl species, mallard populations remain abundant, and they are typically the most commonly seen ducks. **Where found:** lakes, wetlands, rivers, city parks, agricultural areas, sewage lagoons; abundant year-round throughout.

Blue-winged Teal

Anas discors

Length: 14–16 in
Wingspan: 23 in

Many blue-winged teal, our least hardy waterfowl, winter in the tropics of Central America. Quite speedy on the wing, executing sharp twists and turns, they lurk in the dense vegetation of marshes and can be overlooked. Look for a white crescent patch next to the male's bill, visible in all plumages. Females are much duller, as is typical with waterfowl (it allows them to better incubate eggs undetected on their ground nests). • Dabbling ducks' small feet are set near the center of their bodies. Other ducks dive underwater to feed, propelled by large feet set farther back. **Where found:** shallow lake edges, wetlands; prefers short, dense emergent vegetation; common migrant and summer resident throughout; nesters more common northward.

Canvasback

Aythya valisineria

Length: 19–22 in
Wingspan: 29 in

Big and showy canvasbacks prefer deeper water than many other diving ducks. Their scientific epithet refers to eel-grass *(Vallisneria americana)*, an aquatic plant. Canvasbacks congregate where beds of this submergent succulent occur. • Drakes are unmistakable. The much-duller females can readily be recognized by their "ski-slope nose"—the long tapered forehead flowing smoothly into the long bill. Canvasbacks occur in large mixed flocks of diving ducks, and the large drake "cans" stand out from afar by their bright white bodies. **Where found:** marshes, ponds, lakes and other wetlands, open waters of the Great Lakes (flocks can number 10,000 individuals); rare and localized nester.

Ring-necked Duck

Aythya collaris

Length: 14–18 in
Wingspan: 25 in

"Ring-billed duck" might be a better name for this species: the ring around the bill stands out more than the faint cinnamon band encircling the drake's neck. Large flocks of this abundant migrant often collect on roadside borrow ponds and reservoirs. • While most diving ducks require a sprint across the water to become airborne, these ducks practically leap into the air like dabbling ducks. • Females are much less showy and by themselves can be an identification challenge. Fortunately, hens are nearly always with drakes, an excellent clue as to their identity. **Where found:** ponds with lily pads and other surface vegetation, swamps, marshes, borrow ponds, lakes; common migrant and winter visitor; local breeder, more commonly northward.

Common Goldeneye

Bucephala clangula

Length: 16–20 in
Wingspan: 26 in

Common goldeneyes are sometimes called "whistlers"—the drake's wings create a loud, distinctive hum in flight. Goldeneyes overwinter as far north as open water can be found. Big numbers congregate on the Great Lakes where warm water outlets of power plants keep ice from forming. As early as February, testosterone-flooded males begin their crazy courtship dances. Emitting low woodcock-like buzzes, drakes thrust their heads forward, lunge across the water and kick their brilliant orange feet forward like aquatic break-dancers. • Goldeneyes nest in cavities and will readily take to nest boxes, but breed mostly north of our region. **Where found:** open water of lakes, large ponds, rivers; common migrant throughout; winters commonly on the Great Lakes.

Common Merganser

Mergus merganser

Length: 22–27 in
Wingspan: 34 in

Like gleaming white submarines, drake mergansers ride low in the water. Noticeably larger than most other species of ducks, these jumbos can tip the scales at 3½ lbs, making them our heaviest commonly occurring duck. Mergansers have sharply serrated bills like carving knives, the better to seize their fishy prey. Outside of the breeding season, mergansers are highly social, forming large flocks. They commonly overwinter where open water occurs on the Great Lakes, sometimes in flocks numbering into the thousands. **Where found:** large lakes, rivers, reservoirs; breeds along pristine rivers with ample buffering forests in northern parts of the region.

Wild Turkey

Meleagris gallopavo

Length: 3–3½ ft
Wingspan: 4–5½ ft

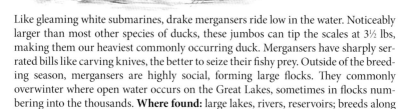

The once common wild turkey suffered habitat loss and over-hunting in the early 20th century. Today, efforts at restoration have re-established the species in many areas. • This charismatic bird is the only widely domesticated native North American animal—the wild ancestors of most other domestic animals came from Europe. • Turkeys are exceedingly popular game birds. The National Wild Turkey Federation has over 500,000 members and has contributed millions of dollars to land conservation. **Where found:** deciduous, mixed and riparian woodlands; occasionally eats waste grain and corn in late fall and winter; common and increasing resident year-round, especially southward.

Common Loon

Gavia immer

Length: 28–35 in
Wingspan: 3½–4 ft

The wild, yodelling cries of loons are
a symbol of North Country wilderness, and evoke images of remote, pristine lakes.
It is a fitting state bird of Minnesota, "Land of 10,000 Lakes." • These excellent
underwater hunters have nearly solid bones that decrease their buoyancy (most
birds have hollow bones), and their feet are placed well back on their bodies to aid
in underwater propulsion. Small bass, perch and sunfish are all fair game—loons
will chase fish to depths of up to 180 ft. • Fall flocks can number into the hundreds.
Where found: large lakes, rivers; of special concern; common spring and fall
migrant throughout; localized breeder more commonly northward.

Pied-billed Grebe

Podilymbus podiceps

Length: 12–15 in
Wingspan: 16 in

Relatively solid bones and the ability to
partially deflate its air sac allow these little birds to seem to vanish below the surface
of the water like tiny submarines (their colloquial name is "hell diver"). Visitors
to marshes that support breeding grebes have no trouble hearing their booming
voices and wild, drawn-out, cuckoo-like calls, which sound better-suited to a
jungle. • Dark plumage, small size and a chicken-like bill distinguish the pied-
billed grebe from other waterfowl. **Where found:** ponds, marshes and backwa-
ters with sparse emergent vegetation; larger lakes in migration; common,
widespread migrant and breeder throughout.

Double-crested Cormorant

Phalacrocorax auritus

Length: 26–32 in
Wingspan: 4¼ ft

Once uncommon in our region, this cormorant is now one
of the most conspicuous species on the Great Lakes. They
are very easy to spot with flocks numbering into the
thousands. • Cormorants out-swim fish, which they
capture in underwater dives. Most water birds have
waterproof feathers, but the structure of the cormorant's feathers allow water in. "Wettable" feathers make
this bird less buoyant and a better diver. It has sealed nostrils for diving, and
therefore must occasionally open its bill while in flight. **Where found:** large
lakes; large, meandering rivers; common migrant and summer resident on the
Great Lakes; local winter populations throughout.

75

Great Blue Heron

Ardea herodias

Length: 4¼–4½ ft
Wingspan: 6 ft

The stealthy heron waits motionlessly for a fish or frog to approach, spears the prey with its bill, then swallows it whole. Herons usually hunt near water, but they also stalk fields and meadows in search of rodents. • Our most common, widespread heron nests in communal treetop rookeries that range from a few nests to hundreds. A massive rookery on West Sister Island in Lake Erie has had up to 2400 nests. • Great blue herons are sometimes incorrectly called "cranes." Not closely related but similar looking, cranes fly with their neck outstretched, whereas herons fly with their neck folded into their body. **Where found:** along edges of rivers, lakes, marshes, fields, wet meadows; common throughout most of the year; rarer in winter but may be found if open water is present.

Great Egret

Ardea alba

Length: 3–3½ ft
Wingspan: 4 ft

The plumes of great egrets and snowy egrets *(Egretta thula)* were used to decorate hats in the early 20th century. An ounce of egret feathers cost as much as $32— more than an ounce of gold at the time—and, as a result, egret populations began to disappear. Some of the first conservation legislation in North America was enacted to outlaw the hunting of these magnificent birds. • The great egret is the symbol for the National Audubon Society, one of the oldest conservation organizations in the United States. **Where found:** marshes, open riverbanks, irrigation canals, lakeshores; common migrant and summer resident near the Great Lakes, although generally rare and local as a breeder.

Green Heron

Butorides virescens

Length: 15–22 in
Wingspan: 26 in

Green herons are less obvious than most of the larger herons, but are common and widespread. They lurk in dense vegetation of stream, pond and lake margins, and when startled blast off with an explosive, somewhat metallic *skeeow* often accompanied by an equally explosive release of feces. • The green heron is one of the few birds known to use tools as a hunting strategy. They have been observed dropping feathers, leaves or other small debris into the water to attract fish, which are then captured and eaten. **Where found:** marshes, lakes and streams with dense shoreline or emergent vegetation; common summer resident throughout.

Turkey Vulture

Cathartes aura

Length: 25–31 in
Wingspan: 5½–6 ft

An almost ubiquitous part of the summer sky, turkey vultures rarely flap their wings, and rock slightly from side to side as they soar. They also hold their wings in a dihedral, or V-shaped position. Endowed with incredible vision and olfactory senses, turkey vultures can detect carrion, their only food source, at great distances. • Vultures often form communal roosts in trees or atop buildings or powerline towers and will use the same roosting sites for decades. They also nest in barn lofts or abandoned buildings. Do not approach a nest; turkey vultures vomit on invaders, and vulture goop is decidedly unpleasant. **Where found:** all manner of habitat; large numbers can be seen soaring in spring and fall migrations; common throughout, but rare in winter.

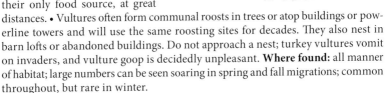

Osprey

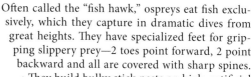

Pandion haliaetus

Length: 22–25 in
Wingspan: 5½–6 ft

Often called the "fish hawk," ospreys eat fish exclusively, which they capture in dramatic dives from great heights. They have specialized feet for gripping slippery prey—2 toes point forward, 2 point backward and all are covered with sharp spines. • They build bulky stick nests on high, artificial structures such as communication towers and utility poles, or on buoys in water. Nesting pairs have increased greatly in recent years, as the chemical DDT has gradually disappeared from the environment. That toxin accumulated in fish, and greatly reduced osprey reproductive abilities. **Where found:** lakes, rivers; common migrant and uncommon localized summer resident, but breeding pairs are increasing.

Bald Eagle

Haliaeetus leucocephalus

Length: 30–43 in
Wingspan: 5½–8 ft

Bald eagles were severely affected by DDT; fortunately that toxin has long been banned and eagle populations have increased dramatically in the Great Lakes region. Usually found near water, they catch fish but are also inveterate scavengers. • Bald eagles do not mature until their fourth or fifth year, when they develop the white head and tail plumage. They mate for life and re-use nests year after year, adding to them each season. Their aeries can grow to mammoth proportions, the largest of any North American bird. One near Vermilion, Ohio, was estimated to be 12 ft tall, 8 ft wide, and weigh nearly 2 tons. Its tree was finally toppled by a storm in 1925. **Where found:** increasingly common and to be expected throughout; nesting pairs have increased dramatically in recent years; overwinters on large lakes and rivers throughout.

Northern Harrier

Circus cyaneus

Length: 16–24 in
Wingspan: 3½–4 ft

A perched northern harrier looks astonishingly like an owl: it has prominent facial discs to better detect and focus sounds. In flight, this graceful raptor is unmistakable. Harriers have a distinctive white rump patch and fly low over the ground on wings held above horizontal. Their sudden appearance startles small prey such as voles, which are quickly pounced on. • Britain's Royal Air Force was so impressed by the northern harrier's maneuverability that it named the Harrier aircraft after this bird. **Where found:** open country, including fields, wet meadows, marshes; breeds sparingly in southern Great Lakes region, more commonly northward; greatest numbers occur in winter.

Cooper's Hawk

Accipiter cooperii

Length: 15–19 in
Wingspan: 27–37 in

These speedy, aggressive raptors are an increasingly common sight in backyards, where they shoot in like kamikazes and snag a songbird caught unawares. Cooper's hawks will even take on squirrels or birds the size of rock pigeons. • This species is the most common of the "bird hawks" *(Accipiters)*, distinguished by relatively short, rounded wings and long, rudder-like tails, which help aerial maneuverability in tight wooded situations. They normally fly with a flap-and-glide style. • Females are typically bigger and bulkier than males in this species. **Where found:** mixed woodlands, riparian woodlands, urban gardens with feeders; common and increasing resident throughout.

Red-tailed Hawk

Buteo jamaicensis

Length: 18–23 in (male); 20–25 in (female)
Wingspan: 4–5 ft

Widespread and ubiquitous, this hawk is probably the most common throughout our region. Red-taileds are often seen along freeways, perched on signs or trees where their white breasts render them conspicuous. They belong to a group of hawks known as *Buteos*, which typically soar in lazy circles or perch prominently watching for prey. Red-tailed hawks have adapted well to urban areas and are commonly seen around cities. • The red-tailed hawk's piercing call is sometimes paired with the image of an eagle in TV commercials and movies. **Where found:** open to semi-open habitats; common year-round with numbers bolstered by migrants in early spring and late fall.

American Kestrel

Falco sparverius

Length: 7½–8 in
Wingspan: 20–24 in

Our smallest falcon can commonly be seen perched along roadside wires or hovering over fields like an avian helicopter. Kestrels take lots of small rodents, and in warmer months switch to a diet heavy in grasshoppers. They nest in cavities, and can be enticed to nest in appropriate nest boxes placed in suitable habitat. Kestrel populations are declining significantly in many areas, and lack of nesting holes may be part of the reason. You could help by erecting suitable nest boxes. **Where found:** open fields, grassy roadsides, agricultural landscapes; common year-round, although numbers may be reduced in harsh winters.

Sora

Porzana carolina

Length: 8–10 in
Wingspan: 14 in

Although you have probably never seen a sora, or any rail, they can be surprisingly abundant. A stone tossed into the dense, inaccessible marshes they inhabit during May migration might elicit a dozen or more rail alarm calls. Our most common rails, soras are easier to hear than to see: loud *kur-ree* or sharp *keek* calls give them away. • Rails have large, chicken-like feet for walking on aquatic vegetation, and they swim quite well over short distances. Their thin, compressed bodies allow them to slip effortlessly through thick cattail stands. **Where found:** wetlands with abundant emergent vegetation; migrant and summer resident throughout.

American Coot

Fulica americana

Length: 13–16 in
Wingspan: 24 in

Sometimes called "mudhens," coots are the extroverts of the rail world. While the rest of the clan is furtive, coots swim in open waters like ducks. In migration, massive numbers often gather on lakes, and they boldly forage for food on the shorelines. Their individually webbed toes make them efficient swimmers and good divers, but they aren't above snatching water celery from another skilled diver. • In marshes where they breed, coots give loud, maniacal, laughing calls. **Where found:** shallow marshes, ponds, wetlands with open water and emergent vegetation; common to abundant migrant; summer resident, becoming more common northward.

Killdeer

Charadrius vociferus

Length: 9–11 in
Wingspan: 24 in

When an intruder wanders too close to its nest, the gifted killdeer puts on its "broken wing" display. It greets the interloper with piteous cries while dragging a wing and stumbling about as if injured. Most predators take the bait and follow, and once the killdeer has lured the predator far away from its nest, it flies off with a loud call. • This species has no doubt increased tremendously in modern times, as human activities have created more habitat suitable for it. **Where found:** open fields, lakeshores, gravel streambeds, parking lots, large lawns; big numbers collect on mudflats in migration; common summer resident throughout; some linger in mild winters.

Spotted Sandpiper

Actitis macularius

Length: 7–8 in
Wingspan: 15 in

In a rare case of sexual role-reversal, female spotted sandpipers are the aggressors. They lay the eggs, but little else—males tend the clutches. She diligently defends her territory and may mate with several males, an unusual breeding strategy known as "polyandry." Each summer, the female can lay up to 4 clutches and may produce 20 eggs. • Spotted sandpipers bob their tails constantly, and fly with rapid, shallow, stiff-winged strokes, like a wire that has been "twanged." **Where found:** shorelines, gravel beaches, swamps, sewage lagoons; common migrant and breeder throughout.

Greater Yellowlegs

Tringa melanoleuca

Length: 13–15 in
Wingspan: 28 in

Greater yellowlegs and lesser yellowlegs (*T. flavipes*) are very similar medium to large sandpipers. Greaters have a longer bill, thicker legs with noticeable "knees" and a louder, more strident series of 3 or more whistles; lessers normally deliver two. The body mass of a greater is nearly twice that of a lesser, something very apparent when the species are together. Yellowlegs are sometimes called "tell-tales": they alert all the shorebirds on a mudflat to invaders such as birders. **Where found:** shallow wetlands, shorelines, flooded fields; common migrant and breeder throughout.

Pectoral Sandpiper

Calidris melanotos

Length: 9 in (female noticeably smaller than male)
Wingspan: 18 in

Pectoral sandpipers get their name from the location of the male's prominent air sacs. When displaying on its Arctic breeding grounds, the male inflates these sacs, causing his breast feathers to rise. Males also emit a foghorn-like hollow hooting during displays. • One of our most common migrants, pectoral sandpipers make spectacular journeys between nesting grounds in the high Arctic and wintering habitats in South America. In spring and fall, large flocks of hundreds or even thousands can occur in wet, grassy fields and along shorelines. **Where found:** lakeshores, marshes, mudflats, sod farms, flooded fields, pastures; abundant migrant throughout.

American Woodcock

Scolopax minor

Length: 11 in
Wingspan: 18 in

Bizarre by shorebird standards, Pinocchio-billed American woodcocks are forest-dwellers that engage in spectacular aerial courtship displays. During breeding season, the male spirals upward, chirping and twittering (a sound made by air rushing past the outer primary flight feathers). He then circles rapidly back to a favored landing pad, where he struts around uttering a series of loud *peent* notes. • Woodcocks use their long bills, which have sensitive "feelers" at the tip, to probe moist soil for earthworms. While populations have declined, this species remains common in many areas. **Where found:** moist woodlands and brushy areas adjacent to grassy clearings or fields; common summer resident throughout; occasional birds attempt to overwinter.

Bonaparte's Gull

Larus philadelphia

Length: 12–14 in
Wingspan: 33 in

Small, buoyant and graceful on the wing, Bonaparte's gulls are very different from their larger, cruder brethren. This species doesn't scavenge in parking lots—largely piscivorous, it snares small fish adeptly from the water's surface. Spring migrants are resplendent with black heads, as if the birds were dunked in dark paint. By late fall, the black is gone, but adult birds still display conspicuous, white, primary wedges on the wings. **Where found:** migrants can turn up on large lakes, rivers; big congregations form in fall at favored Great Lakes harbors (flocks of tens of thousands in November and December).

Ring-billed Gull

Larus delawarensis

Length: 18–20 in
Wingspan: 4 ft

The most abundant gull in our region, this species is the one most likely to be scavenging
waste at malls, landfills and fast-food joints,
although they often forage in freshly plowed fields. They are
3-year gulls; they take 3 full seasons to acquire the characteristic
gray and white plumage of adults. Other gulls take 2 or 4 years. This opportunistic species was nearly eradicated over much of the East 100 years ago—large
numbers were shot to supply feathers for the hat trade. **Where found:** in nearly
any wet habitat; abundant year-round resident throughout; breeding colonies
tend to be scattered and local.

Herring Gull

Larus argentatus

Length: 23–26 in
Wingspan: 4 ft

Populations of large gulls like the herring gull
have soared because of their ability to exploit the
offal of human culture, such as at landfills and
sewage lagoons. As nesting colonies have increased,
so have their predations on vulnerable species such as terns which nest
nearby. • Like many gulls, herring gulls have a small red spot on their lower
mandible. When a chick pecks at the red spot, the parent regurgitates a meal.
• The loud, clear bugling calls of herring gulls is a classic sound of the Great
Lakes. **Where found:** large lakes, wetlands, rivers, landfills, urban areas;
common year-round on the Great Lakes.

Caspian Tern

Sterna caspia

Length: 19–23 in
Wingspan: 4–4½ ft

The largest tern in the world, this jumbo fisher occurs
on every continent but Antarctica. Caspian terns,
named for the Caspian Sea where the first specimen
was collected, appear more like gulls than the graceful
smaller terns. They are often detected by their loud grating *ca-arr* calls, which
carry for some distance. • Juveniles accompany adults in late summer and fall; the
youngsters follow adults begging for food for several months after fledging.
Where found: along large lakes, rivers; common migrant and localized breeder
on the Great Lakes (not found nesting on Lake Erie).

Common Tern

Sterna hirundo

Length: 13–16 in
Wingspan: 30 in

Common terns capture shiners and other small fish in spectacular aerial dives, plunging into the water from heights of up to 100 feet or more. Groups sometimes follow schools of large fish that are feeding, snatching smaller fish that are flushed to the surface. Courting males offer small fish to females; if she accepts the gift they pair up and nest. • In some places, breeding tern colonies have been detrimentally affected by large gulls that prey on their eggs and chicks. **Where found:** large lakes and rivers, most common along the Great Lakes, especially in fall migration; nesting colonies scattered and local.

Rock Pigeon

Columba livia

Length: 12–13 in
Wingspan: 28 in

Formerly called rock doves, these Old World pigeons have been domesticated for about 6500 years; because of their ability to return to far-flung locales, they are often bred as "homing pigeons." In the wild, rock pigeons breed on cliffs; their urban counterparts nest on building ledges or under bridges. • All pigeons and doves feed to their young a nutritious liquid produced in their crop called "pigeon milk" (it's not real milk). • Most commonly encountered is the wild phenotype "blue-bar" pigeon, which is mostly gray with two black bars, but a staggering array of color variation is found. **Where found:** urban areas, railyards, agricultural areas; very common year-round throughout.

Mourning Dove

Zenaida macroura

Length: 11–13 in
Wingspan: 18 in

Although up to 70 million doves are taken by hunters each year, this dove remains one of the most abundant and widespread native birds on the continent. • There are usually only 2 eggs in the average clutch, but each pair of doves raises multiple broods each breeding season, which is nearly all year in warmer climates. • When the mourning dove bursts into flight, its wings create a distinctive whistling sound. Its softly repeated *coo* sounds much like a hooting owl. **Where found:** open and riparian woodlands, agricultural and suburban areas, open parks; common year-round throughout.

Yellow-billed Cuckoo

Coccyzus americanus

Length: 11–13 in
Wingspan: 18 in

Large but quite furtive, cuckoos can be detected by their loud, drawn-out series of jungle-sounding notes. The black-billed cuckoo *(C. erythropthalmus)* is less common in our region. Both lay larger clutches when outbreaks of cicadas or tent caterpillars provide abundant food. • Cuckoos are some of few birds that routinely gorge on spiny tent caterpillars. When its stomach lining becomes packed with spines, it regurgitates it and grows a replacement. **Where found:** a diversity of semi-open to dense deciduous woodlands; common in summer; winters in tropical jungles of Central and South America.

Eastern Screech-Owl

Megascops asio

Length: 8–9 in
Wingspan: 20–22 in

This little owl is suprisingly common, even in treed, suburban neighborhoods. In 1981, the Christmas Bird Count in Toledo, Ohio, recorded 112 owls in a 15-mile diameter circle! • Strictly nocturnal, these birds are best detected by their un-owl-like quavering whistles, although you can occasionally spot one peeking from the entrance of a tree cavity. • Two color morphs occur: the gray form is more common in the Great Lakes region, with reds becoming more frequent southward. **Where found:** mature deciduous forests, riparian areas, cities or orchards with shade trees; common year-round throughout.

Great Horned Owl

Bubo virginianus

Length: 18–25 in
Wingspan: 3–5 ft

Our most common large owl, the great horned owl even occurs in urban sites where it preys on rats. A powerful predator, it is not put off by the smell of skunks and will take mammals as big as small house cats. • Most great horned owls nest on crow or hawk stick nests, and may be spotted by their "ears" projecting above the nest. • Great horned owl courtship begins in January, with females incubating eggs by February and March. **Where found:** everywhere from open agricultural areas to marshes with scattered woodlots, urban areas; scarcest in large, unbroken forests; common, widespread year-round throughout.

Barred Owl

Strix varia

Length: 17–24 in
Wingspan: 3½–4 ft

The maniacal caterwauling of calling barred owls is unforgettable; it is enough to scare the uninitiated out of the woods. Their typical call is a series of hoots that sounds like *Who cooks for you? Who cooks for you all?* • Most barred owls occur in swampy woods, or densely forested ravines; they do best near water. Increasing numbers are turning up in heavily treed suburbia, a sign of their adaptability. **Where found:** mature coniferous and mixed forests, especially near water; locally common year-round throughout.

Common Nighthawk

Chordeiles minor

Length: 8–10 in
Wingspan: 23–26 in

A bird of urban and suburban places, nighthawks mostly nest on gravel rooftops. Males put on dramatic aerial courtship displays. Uttering nasal *peent* notes, he flies high over nesting sites in an odd fluttering flight, then dives with wings extended. At the bottom of the dive, wind rushing through the primary feathers produces a hollow, booming sound. • The nighthawk also feeds in mid-air. Its large, gaping mouth is surrounded by feather shafts that funnel insects into its bill. • When resting, this bird sits lengthwise on tree branches and can be nearly invisible. **Where found:** open country, suburban and urban areas; often near water during migration; breeds and migrates throughout (fall flocks sometimes number in the hundreds).

Whip-poor-will

Caprimulgus vociferus

Length: 9–10 in
Wingspan: 16–20 in

Few birds are easier to hear, yet harder to see, than whip-poor-wills. When at rest on a lichen-speckled limb or leafy forest floor, they blend into the background. But their loud, oft-repeated songs are delivered incessantly and are a near-perfect rendition of their name. One bird was documented singing over 28,000 songs in 1 night! • Ground-nesting whip-poor-wills time their egg laying to the lunar cycle so that hatching occurs during full moons, when their moth prey is readily captured. **Where found:** open deciduous and pine woodlands, often along forest edges; breeds sparingly throughout; in decline.

Chimney Swift

Chaetura pelagica

Length: 5¼ in
Wingspan: 14 in

Resembling flying cigars, chimney swifts are more at home on the wing than perched. Unable to perch like most birds, they prop themselves against a vertical surface using their stiff tails for support. Feeding, drinking, bathing, nest material collection and mating are all done on the wing! • Most swifts nest in chimneys, and during migration, large numbers funnel in en masse at dusk. • Chimney swifts feed solely on insects and retreat to South America for the winter. **Where found:** forages above cities and towns; roosts and nests in chimneys or tree cavities; breeds throughout, more frequent southward.

Ruby-throated Hummingbird

Archilochus colubris

Length: 3½–4 in
Wingspan: 4–4½ in

Aerial extremists, these hummingbirds fly in any direction and can beat their wings up to several dozen times a second. At full tilt, these nickel-weight speedsters have a heart rate of over 1000 beats per minute. Courting males fly a pendulum-like arc, creating a loud hum with their wings. • Feeders can attract dozens of these feisty birds. Their tiny lichen-shingled nests house 2 jellybean-sized eggs. Spiderwebs used in nest construction allow the nest to expand as the youngsters grow. **Where found:** open, mixed woodlands, wetlands, gardens, backyards; breeds throughout the region; winters in Central America, with many flying 500 non-stop miles over the Gulf of Mexico.

Belted Kingfisher

Megaceryle alcyon

Length: 11–14 in
Wingspan: 20–21 in

Antisocial other than during the brief nesting period, kingfishers stake out productive fishing grounds and scold invaders with loud rattling calls. They catch fish with headfirst plunges, and often beat the victim into submission by rapping it against a branch. • Mating pairs nest in a chamber at the end of a long tunnel dug into an earth bank. • With an extra red band across her belly, the female kingfisher is more colorful than her mate. Kingfishers are quite hardy, and may overwinter where open water can be found. **Where found:** lakes, ponds, rivers; common throughout; most move south in winter.

Red-headed Woodpecker

Melanerpes erythrocephalus

Length: 9–9½ in
Wingspan: 17 in

Red-headed woodpeckers are prolific cachers of acorns, which they store in crevices in trees known as granaries. Redheads also flycatch from prominent perches. • Mature forests are less suitable habitat for these woodpeckers as they do best in open country with scattered woodlots. • Family units often stay together over winter, and can be quite conspicuous as they utter loud *queeer* calls and softer *churr* notes. **Where found:** open deciduous woodlands (especially oak woodlands), agricultural areas with groves of scattered trees; locally common year-round throughout.

Red-bellied Woodpecker

Melanerpes carolinus

Length: 9–10½ in
Wingspan: 16 in

These large woodpeckers are common and conspicuous. Frequent visitors to backyard bird feeders, these loud and aggressive birds are near the top of the pecking order. More of a southern species, red-bellies are actively expanding northward into this region. • The "red belly" of this species is faint and can only be seen up close and under good conditions. **Where found:** mature deciduous woodlands, occasionally wooded residential areas; common year-round throughout but absent from northern MI, MN.

Downy Woodpecker

Picoides pubescens

Length: 6–7 in
Wingspan: 12 in

Our most common woodpecker, downies are found everywhere from backyard feeders to dense forest. They resemble the less common hairy woodpecker (*P. villosus*), but are much smaller with a tiny bill, and black spots on the white outer tail feathers. • Downies and other woodpeckers have feathered nostrils that filter out sawdust produced by their excavations, and long barbed tongues that can reach far into crevices to extract grubs. **Where found:** deciduous and mixed forests; common and widespread year-round throughout.

Northern Flicker

Colaptes auratus

Length: 12–13 in
Wingspan: 20 in

Many people have become birders after seeing
one of these beautiful woodpeckers flush from
the ground, revealing a bold white rump and
golden underwings. Northern flickers are inveterate anters, ripping into
ant mounds and gorging on the occupants. Our eastern birds, with their yellow
underwings, are "yellow-shafted flickers"; western birds have salmon-colored
underwings and are "red-shafted flickers." They were once considered separate
species. • Flickers are named for their call, a loud, rolling *flicka-flicka-flicka*.
Where found: open woodlands, forest edges, fields, meadows, treed suburbia;
common year-round throughout.

Pileated Woodpecker

Dryocopus pileatus

Length: 16–19 in
Wingspan: 29 in

These crow-sized birds, the sixth-largest woodpecker in the
world, are an unforgettable sight. Their loud, maniacal laughing
calls give them away, but seeing one of these secretive woodpeckers is more difficult. Their large, distinctively oval-shaped nest
holes also reveal their presence, as do trees that look as if some-
one had taken an axe to them. Pileateds feed heavily on carpenter
ants, and that's what they are digging for. Wood ducks, American
kestrels, owls and even flying squirrels nest in abandoned pileated
woodpecker nest holes. **Where found:** large, mature forests; common
to uncommon and local but becoming increasingly frequent.

Eastern Wood-Pewee

Contopus virens

Length: 6–6½ in
Wingspan: 10 in

One of the most common breeding birds of our deciduous
forests, the wood-pewee is named for its plaintive, whistled
pee-ah-wee sound. In fact, because the pewee sings incessantly, it is easier to detect it by song than to spot it in the dense
shade of its wooded haunts. • Eastern wood-pewees engage in
"yo-yo" flights, darting from a perch in the forest understory, grabbing an insect in
midair, and returning to the same perch. **Where found:** open to dense mixed and
deciduous woodlands; common throughout during summer and migration.

Eastern Phoebe

Sayornis phoebe

Length: 6½–7 in
Wingspan: 10½ in

Phoebes are "people-birds": they often nest on building ledges, bridge trestles, and the eaves of barns and sheds and consequently are close to people. Their loud, emphatic *fee-bee!* is a familiar sound. • Most flycatchers are not very tolerant to cold. In winter they migrate to the tropics, where a good supply of flying insects is assured. But the tough Eastern phoebe routinely attempts to overwinter as far north as the southern Great Lakes; migrants return by March. **Where found:** open deciduous woodlands, forest edges, clearings; often near bridges, culverts and other such structures; common throughout in summer.

Great Crested Flycatcher

Myiarchus crinitus

Length: 8–9 in
Wingspan: 13 in

Loud, raucous *wheep!* calls reveal the presence of the great crested flycatcher. Although easily heard, these large, showy yellow and rufous flycatchers typically remain high in leafy forest canopies and are hard to spot. The only eastern flycatchers to nest in cavities, they often adorn the entrance with a shed snakeskin or translucent plastic wrap. The purpose of this practice is not fully understood, but it probably serves as a deterrent to potential predators. **Where found:** semi-open deciduous and mixed woodlands; common breeder throughout.

Eastern Kingbird

Tyrannus tyrannus

Length: 8½–9 in
Wingspan: 15 in

The eastern kingbird lives up to its scientific name, *Tyrannus tyrannus*. It fearlessly attacks crows, hawks and other large birds that pass through its territory, pursuing and pecking at them until the threat has passed. A bird of very open landscapes, it often perches prominently on roadside wires. • The eastern kingbird is a gregarious fruit eater while wintering in South America, and an antisocial, aggressive insect eater while nesting in North America. **Where found:** fields and agricultural landscapes with scattered trees, large forest clearings, shrubby roadsides, borders of marshes, sometimes treed suburbia; common and widespread summer resident throughout.

Red-eyed Vireo

Vireo olivaceus

Length: 6 in
Wingspan: 10 in

Capable of delivering 40 phrases per minute, male red-eyed vireos drone on all day. A patient researcher once tallied 22,000 individual songs delivered in one day by one of these avian motor-mouths. Such incessant yammering earned these birds the nickname "preacher bird."
• Red-eyed vireos are hard to spot because they sluggishly forage high in the canopy, hidden in dense leafy cover. This species is one of the most common breeding birds in our deciduous forests. **Where found:** deciduous or mixed woodlands; abundant breeder throughout.

Blue Jay

Cyanocitta cristata

Length: 11–12 in
Wingspan: 16 in

This loud, striking and well-known bird can be quite aggressive when competing for sunflower seeds and peanuts at backyard feeders. It rarely hesitates to drive away smaller birds, squirrels or even cats. • Jays cache nuts and are very important to the forest ecosystem. In autumn, one blue jay might bury 1000s of acorns, forgetting where many were hidden and thus planting scads of oaks. • Spectacular numbers of jays may congregate along the shores of the Great Lakes during May migration. **Where found:** all manner of habitats, from dense forests to suburbia; common and widespread year-round throughout.

American Crow

Corvus brachyrhynchos

Length: 17–21 in
Wingspan: 3 ft

One of our most intelligent birds, crows have in recent years occupied urban places in much greater numbers. Here, they are safe from hunters, plus towns offer this opportunistic scavenger abundant food. • Crows will drop walnuts or clams from great heights onto a hard surface to crack the shells, one of the few examples of birds using objects to manipulate food. • Very social, crows sometimes form massive winter roosts numbering into the thousands. **Where found:** nearly ubiquitous; urban areas, agricultural fields, forests; common and widespread year-round throughout.

Horned Lark

Eremophila alpestris

Length: 7 in
Wingspan: 12 in

Mousy and seemingly nondescript, horned larks scurry like mice across the most barren landscapes. They often flush from rural roadsides as cars pass by; watch for the blackish tail that contrasts with the sandy-colored body. A good look at a perched lark reveals a very handsome bird sporting a black mask, twin tiny horns and pale yellow underparts smudged with a dark crescent across the chest. Listen for their clear, tinkling calls in open agricultural lands. In winter, they flock with lapland longspurs and snow buntings. **Where found:** wide open areas; pastures, prairies, cultivated fields; common year-round throughout, although may retreat south in harsh winters.

Purple Martin

Progne subis

Length: 7–8 in
Wingspan: 18 in

Purple martins have been associated with man for centuries. Native North Americans placed hollow gourds around their villages to lure these handsome swallows. Today, probably all martins, at least in this region, rely on nest boxes. Placing appropriate martin houses in suitable sites may lure this species, our largest swallow, to nest near you. Martins sometimes form enormous roosts in migration that can number into the tens of thousands. **Where found:** semi-open areas, often near water; uncommon and local nester throughout.

Tree Swallow

Tachycineta bicolor

Length: 5½ in
Wingspan: 14½ in

The first of these tough swallows return to our region as early as late February, and they are back in force by the end of March. Competition for cavity nest sites is fierce, and the earliest swallows are most likely to secure good cavity nests. Bluebird enthusiasts have greatly benefited this cavity-nesting species, as tree swallows readily adopt bluebird boxes. • When the nestlings hatch, both parents share feeding duties, returning to their young 10 to 20 times per hour. **Where found:** often seen in areas with bluebird nest boxes; a wide range of open habitats with peak numbers around ponds, lakes, wetlands; common summer resident throughout.

Barn Swallow

Hirundo rustica

Length: 7 in
Wingspan: 15 in

Barn swallows are familiar sights around farmsteads, where they nest in barns and other buildings. It is now almost unheard of for them to nest in natural sites such as cliffs, to which they once were restricted. In males, the long forked tail is a sign of vigor; longer-tailed males tend to live longer and have higher reproductive success. This species is probably the most common swallow in the Great Lakes region, and you should find barn swallows on nearly any outing. **Where found:** open landscapes, especially rural and agricultural, often near water; common breeder throughout.

Black-capped Chickadee

Poecile atricapillus

Length: 5–6 in
Wingspan: 8 in

Curious and inquisitive, black-capped chickadees may even land on people and are common and familiar visitors to backyard feeders. Chickadees cache seeds, and are able to relocate hidden food up to a month later. • Small flocks of foraging chickadees join titmice, nuthatches and other small birds to form mixed flocks in winter. These flocks sometimes stumble into Eastern screech-owls *(Megascops asio)*, and the ensuing loud and vigorous scolding can help you find the owl. **Where found:** mixed and deciduous forests, parks, suburban backyards; common year-round throughout.

Tufted Titmouse

Baeolophus bicolor

Length: 6–6½ in
Wingspan: 10 in

This bird's amusing feeding antics and insatiable appetite keep observers entertained at bird feeders. Grasping a sunflower seed with its tiny feet, the dexterous tufted titmouse strikes its dainty bill repeatedly against the hard outer coating to expose the inner core. • A breeding pair of titmice will maintain their bond throughout the year, even when joining small, mixed flocks for the cold winter months. Young often remain with their parents for over a year to help raise the next brood. **Where found:** deciduous woodlands, groves, suburban parks with large, mature trees; common year-round throughout, but absent from northern MI, MN.

93

Red-breasted Nuthatch

Sitta canadensis

Length: 4½ in
Wingspan: 8½ in

This species is much more northerly than the white-breasted nuthatch, occurring throughout boreal forests of northern U.S. and Canada. Red-breasted nuthatches stage periodic southward invasions (irruptions) some winters. Thus, they may be absent at feeders some winters and common the next. Irruptions are triggered by food shortages, not weather. • Nuthatches are attracted to backyard feeders filled with suet or peanut butter. **Where found:** coniferous and mixed forests; common year-round resident in northern reaches of our region, becoming a scarcer breeder southward; can be common throughout in winter.

White-breasted Nuthatch

Sitta carolinensis

Length: 5½–6 in
Wingspan: 11 in

A number of species—creepers, woodpeckers and nuthatches—are specialized tree gleaners, working tree trunks and limbs in search of bark-dwelling insects. Nuthatches typically move headfirst down trunks rather than upwards. This perspective allows them to see into nooks and spot prey that upwardly mobile birds would miss. Nuthatches are common feeder visitors, and their name comes from their habit of lodging nuts and seeds in crevices, and hammering them with their powerful bills, thus "hatching" the fruit to get at the meat within. **Where found:** deciduous and mixed forests; year-round throughout, more common southward.

Carolina Wren

Thryothorus ludovicianus

Length: 5½ in
Wingspan: 7½ in

A little bird with a booming voice, the Carolina wren's year-round, ringing *tea-kettle tea-kettle tea-kettle tea* song can't be missed. • Carolina wrens are southerners but have expanded increasingly north over the past century. They are vulnerable to severe winters; large die-offs occur as a result of brutal winter weather. Carolina wrens occur around homes and have a penchant for nesting in flowerpots, old shoes and mail boxes. • If conditions are favorable, 2 broods may be raised in a single season. **Where found:** shrubby tangles and thickets of forests, around gardens, farms and overgrown brushy areas; common year-round throughout, especially southward.

House Wren

Troglodytes aedon

Length: 4½–5 in
Wingspan: 6 in

A familiar suburban sight and sound, house wrens have loud, bubbly warbles. They typically skulk in dense brush but won't hesitate to express displeasure with intruders by delivering harsh, scolding notes. These cavity nesters are easily lured to nest boxes. House wrens can be aggressive and highly territorial, and are known to puncture the eggs of other birds that nest nearby. This wren ranges all the way from Canada to southern South America—the broadest longitudinal distribution of any wren. **Where found:** thickets, shrubby openings, woodland openings, often near buildings; common during summer in suburban areas.

Golden-crowned Kinglet

Regulus satrapa

Length: 4 in
Wingspan: 7 in

Our smallest songbird, golden-crowned kinglets are impossibly tiny, barely larger than ruby-throated hummingbirds. They are rather tame and can often be coaxed closer by making squeaking or "pishing" sounds. Identify kinglets from afar by their perpetual motion and chronic, nervous wing flicking. Surprisingly hardy, these birds nest throughout the boreal forest and overwinter at northern latitudes throughout the Great Lakes region. Like chickadees, kinglets can lower their body temperature at night to conserve energy. **Where found:** nests in conifers, becoming more common northward; common throughout in migration and winter in wooded habitats.

Blue-gray Gnatcatcher

Polioptila caerulea

Length: 4½ in
Wingspan: 6 in

These beautiful little birds typically remain well up in the trees, and only their squeaky, fussy-sounding banjo-like notes give them away. They are constantly on the move, and foraging gnatcatchers flash their white outer tail feathers, an action that reflects light and may scare insects into flight. • Their nest is a beautiful but minute cup shingled with lichens and held together with spider webs, saddled to a horizontal limb well off the ground. **Where found:** deciduous woodlands and woodland edges, often near water; common summer resident throughout.

95

Eastern Bluebird

Sialia sialis

Length: 7 in
Wingspan: 13 in

Bluebird enthusiasts have erected thousands of nest boxes throughout the range of this cavity-nesting thrush, greatly bolstering populations. Males—a gorgeous deep blue above, contrasting with warm rufous tones below—issue soft, pleasing warbles. Females are duller, and young birds are heavily spotted below, revealing their relationship to the thrushes. • Bluebirds are hardy and often overwinter, eating primarily berries. However, severe weather in late winter of 1895 nearly wiped them out throughout the Great Lakes. • State bird of New York. **Where found:** agricultural lands, fencelines, meadows, forest clearings and edges; common summer resident throughout; overwinters irregularly throughout.

Wood Thrush

Hylocichla mustelina

Length: 8 in
Wingspan: 13 in

The clear, flute-like whistled song of the wood thrush is one of the most characteristic melodies of the eastern deciduous forest—and perhaps the most beautiful of all our bird songs. These rich, rufous-brown thrushes with heavily speckled underparts have a split syrinx, or vocal organ, that enables them to sing two notes simultaneously and thus harmonize with themselves to create the hauntingly ethereal songs that delight listeners. Still common but on the decline, wood thrushes face loss of habitat and other threats, both here and in their Central American wintering habitat. **Where found:** moist, mature and preferably undisturbed deciduous woodlands, mixed forests; common summer resident throughout.

American Robin

Turdus migratorius

Length: 10 in
Wingspan: 17 in

Among our most widely seen, familiar and easily recognized birds, robins occur nearly everywhere. Males are striking birds with black heads, rich brick-red underparts and streaked white throats. • Robins are master earthworm-hunters, adeptly spotting the worm and tugging it from the soil. In winter, they switch to a diet of berries. The proliferation of non-native bush honeysuckles with their copious fruit lure many more robins to stay north for the winter than in the past. • State bird of MI and WI. **Where found:** residential lawns, gardens, urban parks, forests, almost anywhere; abundant year-round throughout; more common southward in winter.

Gray Catbird

Dumetella carolinensis

Length: 8½–9 in
Wingspan: 11 in

A catbird in full song issues a non-stop, squeaky barrage of
warbling notes, interspersed with poor imitations of other birds.
Occasionally they let go with loud, cat-like meows that could even fool
a feline. • Gray catbirds occupy thick brushy habitats and can be difficult
to glimpse. Perseverance pays off; these are very handsome birds in tones
of gray set off by a dark cap and striking cinnamon undertail coverts. Curious
by disposition, catbirds can be lured into view by making squeaking sounds.
Where found: dense thickets, brambles or shrubby areas, hedgerows, often near
water; common and widespread summer resident throughout.

Northern Mockingbird

Mimus polyglottos

Length: 10 in
Wingspan: 14 in

The undisputed master of avian mimicry, at least
in our region, mockingbirds can have a vocal repertoire of over 400 different song types. They imitate
a wide array of sounds flawlessly, including crows,
chickadees, human wolf-whistles, even fire truck sirens and
the backup beeps of garbage trucks. Unmated males often sing
throughout the night in summer, sometimes from the tops of
chimneys to the displeasure of homeowners trying to sleep. This
southern bird has expanded northward over the last century, but barely reaches the
southern Great Lakes. **Where found:** hedges, fencerows and suburban gardens and
parks; year-round resident, but rare near the Great Lakes.

Brown Thrasher

Toxostoma rufum

Length: 11½ in
Wingspan: 13 in

Looking somewhat thrush-like with their rufous backs
and spotted underparts, brown thrashers are mimics
(along with the gray catbird and northern mocking-
bird). Thrashers have the most expansive repertoire of all; some 3000 distinct
phrases have been catalogued. This species sounds a bit like a mockingbird, but
thrashers have a more uniform mechanical delivery and sing phrases in repeated
couplets. Singing thrashers often deliver their songs from near the tip of a small tree.
Where found: open areas interspersed with fencerows, dense thickets, dry brushy
fields, woodland edges; common breeder throughout; rare in winter.

European Starling

Sturnus vulgaris

Length: 8½ in
Wingspan: 16 in

We can thank the Shakespeare Society for this species, which is perhaps the most damaging non-native bird introduction in North America. About 60 European starlings were released in New York City in 1890 and 1891 as part of an ill-fated effort to establish all birds mentioned by Shakespeare. Now abundant throughout North America, starlings often drive native species like Eastern bluebirds from nest cavities. Starlings are one of our longest-lived songbirds—one survived for nearly 18 years. **Where found:** cities, towns, farmyards, woodland fringes, clearings; abundant year-round throughout.

Cedar Waxwing

Bombycilla cedrorum

Length: 7 in
Wingspan: 12 in

Graceful and dapper, cedar waxwings have a decidedly suave look. They also display impeccable manners—sometimes engaging in communal feeding, passing fruit from bird to bird. Although largely frugivorous (fruit eating), waxwings engage in lots of flycatching in the summer along the riparian areas where they often nest. In winter, large flocks form nomadic groups that wander about plundering berries from fruiting trees. A favored tree that you can plant is the serviceberry. **Where found:** wooded residential parks and gardens, overgrown fields, riparian areas; common and nomadic year-round resident; more common southward in winter.

Yellow Warbler

Dendroica petechia

Length: 5 in
Wingspan: 8 in

Warblers are among our most beautiful birds. Thirty-seven species occur in this region annually, but space precludes describing them all. The yellow warbler is one of our showiest and most common species. Their loud, ringing *sweet-sweet-I'm-so-sweet* song is easily heard in wetlands, especially those with willows. Like most of our warblers, yellows are neotropical: they breed in northerly latitudes but winter several thousand miles to the south in very different Central and South American habitats. **Where found:** peak numbers occur in wetlands, but also in brushy fields, pond margins, scruffy woodland borders; common breeder throughout.

Magnolia Warbler

Dendroica magnolia

Length: 4½–5 in
Wingspan: 7 in

Magnolia warblers breed in boreal forests dominated
by conifers; a far cry from what their moniker suggests
(the first specimen was a migrant shot out of a magnolia tree
in Mississippi in 1810). One of our most striking warblers, males
are adorned with nearly every field mark one could want: wing bars, tail spots,
breast stripes, eyeline and face mask. • This active feeder often fans its tail to
reveal the distinctive white band on the uppertail, and the equally distinctive
undertail pattern of white basal half and black distal half. **Where found:** any
wooded habitat in migration; conifer woodlands for breeding; common migrant
throughout; breeders more common northward.

Yellow-rumped Warbler

Dendroica coronata

Length: 5½ in
Wingspan: 9¼ in

Yellow-rumped warblers are the most abun-
dant and widespread wood-warblers in North America. East-
ern and western forms are distinctive and once were considered separate species.
Our birds were formerly known as "Myrtle warbler," while the yellow-throated
westerners were called "Audubon's warbler." The latter is a rare vagrant to our
region. Blizzards of yellow-rumped warblers occur during April-May migration,
typically far outnumbering other warblers. They are hardy and will overwinter,
eating berries such as the fruit of poison ivy. **Where found:** mature coniferous
and mixed woodlands; abundant throughout during migration, nesting in northern areas of the region; uncommon winter resident; more frequent southward.

American Redstart

Setophaga ruticilla

Length: 5 in
Wingspan: 8½ in

Hyperactive American redstarts chronically
flick their wings and fan their tails. It is thought
that by flashing the bright orange or yellow spots in their
plumage, they flush insects from the foliage. A broad bill and
rictal bristles (the short, whisker-like feathers around its mouth) help it
capture insects in the manner of a flycatcher. Females and first-year males have the
orange marks replaced with yellow, so if a "yellowstart" is seen singing, it is a young
male. **Where found:** dense shrubby understory of deciduous woodlands, often near
water; common throughout during summer and migration.

Ovenbird

Seiurus aurocapilla

Length: 6 in
Wingspan: 9½ in

Ovenbirds get their name from the shape of their nests, which resemble old-fashioned Dutch ovens. Finding an expertly concealed nest on the forest floor is nearly impossible, but hearing this bird is easy. Issuing a loud *tea-CHER tea-CHER tea-CHER* song that ascends in volume, ovenbirds are conspicuous singers. Ovenbirds are unusual in the warbler world: they are primarily ground feeders and walk about poking through leaf litter for food. **Where found:** undisturbed, mature forests, often with little understory; common throughout during summer and migration.

Common Yellowthroat

Geothlypis trichas

Length: 5 in
Wingspan: 7 in

The loud *witchity witchity witchity* song bursting from the cattails gives away this skulker. These little masked bandits are probably our most common breeding warblers, reaching peak numbers in wetlands and damp overgrown fields. They have wren-like curiosity and you can coax them into view by making squeaking or "pishing" sounds. Females can be confusing but share the male's big-headed, slender-bodied, long-legged dimensions. Surprisingly hardy, common yellowthroats occasionally linger well into winter in milder years. **Where found:** wetlands, riparian areas, wet, overgrown meadows; common and widespread throughout during summer and migration.

Scarlet Tanager

Piranga olivacea

Length: 7 in
Wingspan: 11½ in

Many people have become interested in birds after stumbling across one of these stunners. Almost shocking in appearance, a male scarlet tanager glows neon red, its scarlet contrasting with shiny black wings and tail. Tanagers spend most of their time high in the forest canopy, thus knowing their song helps tremendously in locating them. Their tune is a raspy, whistled series of phrases, sounding like an American robin with a sore throat. Most winter in the jungles of South America. **Where found:** dense, mature forest; common throughout during summer and migration.

Eastern Towhee

Pipilo erythrophthalmus

Length: 7–8½ in
Wingspan: 10½ in

Towhees are large, colorful, chunky sparrows with long tails. These noisy birds are often heard before they are seen as they rustle about in dense undergrowth. They employ an unusual 2-footed shuffling technique to uncover food items. Eastern towhees have an easily learned song: a loud whistled *drink your teeee.* • Formerly the rufous-sided towhee, it was reclassified as separate from western birds in 1995, with the latter known as spotted towhee *(P. maculatus).* **Where found:** open woods, brushy fields, woodland borders, overgrown gardens and parks; common summer resident throughout; winters sparingly in north, more commonly southward.

American Tree Sparrow

Spizella arborea

Length: 6¼ in
Wingspan: 9½ in

These rufous-capped, spot-breasted sparrows are winter visitors to agricultural fields and backyard feeders, though their numbers fluctuate depending on the year and location. • Not actually tree dwellers, American tree sparrows are birds of treeless fields and semi-open, shrubby habitats. They breed at or above the treeline at northern latitudes, then return to weedy fields in the northern states and southern Canada to overwinter. **Where found:** brushy thickets, semi-open fields, especially fields filled with goldenrod and other prolific seed producers; common winter resident throughout and frequent feeder visitor.

Song Sparrow

Melospiza melodia

Length: 6–7 in
Wingspan: 8 in

Our most common and adaptable sparrow, ubiquitous song sparrows will fill your backyard with one of the most beautiful songs of any bird; a bright, variable series of clear notes and trills. • Margaret Morse Nice of Columbus, Ohio, studied this species extensively and published groundbreaking research on song sparrows in the 1930s and 40s, a time when the role of women in biology was largely non-existent. • The song sparrow may be identified by its bold, central breast spot and its long, rounded tail, which is conspicuous as the bird is flying away. **Where found:** shrublands, riparian thickets, suburban gardens, forest openings, fields; common year-round throughout.

White-throated Sparrow

Zonotrichia albicollis

Length: 6½–7½ in
Wingspan: 9 in

White-throated sparrows sing in a distinctive, somewhat mournful minor key: a clear whistled *Old Sam Peabody, Peabody, Peabody* very characteristic of boreal forests. • Large numbers of white-throated sparrows pass through in migration, and many overwinter. They are unique among sparrows in that there are two color morphs: one has black and white stripes on the head; the other has brown and tan stripes. So, a duller tan-colored bird is not necessarily a female, nor is a bright white-striped bird always a male. **Where found:** coniferous and mixed forests; common migrant throughout and often found in winter; breeds in northern Great Lakes region, rarely southward.

Dark-eyed Junco

Junco hyemalis

Length: 6–7 in
Wingspan: 9 in

Sometimes called "snowbirds," juncos are familiar to many people as wintertime visitors to backyard feeders. This songbird is one of North America's most abundant, with a total population estimated at 630 million. When flushed, dark-eyed juncos flash prominent white outer tail feathers. These feathers may serve as "lures" for raptors; a pursuing hawk fixates on the white flashes and will grab only a few tail feathers, enabling the junco to escape. • Five closely related subspecies occur in North America. **Where found:** breeds in northern boreal forests, more commonly northward; abundant in winter and migration throughout.

Northern Cardinal

Cardinalis cardinalis

Length: 8–9 in
Wingspan: 12 in

One of the most popular and widely recognized eastern North American birds, the Northern cardinal is the state bird of seven states, including Illinois, Indiana and Ohio. It is a southerner that has continued to expand northward over the last century. • Cardinals maintain strong pair bonds. Some couples sing to each other year-round, while others join loose flocks, re-establishing pair bonds in spring during a "courtship feeding": a male will offer a seed to the female, which she then accepts and eats. **Where found:** woodland edges, thickets, backyards, parks; common year-round throughout.

Rose-breasted Grosbeak

Pheucticus ludovicianus

Length: 7–8½ in
Wingspan: 12½ in

The rose-breasted grosbeak sounds like a robin that has taken singing lessons. Its call note is a squeaky sound reminiscent of a sneaker on a basketball court. Listen for grosbeaks to find them—they remain high in leafy canopies and are rather sluggish. Males have beautiful black-and-white plumage and bold, inverted "V" of crimson-pink on the breast. Females are muted and resemble big sparrows, but are unusual for songbirds in that they also sing. • Rose-breasted grosbeaks visit bird feeders and are increasingly seen in backyards. **Where found:** deciduous and mixed forests; fairly common migrant and summer breeder throughout.

Indigo Bunting

Passerina cyanea

Length: 5½ in
Wingspan: 8 in

These abundant birds often sing from roadside wires looking like small black birds. But catch one in good light and the vivid electric-blue males will knock your socks off, looking every inch the tropical exotic—which they are. Indigo buntings spend more time wintering in the Caribbean and Central America than with us. • Males are persistent singers, vocalizing throughout the hottest summer days. Females look like plain brown sparrows. **Where found:** deciduous forests, woodland edges, agricultural areas with fencerows, orchards, shrubby fields; common during spring and summer.

Bobolink

Dolichonyx oryzivorus

Length: 6–8 in
Wingspan: 11½ in

William Cullen Bryant wrote "*Bob-o-link, bob-o-link, Spink, spank, spink*" in his poem "Robert of Lincoln." Small wonder this beautiful blackbird inspired the poet—bobolinks enrich a meadow like few others. Males deliver their bubbly, banjo-like twangs on the wing, and large numbers will occupy favored fields. • Most bobolinks winter in Argentina, a round trip of 12,000 miles! One banded female made the round trip 9 times during her lifetime, the equivalent of circling the Earth at the equator 4 times! **Where found:** prairies, hayfields, grassy fields; locally common throughout.

Red-winged Blackbird

Agelaius phoeniceus

Length: 7½–9 in
Wingspan: 13 in

This is one of North America's most abundant birds. The stunning-looking males court females by thrusting their wings forward to flare their brilliant scarlet-orange epaulets. • Males may have 15 females in their territory. • True harbingers of spring, they make loud, raspy *konk-a-ree* calls that can be heard by late February. In late fall, flocks numbering into the tens of thousands can form. **Where found:** cattail marshes, wet meadows, ditches, agricultural areas, overgrown fields; abundant breeder throughout; overwinters in varying numbers throughout, more commonly southward.

Eastern Meadowlark

Sturnella magna

Length: 9–9½ in
Wingspan: 14 in

The clear, ringing, whistled songs of eastern meadowlarks sound like *Spring of the Year!* and are characteristic of grasslands and fields. From above, meadowlarks blend with the vegetation with their muted, somber hues of speckled brown. From below, their striking, lemon-yellow breast is struck across with a bold, black chevron. When flushed, meadowlarks reveal conspicuous, white outer tail feathers, and they fly with distinctive stiff, shallow wingbeats. **Where found:** grassy meadows, roadsides, pastures, old fields, agricultural areas; common summer resident throughout in appropriate habitat; winters in variable numbers, more commonly southward.

Common Grackle

Quiscalus quiscula

Length: 11–13½ in
Wingspan: 17 in

Our largest blackbirds, common grackles are abundant and are seen in numbers on every outing. Although not popular owing to their aggressive bullying at the feeder, males are striking birds with a colorful iridescence that gleams in sunlight. Farmers detest grackles because they pull up new corn shoots. • Grackles form enormous roosts in fall and winter with other blackbirds and European starlings; some number into the hundreds of thousands. **Where found:** nearly all habitats, especially in open to semi-open areas; abundant breeder throughout; winters irregularly, more commonly southward.

Brown-headed Cowbird

Molothrus ater

Length: 6–8 in
Wingspan: 12 in

Cowbirds are often reviled as nest parasites: they lay their eggs in other birds' nests and are known to parasitize more than 140 bird species. Upon hatching, baby cowbirds out-compete the host's young, leading to nest failure. This habit evolved with the birds' association with nomadic bison herds—cowbirds were not in one place long enough to tend their own nests. Today, cowbirds haven't forgotten their roots and still commonly forage around cattle. **Where found:** agricultural and residential areas, woodland edges, now nearly ubiquitous; common summer resident throughout; winters irregularly, more commonly southward.

Baltimore Oriole

Icterus galbula

Length: 7–8 in
Wingspan: 11½ in

The clear, flute-like whistles of this tropical blackbird are common sounds where large trees are found, even in suburbia. Even a crude whistled imitation can send the male oriole rocketing down to investigate. Baltimore orioles make interesting hanging, pouch-like nests woven of plant fibers, which become conspicuous once the leaves have fallen. Formerly associated with mature American elms, orioles have shifted to eastern cottonwoods, Dutch Elm Disease having largely eliminated large elms. **Where found:** open deciduous and mixed forests, particularly riparian woodlands around large eastern cottonwoods; common summer resident throughout.

Purple Finch

Carpodacus purpureus

Length: 5–6 in
Wingspan: 10 in

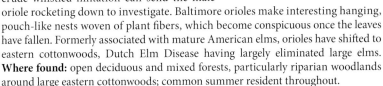

Male purple finches are more raspberry red than purple. They are often confused with house finches, but the latter is more reddish and prominently streaked below. Female purple finches have a bolder eyeline and face pattern than do female house finches. • Purple finches are attracted to sunflower seeds; large numbers can be lured to feeders in winter. However, during some winters many more move south than in other years. **Where found:** coniferous and mixed forest; becoming a more common breeder northward; winter resident in variable numbers throughout.

House Finch

Carpodacus mexicanus

Length: 5–6 in
Wingspan: 9½ in

A native to western North America, house finches were cage birds released in small numbers in New York City in 1940. They colonized much of eastern North America and are now abundant in many areas. House finches are especially common in suburbia and around dwellings. Occasionally, yellowish or pinkish males are seen; this color variation results from the amount of carotenoid pigments available in their food. **Where found:** cities, towns, agricultural areas; common year-round throughout.

American Goldfinch

Carduelis tristis

Length: 4½–5 in
Wingspan: 9 in

If you want "wild canaries," put up a thistle feeder—these seeds are irresistible to goldfinches. • Few birds have as conspicuous a molt as male American goldfinches; their drab winter plumage miraculously changes to brilliant yellow in April. • Adaptive and opportunistic, goldfinches exploit all open habitats and are one of our most abundant native birds. They often do not begin nesting until mid-summer, when the down of ripened thistles and other sunflower family members is available for nest construction. **Where found:** weedy fields, agricultural areas, parks, gardens, suburbia; nearly ubiquitous; abundant year-round throughout.

House Sparrow

Passer domesticus

Length: 5½–6½ in
Wingspan: 9½ in

House sparrows depend completely on humans and our habitations, and will rarely be seen far from dwellings or structures. This species was introduced to North America in the 1850s in an ill-advised attempt to control insect pests. They often nest in cavities and aggressively displace native species such as eastern bluebirds. Resilient and adaptable, populations of house sparrows can even live in large box stores where they forage among the aisles. Although house sparrows are still abundant, evidence suggests that they are in decline. **Where found:** any human environment; generally abundant year-round throughout.

AMPHIBIANS & REPTILES

Amphibians and reptiles are commonly referred to as cold-blooded. They lack the ability to generate their internal body heat, but are not necessarily cold-blooded. These animals are ectothermic or poikilothermic, meaning that the temperature of the surrounding environment governs their body temperature. The animal will obtain heat from sunlight and from warm rocks, logs and earth. Amphibians and reptiles hibernate in winter in cold regions; some species of reptiles aestivate (are dormant during hot or dry periods) in summer in hot regions. Both amphibians and reptiles molt (shed their skins) as they grow.

Amphibians are smooth skinned and most live in moist habitats. They are represented by the salamanders, frogs and toads. These species typically lay eggs lacking shells in jelly-like masses in water. The eggs hatch into gilled larvae (larvae of frogs and toads are called tadpoles), which later metamorphose into adults with lungs and legs. Amphibians can regenerate their skin and sometimes even entire limbs. Male and female amphibians often differ in size and color, and males may have other specialized features when sexually mature, such as the vocal sacs in many frogs and toads.

Reptiles are mostly terrestrial vertebrates with scaly skin. In this guide, the representatives are turtles, skinks and snakes. Most reptiles lay eggs buried in loose soil, but some snakes and lizards give birth to live young. Reptiles do not have a larval stage.

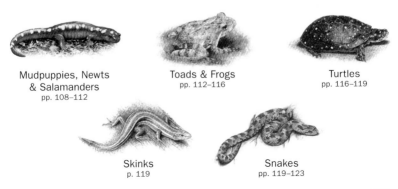

Mudpuppies, Newts
& Salamanders
pp. 108–112

Toads & Frogs
pp. 112–116

Turtles
pp. 116–119

Skinks
p. 119

Snakes
pp. 119–123

Handling Amphibians and Reptiles

To safely handle amphibians and reptiles, make sure your hands are wet and all lotion or bug spray has been washed off. Observe small frogs and salamanders through a water-filled, clear plastic bag to avoid drying out their skin and to reduce stress levels. For larger species, ensure their entire body is supported. Grasp a large frog's thighs with one hand and support its body with the other hand. Pick up a snake at both ends. Do not handle venomous snakes at all. Also be aware that some large reptiles, such as snapping turtles and northern water snakes, are by nature ill-tempered and can inflict unpleasant bites. These species, and wild animals in general, are best left uncaught and admired from a respectable distance. If you do capture one, be sure to return it to the exact spot from where you got it.

Mudpuppy

Necturus maculosus

Length: to 19 in

These huge salamanders inhabit deep, muddy water and are largely nocturnal; thus they are seldom seen. They can go deep; an especially intrepid "water-dog" was caught 90 ft down in a lake near Green Bay, Wisconsin. Unlike other salamanders, mudpuppies keep their feathery external gills throughout their adult lives. These bottom-dwellers spend much of their time eating aquatic insects, crayfish and small fish or hiding under debris on the bottom of lakes and streams. **Where found:** river and lake bottoms; locally common year-round throughout.

Red-spotted Newt

Notophthalmus viridescens

Length: 2½–5 in

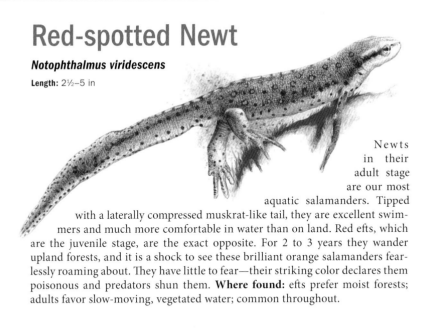

Newts in their adult stage are our most aquatic salamanders. Tipped with a laterally compressed muskrat-like tail, they are excellent swimmers and much more comfortable in water than on land. Red efts, which are the juvenile stage, are the exact opposite. For 2 to 3 years they wander upland forests, and it is a shock to see these brilliant orange salamanders fearlessly roaming about. They have little to fear—their striking color declares them poisonous and predators shun them. **Where found:** efts prefer moist forests; adults favor slow-moving, vegetated water; common throughout.

Blue-spotted Salamander

Ambystoma laterale

Length: 4–6 in

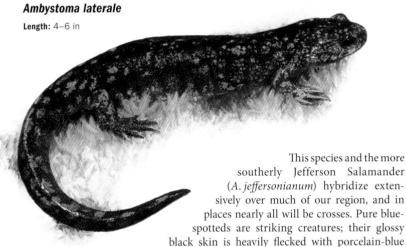

This species and the more southerly Jefferson Salamander (*A. jeffersonianum*) hybridize extensively over much of our region, and in places nearly all will be crosses. Pure blue-spotteds are striking creatures; their glossy black skin is heavily flecked with porcelain-blue spots. This secretive amphibian is one of 6 mole salamander species in our area. They are so named because most of their life is lived subterraneously, and they rarely venture above ground. **Where found:** moist deciduous forests near fish-free wetlands; hibernates underground; uncommon throughout.

Smallmouth Salamander

Ambystoma texanum

Length: 4½–5½ in

Mole salamander (genus *Ambystoma*) biomass may exceed all other amphibians combined in a given area, but few people ever see these secretive but fascinating animals. They live underground, consuming earthworms and other invertebrates, occasionally wandering about on rainy nights. With the first warm spring rains, Ambystomids stage a mass migration to favored breeding pools, where they sometimes swarm by the hundreds, mating and laying eggs. At this season, large numbers may sometimes be encountered crossing roads or purposefully marching overland. **Where found:** swamps, wet woods, river bottoms; congregates in breeding pools in early spring; southern Great Lakes, barely reaching MI.

Spotted Salamander

Ambystoma maculatum

Length: 5–8 in

This handsome amphibian is one of our most striking salamanders, and first-time viewers will be shocked by the canary-yellow round spots. • A visit to their breeding pools in late February or early March can produce hundreds, gathered in groups to mate. Females lay jelly-like clumps of up to 300 eggs that hatch in about 2 weeks. Juveniles remain in the breeding ponds until August, then crawl onto dry land and burrow into the forest floor. • The spotted salamander may live for over 30 years. **Where found:** forested regions near wetlands; hibernates underground; abundant throughout; common from MI south and east, including Ohio Valley and southern Great Lakes basin.

Eastern Tiger Salamander

Ambystoma tigrinum

Length: 7–11 in

These whoppers can reach 1 ft in length, and resemble mini komodo dragons as they swagger along. Tiger salamanders are richly patterned in dull yellow blotches that contrast with their grayish-black ground color. They prefer more open landscapes than other mole salamanders and are often found far from woods or water during early spring migrations. They lay their eggs in shallow pools and even farm ponds, but will vanish if fish are introduced. Most salamanders require fishless ponds—fish are voracious predators that quickly consume amphibian eggs and young. **Where found:** farms, prairies, wet woods near water; hibernates underground; common throughout western half of region, becoming more frequent westward.

110

Northern Two-lined Salamander

Eurycea bislineata

Length: 2½–4 in

You can often find this species by turning over flat rocks at the edge of rocky streams. Northern two-lined salamanders are lungless salamanders, which are generally smaller, slimmer and have shorter legs than mole salmanders. Adults have no lungs but breathe through their skin. Handling a salamander can dry its skin and cause suffocation, so observe them through a water-filled, clear plastic bag. • This salamander's sleek shape allows it to swim smoothly through fast-moving water. To identify it, look for 2 dark lines running down the adult's yellow or golden back. **Where found:** fast-moving streams, adjacent woodlands; hibernates under streambeds; throughout eastern Great Lakes basin.

Four-toed Salamander

Hemidactylium scutatum

Length: 2–3½ in

Four-toed salamanders are more habitat-specific than many other salamanders and have a scattered and spotty distribution. They prefer boggy sites or woodland pools with rotting, moss-covered logs. Females lay eggs under a loose wrap of moss and then remain to guard them from predators. This species has only 4 toes on its hind feet (except for the mudpuppy, our other species have 5 toes) and a unique white belly covered with black spots. The tail base is constricted; it breaks off at this point if grabbed by a predator. **Where found:** sphagnum bogs, moist forests; hibernates under soil; uncommon and scattered throughout.

Redback Salamander

Plethodon cinereus

Length: 2¼–4 in

You can often find this amazingly abundant species by turning rotting logs and rocks in woodlands. Sometimes dozens can be found in short order. Two variable color forms occur: the typical red-backed form and a less common lead-backed (gray) form. Some redbacks have black dots or a black line running down the centre of their backs. • This salamander catches aphids, worms and other small invertebrates by thrusting out its sticky tongue. **Where found:** moist, forested areas; hibernates communally in underground burrows; abundant throughout, but scarce in IL and southern MN.

Northern Dusky Salamander

Desmognathus fuscus

Length: 2½–4½ in

To locate one of these secretive sala-manders, find a clean stream flowing through woodlands and look under stones and logs. Although not boldly marked, this rather plain salamander can be identified by the pale line that extends down and back from the eye to the rear of the mouth. Dusky Salamanders also have rear legs that are much larger than the front legs. If you see one, look quick! It is fast and slippery as an eel, and jumps well to boot. **Where found:** wooded streams, springs and seeps; NY, PA and the eastern half of OH.

American Toad

Anaxyrus americanus

Length: 2–4 in

One of spring's great amphibian spectacles is the mass chorus of trilling American toads. For about a month, these warty songsters deliver loud, lengthy, monotonous but semi-musical trills from almost any patch of water. Left in their wake are long strings of egg masses that soon hatch tiny black tadpoles. We are not likely to bite into a toad, but dogs sometimes aren't so wise—toads have parotoid glands behind the eyes that contain a toxin that can sicken predators. **Where found:** various habitats, including forests, meadows, suburban backyards, gardens; hibernates under soil; common throughout.

Fowler's Toad

Anaxyrus fowleri

Length: 2½–4 in

This species resembles the American toad but its "song" is completely different. It sounds like a short, terror-stricken scream; an explosive nasal *waaaahhh!* given by breeding males. • Fowler's toads like sandy soils, and will often hibernate in groups, burrowing up to 1 ft underground. • This species has a marbled pattern; 3 or more warts in the larger, dark blotches; and a pale, unmarked belly, often with a single belly spot. • Fowler's toad sometimes hybridizes with the American toad. **Where found:** sandy beaches, meadows, forests; hibernates underground; occurs along eastern shores of Lake Michigan and throughout much of southern Great Lakes region.

Gray Treefrog
Hyla versicolor
Length: 2½ in

Many people have heard this diminutive tree dweller, but probably thought the sound came from a bird. Quite arboreal, gray treefrogs frequently deliver a loud, rather coarse trill from high in the foliage that carries some distance. Tiny suction-cup grippers on their toes allow for Spiderman-like climbing ability. Gray treefrogs can change color like chameleons to perfectly match their background, morphing from a rather bright gray-green to dull pearly-gray. • Treefrogs breed in vegetated ponds, depositing clumps of floating eggs. **Where found:** woodlands near water; hibernates under soil or leaves; common throughout.

Blanchard's Cricket Frog
Acris crepitans blanchardi
Length: ¾–1½ in

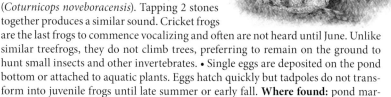

Cricket frogs are most easily detected by their song: a loud, metallic series of rapid clicking notes remarkably similar to the yellow rail (*Coturnicops noveboracensis*). Tapping 2 stones together produces a similar sound. Cricket frogs are the last frogs to commence vocalizing and often are not heard until June. Unlike similar treefrogs, they do not climb trees, preferring to remain on the ground to hunt small insects and other invertebrates. • Single eggs are deposited on the pond bottom or attached to aquatic plants. Eggs hatch quickly but tadpoles do not transform into juvenile frogs until late summer or early fall. **Where found:** pond margins, marshes, wet meadows; southern Great Lakes from western OH west.

Northern Spring Peeper
Pseudacris crucifer
Length: 1½ in

A distinctive sound of early spring is the loud, bird-like peeps of this tiny frog. It is amazing how loud their calls are; standing amidst a pack of peepers chorusing in a wetland will almost cause your ears to hurt. Spring peepers begin calling and mating as soon as ice thaws from ponds and wetlands, and they are only conspicuous at this time. For much of the rest of the year, they forage in low shrubs and leaf litter, and are much less likely to be detected. Peepers are easily identified by the dark, X-shaped mark on their tan to gray backs. **Where found:** forest floors near water; hibernates under leaf litter; common throughout.

Western Chorus Frog

Pseudacris triseriata

Length: ¾–1½ in

In early spring, you can hear chorus frogs calling from wetlands, often along with spring peepers. The chorus frog's commonly heard sound resembles the sound made by running a finger down the teeth of a comb—but projected through a stack of Marshall amps. • In northern Minnesota and Wisconsin, the western chorus is replaced by the similar-looking boreal chorus frog (*P. maculata*). Both these tiny frogs have a gray-brown body, a dark eye stripe and 3 darker, sometimes broken, stripes running along their backs. **Where found:** breeds in ponds, marshes, ephemeral water bodies; hibernates under leaf litter; common throughout except northeastern WI and northern MN.

Wood Frog

Lithobates sylvatica

Length: 1½–2¾ in

Wood frogs are amphibians with antifreeze. At below-zero temperatures, their heart rate, blood flow and breathing stop, turning them into froggy ice cubes. Special compounds, mainly glucose, allow them to survive partial freezing and thawing of their tissues. Thus, they are able to range north of the Arctic Circle, further north than any amphibian. In early spring, when ice still fringes woodland pools, vernal wetlands explode to life as wood frogs invade to mate and lay eggs. Their collective calls sound like distant ducks quacking. **Where found:** moist woodlands, sometimes far from water; common throughout.

Northern Leopard Frog

Lithobates pipiens

Length: 3–4 in

Leopard frogs are often seen when flushed from grass in wet meadows or near wetlands. But you won't see much—just a froggy blur shooting off in huge, zigzagging bounds. With a bit of patience, the leaper can usually be tracked down and admired. It's easy to see where the name comes from: these frogs are patterned with very distinctive leopard-like spots. They are often heard, too, but it's likely that most people don't recognize the calls as a frog. They emit a curious low snoring sound, sometimes even delivered under water. **Where found:** in summer in meadows, fields, marshes; hibernates on lake bottoms; common but possibly declining throughout.

Pickerel Frog

Lithobates palustris

Length: 2–3½ in

This species resembles the leopard frog, but differs in its rectangle-shaped spots, overall brownish rather than green color, and bright yellow under the hind legs. Pickerel frogs also inhabit cooler waters such as brooks and streams, fens and other springy places. In general, leopards prefer open, marshy haunts while pickerels favor cooler, forested places. • Toxic skin secretions cause many predators to avoid this species, and it is said that these toxins are potent enough to kill other frogs kept in the same aquarium with a pickerel frog. **Where found:** throughout Great Lakes region but generally uncommon and local; absent from northern OH, IL, WI; special concern in MN.

Green Frog

Lithobates clamitans

Length: 2½–3½ in

The explosive, nasal, banjo-like twangs of the green frog are one of our most characteristic wetland sounds. And when flushed from the water's edge, the green frog utters a high-pitched *eek!* as it leaps in. • This species is the most widespread, abundant frog in the Great Lakes region and might be encountered anywhere there is water. As with bullfrogs, males are told from females by the size of the tympanic membrane—the large round disk behind the eye. In males it is much larger than the eye; in females, about the same size as the eye. **Where found:** adults in or near permanent water; hibernates underwater; common throughout.

Mink Frog

Lithobates septentrionalis

Length: 2–3 in

This species looks somewhat like a leopard frog with spots that got wet and ran together before the ink could dry. Blotchy-patterned mink frogs smell like mink (like rotting onions). • This pungent frog prefers ponds full of lily pads to use for hunting, cover and escape. Try searching for mink frogs after dark, as they are primarily nocturnal and will usually sit motionless under a flashlight beam. • The male's raspy metallic *tuk tuk tuk* breeding call is heard mostly in spring. **Where found:** adults in or near permanent water with abundant lilypads or vegetation; locally common in northernmost Great Lakes region.

American Bullfrog

Lithobates catesbeiana

Length: 4–6 in

The American bullfrog is our largest frog—whoppers can tape out at 8 in. Bullfrogs are the primary source of frog legs, a delicacy for some. • This abundant species is probably far more common now than historically. Voracious predators, they snap up other frogs, small snakes and even birds and mice! Their loud *jug-a-rum* call is easily identified and can carry up to a mile across open water. Females lay large, floating mats of 8000 to 25,000 eggs, a reason this species is so common. **Where found:** large, permanent water bodies with cover; hibernates underwater; common throughout.

Common Snapping Turtle

Chelydra serpentina

Length: up to 19 in

Mess with one of these prehistoric-looking beasts when it's on land and you'll quickly learn how it got its name. Quicker than Ali could throw a jab, the hostile turtle lunges its neck out a surprising distance and snaps menacingly with powerful jaws. Tales of them snapping broomsticks are greatly exaggerated but snappers can inflict a nasty bite. • This turtle spends most of its time underwater, walking along lake or pond bottoms eating weeds and scavenging for carrion. In early summer, females emerge on land to seek sites to bury their white, spherical eggs (our other turtles lay oval eggs). **Where found:** lakes, ponds, marshes; common throughout.

Common Musk Turtle

Sternotherus odoratus

Length: 3–5½ in

Aggressive and feisty, this little turtle won't hesitate to bite and can extend its rubbery neck backward nearly to its hind legs. Another name for the musk turtle is "stinkpot"; when grabbed, it expels a nasty, yellowish liquid from glands under the shell. • This turtle inhabits still, shallow water bodies, walking along the bottom in search of aquatic invertebrates and carrion or basking at the water's surface. • A captive musk turtle lived for 55 years. **Where found:** common but perhaps declining; Mississippi River and southeastern WI, southern MI, IN, OH and lower Great Lakes basin.

Painted Turtle

Chrysemys picta

Length: 5–9 in

This species is typically the most common turtle in our region. Often, most of the turtles basking on a log will be painteds—favored logs may harbor dozens of these showy little turtles. • These turtles may live for up to 40 years. • Two subspecies occur within the Great Lakes region. The midland painted turtle has a dark green or black carapace with yellow, orange or red underside borders. The larger western painted turtle has an olive green carapace with orange or red underside borders. **Where found:** marshes, ponds, lakes, slow-flowing streams; *midland*: common in MI, IL and east; *western*: common in MN, WI.

Northern Map Turtle

Graptemys geographica

Length: Female: to 11 in; Male: 5–6 in

Fine, pale lines give this turtle's shell the look of a topographical map. • The females are larger and have powerful jaws capable of cracking open freshwater mussels, a staple food. The smaller males' less powerful mandibles can easily handle the less sturdy shells of snails. • These inveterate baskers may pile on each other, forming stacks of sleepy reptiles on basking logs. • Two other map turtles are found in southern Minnesota and Wisconsin along the Mississippi River: the locally common Ouachita map turtle (*G. ouachitensis)* and the rare false map turtle (*G. pseudogeographica*). **Where found:** large lakes and rivers; locally common throughout but absent from northern MN, WI, MI.

Blanding's Turtle

Emydoidea blandingii

Length: 6–10½ in

Probably no turtle is more intimately associated with the Great Lakes than Blanding's turtle; most populations are found along the lakes. Bring your binoculars to view turtles: this species is fond of basking on logs, and can be identified from afar by the tall domed shell and especially by the bright yellow throat. • The tall, top-heavy shell makes the Blanding's turtle a poor swimmer. It prefers to walk along pond bottoms, feeding on aquatic invertebrates and vegetation. **Where found:** ponds, marshes, lake margins with aquatic vegetation, sometimes swamp woods; uncommon to rare throughout; absent from northern MN, WI.

Spotted Turtle

Clemmys guttata

Length: 4–5 in

This species is our smallest turtle and one of the most secretive and habitat-specific. It primarily inhabits peatlands such as bogs and fens, often foraging out of sight under bog mats or sedge duff. If luck brings one across your path, you'll admire a striking black turtle sprinkled with canary yellow dots. • Spotted turtles hibernate communally in favored burrows known as hibernacula; over a dozen might occupy one of these dens. Habitat loss has greatly reduced many populations of this charming little turtle. **Where found:** bogs, fens and wet prairies; sometimes beaver ponds and other high-quality wetlands; southern MI and lower Great Lakes basin.

Wood Turtle

Clemmys insculpta

Length: 5–9 in

We do not often think of turtles as arboreal, but wood turtles are excellent climbers. They have been known to scale tall chain-link fences! • The upper shell, or carapace, of this species is quite striking. Each scute, or individual plate, extends upward owing to the growth of concentric ridges, creating an irregular shell as if made from tiny pyramids. • Wood turtles feed mainly on berries and leaves. As a result, they spend more time on land than other turtles. • Wood turtles have an orange neck and feet. Their undersides are yellow with black markings. **Where found:** rivers, streams, meadows, wooded areas; usually hibernates on stream bottom, occasionally buries into soil on land; throughout most of region, but rather scattered distribution and rare in some areas.

Spiny Softshell Turtle

Apalone spinifera

Length: 9–18 in

Easily our most graceful turtle, this dinner plate-sized reptile effortlessly courses about under water with its large, paddle-like feet. It uses its tubular snout like a snorkel, extending it above the surface to breathe. • Pancake-shaped and leathery, the carapaces of softshells are quite unlike the hard armor of other turtles. • Spiny softshells feed on molluscs, fish and crustaceans. Look for them basking on muddy shores, but you won't see them for long. Hyper-alert and very wary, softshells bolt into the water at the first sign of intruders. **Where found:** large lakes, rivers; common from MI south and east to lower Great Lakes.

Eastern Box Turtle

Terrapene carolina

Length: 5–8 in

Help a box turtle cross a road by placing it off
the road on the side it was headed for. You may
save a fascinating little beast documented to live
for over 100 years! • Box turtles "box themselves in"
by pulling in their limbs and head, then tightly closing the shell. Their lower shell,
or plastron, is hinged and can be brought up securely against the domed carapace to
exclude predators. • It is thought that Native peoples largely eliminated box turtles
from much of the East by overharvesting for ceremonial purposes. Today, many are
caught for the pet trade. **Where found:** varied habitats from wooded wetlands to
fields; hibernates in soil; common but declining; found east of the Mississippi River
north to the lower Great Lakes; absent from northern IL and WI.

Five-lined Skink

Eumeces fasciatus

Length: 5–8½ in

Many people are surprised that a
lizard roams the Great Lakes landscape. Often seen are young skinks, with
conspicuous bright blue tails that draw the eye of predators. When seized,
the tail snaps free, allowing the skink to escape. The tail eventually regenerates.
Quick and secretive, skinks are best observed as they bask in the sun. With
patience, close approaches can be made. **Where found:** wooded habitats with
ground cover; cut-over woods with lots of stumps, rocky areas, railroad rights-
of-way, sometimes damp woods; generally uncommon to rare and probably
declining; throughout all but northernmost regions.

Eastern Garter Snake

Thamnophis sirtalis

Length: 18–26 in (exceptional individuals
can be over 3 ft)

This species is probably our most
commonly encountered snake,
and likely the most common serpent
in our region. Although somewhat variable, garters are normally prominently
striped with alternating bands of yellow and dark. Their name comes from the
longitudinally striped pattern, suggestive of garters once used to support socks.
Garter snakes are efficient hunters of amphibians, fish, small mammals, slugs and
leeches. • A single female can have 3 to 83 live young in a single litter. **Where found:**
all manner of habitats; meadows, marshes, gardens, suburban and urban areas;
common throughout.

Northern Ribbon Snake

Thamnophis sauritus septentrionalis

Length: 18–26 in

Graceful of movement and sleek of body, ribbon snakes are among our most beautiful reptiles. Their blackish bodies are adorned with 3 bright yellow stripes running from head to tail, and a crescent moon-shaped marking in front of each eye. They resemble garter snakes but are much more slender and whip-like. • Ribbon snakes are often found in or near water, basking on logs or hunting for prey. They feed on fish, frogs and terrestrial invertebrates. • These snakes mate in spring and give birth to live young. **Where found:** wet meadows, wetlands, weedy lakeshores, creeks; locally common east of Lake Michigan.

Northern Water Snake

Nerodia sipedon

Length: 25–45 in

Almost always found near water, this species is our most common "water snake." Northern water snakes are better admired from afar; they bite fiercely and expel an unpleasant musk from glands near the tail. • These thick-bodied snakes are variable in color and pattern. The background ranges from gray to brown, with darker bands near the head, followed by alternating back and side blotches. • Prey includes small vertebrates such as frogs and fish, and invertebrates. • The Lake Erie water snake, an endangered subspecies, is endemic to islands in Lake Erie. **Where found:** near or in water; hibernates underground; common throughout, but absent from northern MN.

Queen Snake

Regina septemvittata

Length: 15–24 in

Queen snakes are highly aquatic and are sometimes found basking in shrubs near the water's edge, alongside northern water snakes. Unlike water snakes, queen snakes are ordinarily docile and don't bite when handled. • They feed mainly on crayfish and reach peak abundance in sites where these crustaceons are common. They especially prefer newly molted crayfish that have not yet developed hardened shells. • Female queen snakes give birth to 7 to 15 live young in late summer. **Where found:** stream banks, small rivers, wetlands; uncommon; from IL east and south.

Northern Brown Snake

Storeria dekayi

Length: 9–13 in (occasionally to 19 in)

Small and beautiful, this common species
is one of the best snakes to introduce a
"newbie" to the wonderful world of serpents.
Brown snakes are gentle, easy to handle, and almost never
bite. Even if they did, their small jaws would cause no harm. They
often live in towns and cities, but can be hard to find. They are burrowers, digging
into leaf litter, or hiding under flat rocks and boards. Snails, slugs and earthworms are their main food items. • Snakes smell with their tongues, collecting
scents from the air and then interpreting them using a special organ located in their
mouths. **Where found:** various habitats, including suburban and urban sites; hides
under objects; common throughout but absent from northern WI, MN.

Smooth Green Snake

Liochlorophis vernalis

Length: 12–20 in

The smooth green snake is so gentle and beautiful
that even a person with ophidiophobia (fear of snakes)
might not mind it. Small, painted in exquisite hues of emerald and often washed
with a pale lemon color below, a smooth green snake will not bite even when
picked up. • Smooth green snakes' extraordinary color allows them to blend well
with the grasses in which they forage. Road-killed ones stand out—they quickly
turn blue upon death. • A number of female smooth green snakes may share
a single nesting site, where each female lays 3 to 12 eggs under rocks, in loose soil.
Groups sometimes hibernate in anthills. **Where found:** moist meadows, grasslands, prairies; found throughout but often localized.

Northern Ringneck Snake

Diadophis punctatus

Length: 10–15 in (occasionally to 24 in)

A more charming serpent could not be imagined,
and anyone's life will be enriched by experienc-
ing one firsthand. Docile ringneck snakes are
gorgeous; they have a shiny, blue-black ground
color that contrasts startlingly with a brilliant, orange-
yellow collar and underparts. • Mostly nocturnal, ringnecks hide during the day under
rocks and logs; turning over such objects is the way to find them. They are salamander
hunters; small woodland species like redback salamanders form the bulk of their diet.
Where found: a variety of woodlands, particularly where there are plenty of rocks and
logs; uncommon to locally abundant throughout most of the region.

Eastern Hognose Snake

Heterodon platirhinos

Length: 20–36 in (occasionally to 48 in)

An extraordinary actor, the eastern hognose snake is a master of the bluff. If threatened, it will hiss and expand its neck, giving it the look of a cobra. If this response fails to frighten, it will flip over and play dead, even lolling its tongue out the side of its mouth for effect. • This snake favors sandy soil and uses its upturned snout to dig for toads, its favorite prey. • It has dark blotches on a lighter background and distinctive large, dark patches on each side of the head. There is also a black-phase of hognose snake. **Where found:** open forests, meadows, especially where there is sandy soil; fairly common throughout; absent from northern MN, WI.

Eastern Milksnake

Lampropeltis triangulum

Length: 24–36 in (occasionally to 50 in)

The common name of this beautiful reptile is steeped in folklore. Because milksnakes frequently enter barns, it was assumed that they were milking the cows—which, of course, is absurd. They sometimes enter barns and old buildings because they are after mice and rats, an entirely beneficial role. They also eat frogs, bird eggs and invertebrates. • This aggressive snake will bite when handled and will shake the tip of its tail like a rattlesnake when threatened. • To identify a milksnake, look for a pale "Y" or "V" marking on the head and the bold pattern. **Where found:** forests, meadows, edge habitat, agricultural areas; common throughout.

Eastern Fox Snake

Elaphe gloydi

Length: 3–4½ ft (can reach 6 ft)

Eastern fox snakes are big and beautiful but are sometimes killed when mistaken for poisonous copperheads (*Agkistrodon contortrix*), which don't range into our region. Fox snakes are very docile and almost never bite, even when picked up. • The eastern fox snake was recently determined to be a separate species from the western fox snake (*E. vulpina*), which occurs in the western Great Lakes area (IN, IL and west). Easterns are most commonly found near the shorelines of Lakes Erie and Huron. They often hide in rocky riprap or shoreline woods. **Where found:** wetlands, forests, near human habitation; hibernates underground in hibernacula; uncommon in MI and northern OH.

Black Rat Snake

Elaphe obsoleta

Length: 3¾–6¼ ft (exceptional individuals reach 8⅓ ft)

An 8-ft long snake is an impressive sight, and some black rat snakes tape out to such extraordinary lengths. This species is our largest snake, but like most other snakes it is not normally aggressive and can be handled readily. • Rat snakes prey on many small animals, including birds, rodents, amphibians and other snakes. They are excellent climbers—often taking to the trees to raid bird nests, and commonly holing up in tree cavities. **Where found:** variable, from flat farmland to rocky hillside; locally common to rare throughout southern Great Lakes region.

Eastern Racer

Coluber constrictor

Length: 30–60 in

This snake is a real speedster—a racer at full tilt can briefly hit 12 mph! It is an active hunter, and will often take to trees and shrubs, especially if pursued. When alarmed, the racer sometimes vibrates its tail rapidly, creating a rattlesnake-like buzz. Corner one, and you'll find that it can be aggressive, sometimes rearing up like a cobra. • Two subspecies occur in our region, the northern black racer and the blue racer. The former ranges from eastern Lake Erie east, and the latter occurs westward throughout most of our region. **Where found:** open habitats including fields, prairies, forest edges, wetlands; common throughout except northern MN, WI, MI.

Eastern Massasauga

Sistrurus catenatus

Length: 18–30 in

Encountering a venomous snake in the Great Lakes region is unlikely; this small rattler is the only one that might be expected. Timber rattlesnakes (*Crotalus horridus*) are rare and local, and have been extirpated from nearly all former sites. Few bites and only one death from massasaugas have been reported in our region. The poison acts slowly, but all victims should be hospitalized. • Massasaugas are normally shy and retiring, and typically non-aggressive. However, they can become agitated, especially in hot weather, and will rattle their tail furiously, creating a loud buzz. **Where found:** wet prairies and fens, especially westward; bogs and swampy woods in eastern locales; sometimes ranges into drier forested habitats; generally rare and local throughout.

FISH

Fish are ectothermic vertebrates that live in the water, have streamlined bodies covered in scales, and possess fins and gills. A fundamental feature of fish is the serially repeated set of vertebrae and segmented muscles that allow the animal to move from side to side, propelling it through the water. A varying number of fins, depending on the species, further aid fish to swim and navigate. Most fish are oviparous and lay eggs that are fertilized externally. Eggs are either produced in vast quantities and scattered or they are laid in a spawning nest (redd) under rocks or logs. Parental care may be present in the defense of such a nest or territory. Spawning can involve migrating long distances from inland rivers where reproduction occurs, back to the open waters of the Great Lakes.

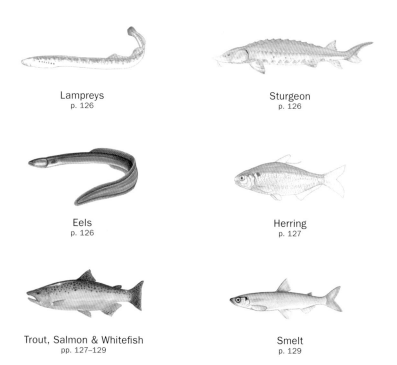

Lampreys
p. 126

Sturgeon
p. 126

Eels
p. 126

Herring
p. 127

Trout, Salmon & Whitefish
pp. 127–129

Smelt
p. 129

Pike
p. 129

Carp & Minnows
p. 130

Suckers
p. 130

Catfish
p. 131

Killifish
p. 131

Burbot
p. 132

Stickleback
p. 132

Sunfish & Bass
pp. 132–133

Walleye, Perch & Darters
pp. 133–134

Drums
p. 135

Gobies
p. 135

Sculpin
p. 135

Sea Lamprey

Petromyzon marinus

Length: 25–46 in

Like creatures from a cheap sci-fi horror flick, sea lampreys are long and eel-like. Their business end is capped with a ferocious sucker mouth like a vacuum cleaner with grinding teeth. The lamprey firmly attaches to a suitable host fish such as lake trout and whitefish, then rasps a hole into the fish and draws out vital liquids. These parasitic fish, native to oceans, gained access to the Great Lakes through the Welland Canal, first being detected in Lake Erie in 1921. • Sea lampreys spend much of their lives as larvae in Great Lake tributary rivers. After 4 to 6 years, the parasitic adults emerge and enter the lakes. **Where found:** Great Lakes and St. Lawrence River.

Lake Sturgeon

Acipenser fulvescens

Length: 2½–4¾ ft
(occasionally over
6½ ft)

For 100 million years, the lake sturgeon has nosed along lake bottoms, using the 4 barbels that surround its mouth to detect prey. This scaleless relic has 5 rows of hard plates called "scutes" running down its body. • Formerly abundant, it is now threatened by overharvesting of eggs for caviar, overfishing and habitat degradation. Recently, sturgeon numbers have been expanding. • Lake sturgeon live up to 80 years; individuals once grew to over 6 ft, making it the largest freshwater fish in the Great Lakes. **Where found:** large lakes and rivers; throughout. **Also known as:** black sturgeon, rock fish, bony sturgeon.

American Eel

Anguilla rostrata

Length: 12–35 in (maximum 60 in)

Historically, American eels migrated up the St. Lawrence to Lake Ontario, but the Welland Canal allowed them access to Lake Erie and beyond. Mature eels swim 2500 miles from Lake Ontario downstream to the Sargasso Sea in the Atlantic Ocean, where they spawn and likely die. Larvae drift with the Gulf Stream and eventually change into young eels and migrate back to the coastal streams of eastern North America, a journey that takes a year or more. **Where found:** Lake Ontario and tributaries; occasionally in lakes Erie, Huron and Superior.

Gizzard Shad

Dorosoma cepedianum

Length: 10 in (maximum 22½ in)

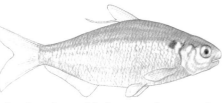

These schooling fish, known for skipping or leaping along the water, are an important and abundant forage fish for many larger species. Extremely prolific, shad produce several hundred thousand eggs per year. Outside their native range of eastern North America they are commonly stocked as forage fish for other introduced fishes such as walleye. • Enormous die-offs, which often occur in winter around warm water outlets of Great Lakes power plants, are caused by de-oxygenated water from temperature changes. **Where found:** large lakes and reservoirs; throughout. **Also known as:** skipjack, herring shad, herring.

Chinook Salmon

Oncorhynchus tshawytscha

Length: 12–40 in (landlocked fish)

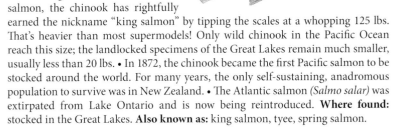

As the largest Pacific salmon, the chinook has rightfully earned the nickname "king salmon" by tipping the scales at a whopping 125 lbs. That's heavier than most supermodels! Only wild chinook in the Pacific Ocean reach this size; the landlocked specimens of the Great Lakes remain much smaller, usually less than 20 lbs. • In 1872, the chinook became the first Pacific salmon to be stocked around the world. For many years, the only self-sustaining, anadromous population to survive was in New Zealand. • The Atlantic salmon *(Salmo salar)* was extirpated from Lake Ontario and is now being reintroduced. **Where found:** stocked in the Great Lakes. **Also known as:** king salmon, tyee, spring salmon.

Rainbow Trout

Oncorhynchus mykiss

Length: to 45 in

Because of anglers' love of the rainbow trout, it has spread from western North America to six continents, becoming the most widely introduced species in the world. Its colorful appearance and spotted back and sides vary in hue with lifestyle and habitat. • Rainbow trout in streams are bottom feeders, but will rise to the surface to leap for a struggling insect. Fly fishermen love their spectacular jumps and fighting strength. **Where found:** cool, well-oxygenated waters; near swift currents in streams; introduced throughout in suitable habitat. **Also known as:** steelhead trout, redband trout, silver trout.

Brown Trout

Salmo trutta

Length: 7–14 in (reaches 40 in where indigenous)

The "brownie" was so much a part of European heritage that early settlers introduced "their" fish to North America and many other regions of the world. Many of the fish were either von Behr trout from Germany or Loch Leven trout from Scotland. Today, the populations are mixed and indistinguishable. • Brownies are drift feeders, preferring streams with cover and an intermediate water flow. They can handle warmer water temperatures and higher turbidity than other members of the trout family, so may be introduced to streams disturbed by logging or industrial activity. **Where found:** various water bodies; throughout.

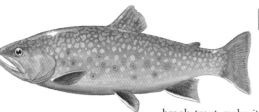

Brook Trout

Salvelinus fontinalis

Length: 6–12 in (maximum 33 in)

The unique patterns of the brook trout make it hard to confuse with any other species. The vermiculations, or "worm tracks," on their backs set these handsome fish apart from other fish. • The brook trout is actually a char, distinguishable from other char by the "jelly doughnuts" (red or yellow dots with blue halos) on its sides. Another fish with "jelly doughnuts," the brown trout, is a true trout and has a light body with black spots. • Native to eastern North America, brook trout were among the first fish introduced to other areas and have spread widely. **Where found:** cold, clear, slow-moving waters; clear shallow areas of lakes; sporadically throughout. **Also known as:** speckled trout, spotted trout, brook char.

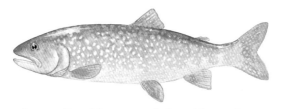

Lake Trout

Salvelinus namaycush

Length: 18–26 in (maximum 50 in)

Large, solitary lake trout prefer ice-cold water. In summer, they follow the retreat of colder water to the bottom of a lake, rarely making excursions into the warm surface layer. • Lake trout can reach old ages and large sizes. Large trout are often over 20 years old, with one granddaddy reaching 62 years old! • They can take 6 years or more to reach maturity and may spawn only once every 2 to 3 years, making recovery from overfishing difficult. • Lake trout are native to the Great Lakes region. **Where found:** usually in deep, cooler lakes; rare to uncommon throughout and sometimes only maintained by stocking. **Also known as:** laker, Great Lakes trout.

Lake Whitefish

Coregonus clupeaformis

Length: 16 in (maximum 25 in)

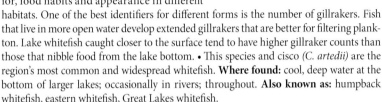

Lake whitefish is what biologists call a "plastic species":
some fish change their behav-
ior, food habits and appearance in different
habitats. One of the best identifiers for different forms is the number of gillrakers. Fish
that live in more open water develop extended gillrakers that are better for filtering plankton. Lake whitefish caught closer to the surface tend to have higher gillraker counts than
those that nibble food from the lake bottom. • This species and cisco (*C. artedii*) are the
region's most common and widespread whitefish. **Where found:** cool, deep water at the
bottom of larger lakes; occasionally in rivers; throughout. **Also known as:** humpback
whitefish, eastern whitefish, Great Lakes whitefish.

Rainbow Smelt

Osmerus mordax

Length: 7–9 in (maximum 13 in)

Introduced into the Great
Lakes in the early 1900s as
a forage fish for salmonids, the rainbow smelt now threatens those and other
native fish. In addition to small fish, smelt eat crustaceans and aquatic and
terrestrial insects. • In 1948, a commercial smelt fishery began in the Great Lakes
which soon grew to exceed the Atlantic Coast fishery in both weight and market
value. A year-round sport fishery is also active. **Where found:** cool, deep, offshore
waters; Great Lakes and tributaries. **Also known as:** American smelt.

Northern Pike

Esox lucius

Length: 18–30 in
(maximum 52 in);
females larger than
males

If you canoe, watch for adult
pike hanging motionless among the reeds or along the edges of a dense aquatic
plant bed. This carnivorous fish lies in wait of prey—other fish, ducklings or shorebirds—then attacks with a quick stab of its long snout, clamping down on its victim
with heavily toothed jaws. • A close relative, the muskellunge *(E. masquinongy)*
or "muskie," is the largest member of the pike family found in the Great Lakes
region. Muskies can reach 6 ft. **Where found:** vegetated edges of warmer lakes
and rivers; throughout. **Also known as:** jackfish, pickerel, water wolf.

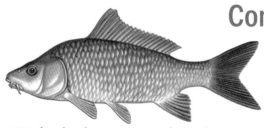

Common Carp

Cyprinus carpio

Length: 15–18 in
(maximum 48 in)

An omnivorous Eurasian fish that was introduced to North America in 1831, this abundant aquatic pest thrives throughout much of the continent. This fish, our largest minnow, roots along the bottom for food, uprooting and sucking in aquatic vegetation, then expelling it back into the water to separate edible items. These destructive feeding habits increase turbidity and destroy spawning, rearing and feeding grounds important for native fish and wildlife. Carp can greatly reduce or eliminate aquatic plant communities, thus affecting everything from dragonflies to nesting birds. **Where found:** eutrophic lakes, irrigation ditches, sewage outlets, ponds, rivers; warm, weedy, fairly shallow waters; abundant throughout. **Also known as:** carp, scaled carp, mirror carp, leather carp.

Emerald Shiner

Notropis atherinoides

Length: 2–3 in
(maximum 5 in)

This baitfish is abundant in larger rivers and lakes and is important to many predators, both aquatic and avian. Populations fluctuate greatly, thus influencing the populations of many fish in the process. • These minnows spend much of their time in open water feeding on plankton, which they follow up to the surface at dusk. In fall large schools of these little jewels gather near shorelines and docks. **Where found:** open water of lakes, large rivers, shallow lakeshores in spring and autumn; throughout. **Also known as:** lake shiner, common shiner, buckeye shiner.

White Sucker

Catostomus commersonii

Length: 10–16 in
(maximum 24 in)

This generalist species lives in habitats ranging from cold streams to warm, even polluted, waters. It avoids rapid currents and uses shallow areas to feed. • During the spring spawning season, mating white suckers splash and jostle in streams or shallow lakeshores. The suckers migrate upstream shortly after the ice breaks up, providing an important food for other fish, eagles and bears. Once hatched, the fry provide critical food for other young fish. **Where found:** variable habitats; prefers cool, clean waters with sandy or gravel substrate; throughout. **Also known as:** common sucker, mud sucker, brook sucker.

Channel Catfish

Ictalurus punctatus

Length: 15–21 in
(maximum 51 in)

The channel catfish is one of the largest and most sought-after members of the catfish family. • A slender fish with small eyes and a long, wide head, its characteristics change considerably with size, sex, season and geographic location. • The specific epithet *punctatus* means "spotted" in Latin and refers to the spots that cover most of its body, though fish over 1 ft long often do not have spots. **Where found:** cool, clear, deep water; sometimes brackish water or lakes; larger rivers; throughout. **Also known as:** channel cat, spotted catfish, northern catfish, lake catfish.

Stonecat

Noturus flavus

Length: 6-8 in
(maximum: 12 in)

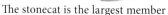

The stonecat is the largest member of the "madtom" group of catfish, notorious for their stinging pectoral fins. A poison gland at the base of the first few spines on this fin delivers a wasp-like sting if the fish is not handled properly. • Stonecats are "feeler feeders" that use their 8 barbels to sense bottom-dwelling invertebrates. They feed mainly at night, rarely using their sense of sight. In fact, 3 species in the madtom family are completely blind, relying entirely on their barbels to find food. • Stonecats, like other catfishes, do not have scales—they have a smooth skin. **Where found:** slow-moving waters with large rocks or boulders and gravel or silty bottoms; throughout; abundant in Lake Erie.

Banded Killifish

Fundulus diaphanus

Length: 2–4 in (maximum 5 in)

These small, schooling fish provide important food for mudpuppies, birds and larger fish including bass and northern pike. They are named for the vertical stripes or "bands" that run along their bodies. • Their scientific name stems from the Latin *fundus,* meaning "bottom," and the Greek *diaphanous* for "transparent." Killifish are in the topminnow family, so named because these species typically forage at or near the water's surface where they can easily be observed. **Where found:** shallows of warmer lakes and slow-moving rivers; throughout Great Lakes drainage.

Burbot
Lota lota
Length: 12–31 in
(maximum 40 in)

The burbot is the only member of the cod family confined to freshwater. • The single chin barbel and the pectoral fins contain taste buds. As these fish grow, they satisfy their ravenous appetite for whitefish and suckers by eating larger fish instead of increased numbers of smaller ones, sometimes swallowing fish almost as big as themselves. A 1-ft-long walleye was found in the stomach of a large burbot. • Once considered by anglers to be a "trash" fish, the burbot is gaining popularity among sport fishers. **Where found:** bottom of cold lakes and rivers; throughout. **Also known as:** freshwater cod, eelpout, ling, lawyer, loche.

Brook Stickleback
Culaea inconstans
Length: 2 in
(maximum 3½ in)

This plentiful little fish is distinguished by 4 to 6 spines along its back. It is one of the easiest fish to see and can be found along the vegetated edges of water bodies. • Brook sticklebacks tolerate low oxygen levels and can live in waters where other fish cannot, even spreading into flooded fields that may eventually leave them high and dry. **Where found:** varied; ponds, saline sloughs, rivers, creeks, lake edges; aquatic vegetation required for breeding; throughout. **Also known as:** black stickleback, five-spined stickleback, pinfish.

White Bass
Morone chrysops
Length: 8–12 in
(maximum 17 in)

Schools of these important native game fish feed near the surface using visual clues to locate crustaceans, smaller fish or other prey. • In spring, schools separate into sex-specific groups and return to spawn in the stream where they were born. • The related white perch *(M. americana)* invaded the Great Lakes through the Welland and Erie canals, and may be responsible for declines of native fish populations including walleye and white bass. **Where found:** clear water and rocky reefs in the lower Great Lakes and St. Lawrence River. **Also known as:** silver bass, white lake-bass, striped bass.

Pumpkinseed

Lepomis gibbosus

Length: 8–12 in (maximum 16 in)

Pumpkinseed are schooling fish that swim through sunny shallows in large numbers. Their gold-flecked bodies reflect sunlight, so they appear to shimmer as they move. • Native to Atlantic drainages of east-central North America, this fish has been widely introduced elsewhere. • These small fish are ideal forage food for predatory fishes such as bass, walleye or yellow perch. **Where found:** clear, shallow lakes; slow-moving waters; near cover such as submerged logs or weeds; all Great Lakes except Lake Superior. **Also known as:** common sunfish, sun bass, yellow-belly, yellow sunfish.

Smallmouth Bass

Micropterus dolomieui

Length: 8–12 in (maximum 27 in)

Often sought by anglers, smallmouth and largemouth bass (*M. salmoides*) are native to east-central North America. • Spawning smallmouth males return to almost the exact same nesting spot each year. They aggressively guard their nests, sometimes even driving less-persistent females away. When the male finally accepts her, the pair remains in the nest for almost 2 hours, releasing eggs and sperm about every 30 seconds. **Where found:** lakes, reservoirs and streams with rocky or sandy bottoms; throughout. **Also known as:** smallmouth blackbass, brown bass.

Yellow Perch

Perca flavescens

Length: 5–12 in (maximum 16 in)

The yellow perch is often pictured in biology textbooks and dissected in science labs. It also falls prey to many predators, including fish and birds. • Yellow perch lay accordion-folded eggs in gelatinous ribbons that can be as long as a human is tall! These zigzag ribbons are draped over aquatic vegetation that keeps them away from suffocating bottom silt. Winds or waves may cast segments, a unique find for beachcombers. • This major game species is a favorite of sport and commercial fishermen. **Where found:** common in lakes, including all Great Lakes, less common in rivers; throughout.

Walleye

Sander vitreus

Length: 15–24 in
(maximum 35 in)

Lake Erie is sometimes called the "walleye capital of the world," and with good reason: visiting fishermen generate millions in income annually for the local economies. Walleye, prized for its tasty flesh and sporting qualities, has black and gold flecks all over its body and two dorsal fins. The first dorsal fin is spiny, the second is fleshy. The name comes from the milky, clouded appearance of their eyes. • In "2-story" lakes, brown trout inhabit the cool bottom "story," while walleye stick to the warmer surface waters and shallows. **Where found:** large rivers, relatively deep lakes; prefers low amounts of light; throughout. **Also known as:** pickerel, pike-perch, wall-eyed pike.

Rainbow Darter

Etheostoma caeruleum

Length: 1½–3 in

Darters are the warblers of the underwater world— many species are unbelievably brightly colored. These tiny members of the perch family lack air bladders and thus don't float. This adaptation allows them to better anchor on graveley stream bottoms in fast-flowing riffles, where they seek small macro-invertebrate prey. In late winter, the colored pigments in male darters become much more vibrant, corresponding with the breeding season. At this time of year species like the rainbow darter rival anything found in tropical aquaria. **Where found:** fast-flowing riffles in rivers and creeks; throughout.

Logperch

Percina caprodes

Length: 3–6 in (maximum 7 in)

Logperch usually remain in water deeper than 3 ft, except during spawning season when large groups of males gather at shallow tributaries of lakeshores to prowl for mates. Competition is fierce, because only 1 or 2 females at a time will join the group. • The logperch is smaller than the yellow perch, and its genus name, *Percina*, means "little perch." *Caprodes* means "pig-like" and refers to the protruding upper jaw, which the logperch uses to flip over rocks and debris when searching for invertebrates. **Where found:** cool lakes and rivers; prefers gravel or sandy bottoms; throughout.

Freshwater Drum

Aplodinotus grunniens

Length: 16–20 in
(maximum 35 in)

The freshwater drum is occasionally encountered but often not recognized. It is silver-colored in turbid waters but bronze in clearer waters. It has two dorsal fins: a spiny front fin joined by a small membrane to a soft posterior fin. • Mature males develop specialized muscles that vibrate against their swim bladders to produce odd grunting noises, giving rise to the species name *grunniens*, meaning "grunting." **Where found:** large water bodies with sandy bottoms, mainly in lower Great Lakes. **Also known as:** croaker, grinder, grunt, sheepshead, thunder pumper.

Round Goby

Neogobius melanostomus

Length: to 10 in

Gobies have a worldwide distribution but were not found in the Great Lakes until 1995, likely introduced via the ballast water of marine vessels. These voracious bottom feeders have undergone rapid expansions in both population and range. Their well-developed sensory organs allow them to feed in darkness and out-compete native benthic species. Gobies are also extremely aggressive at spawning sites, limiting access of native fish. They quickly consume eggs at unguarded smallmouth bass nests, causing localized declines. • Unlike similar sculpins, gobies have a fused pelvic fin. **Where found:** bottom dweller; in lakes Michigan, Erie, Huron and Superior.

Mottled Sculpin

Cottus bairdii

Length: 3 in (maximum 5 in)

Female mottled sculpins literally fall "head over tails" in love. After entering the burrow, the female turns upside down to deposit her sticky eggs on the underside of the rock or ledge that covers the den. Topsy-turvy females must also be tactical, because cannibalistic males will swallow small females. Once she has released her eggs, the swollen-headed male drives her off, intent on attracting other mates to his burrow. With a view box to eliminate surface riffles, you may be able to find a mottled sculpin on the nest. **Where found:** bottom dweller; usually in cool, clean streams and lakes with rocky substrate; throughout. **Also known as:** bullhead, blob, miller's thumb.

INVERTEBRATES

More than 95 percent of all animal species are invertebrates, and there are thousands of invertebrate species in the Great Lakes region. The few mentioned in this guide are frequently encountered and easily recognizable. Invertebrates can be found in a variety of habitats and are an important part of most ecosystems. They provide food for birds, amphibians, shrews, bats and other insects, and they also play an important role in the pollination of plants and aid in the decay process.

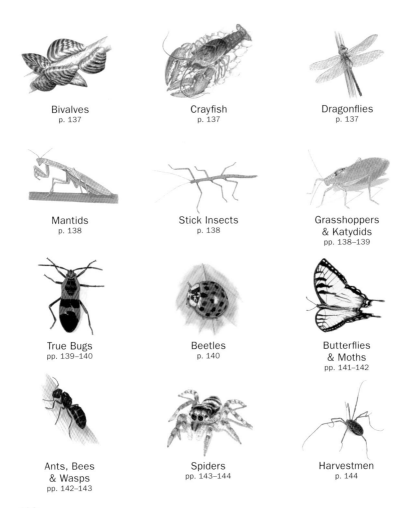

Bivalves
p. 137

Crayfish
p. 137

Dragonflies
p. 137

Mantids
p. 138

Stick Insects
p. 138

Grasshoppers
& Katydids
pp. 138–139

True Bugs
pp. 139–140

Beetles
p. 140

Butterflies
& Moths
pp. 141–142

Ants, Bees
& Wasps
pp. 142–143

Spiders
pp. 143–144

Harvestmen
p. 144

Zebra Mussel

Dreissena polymorpha

Length: ¼–1½ in (maximum 2 in)

A native of Eurasia, zebra mussels were first noticed in the Great Lakes in 1988, having likely hitchhiked on an ocean-going freighter and inadvertently released. Their population has exploded, and they are now incredibly abundant. • Estimates are that all of Lake Erie's water is cycled through their collective bodies in a week's time. Zebra mussels filter-feed—they remove suspended solids from the water column—and consequently have greatly reduced water turbidity. They've also largely out-competed and eliminated native mussels in many areas. • Zebra mussels have since been joined by a similar species, the quagga mussel (*D. rostriformis*). **Where found:** the Great Lakes, some other lakes, rivers; throughout.

Virile Crayfish

Orconectes virilis

Length: up to 8¼ in

Crayfish are fearsome crustaceans with large, lobster-like pincers. As big and distinctive as they are, crayfish are mostly nocturnal and thus difficult to see. Long, sensitive antennae help them feel their way as they range overland, especially on rainy nights. Virile crayfish also tunnel into soft, muddy ground. • This species, along with other crayfish, has been spread by anglers who use them as bait. Introduction of non-native crayfish has led to localized declines in some native crayfish. **Where found:** ponds, lakes, streams, wetlands; throughout.

Common Green Darner

Anax junius

Length: 2¾–3⅛ in
Wingspan: 4⅕ in

Like monarch butterflies, green darners are highly migratory, but their movements are not as well understood. Sometimes massive swarms, numbering into the thousands, are seen moving in fall on a steady south-west trajectory that probably ends in the southern states or Mexico. • Green darners, like all dragonflies, are voracious hunters. Each time they zig and zag in the air, they seize small insect prey. Darners have incredible vision: each compound eye is composed of thousands of tiny facets; each, in effect, a tiny eyelet. **Where found:** any open water; migrants can be seen anywhere; abundant throughout.

Chinese Mantis

Tenodera aridifolia sinensis

Length: 2½–3½ in

These large, rather terrifying-looking Asian imports are common throughout much of the eastern U.S. They are often called "praying" mantises because of the typical posture of their forelegs—they appear to be praying. Actually, they are *preying*; these mantises are formidable predators and seize prey the size of swallowtail butterflies with their powerful, serrated legs. They have even been documented capturing ruby-throated hummingbirds! Their egg cases are brown, foamy masses that overwinter; in spring, dozens of tiny mantises emerge. **Where found:** gardens, weedy fields, meadows, brushy areas; throughout southern Great Lakes region.

Walkingstick

Diapheromera femorata

Length: 3–3¾ in

We can probably thank birds for the incredible camouflage diversity that insects display—after all, bugs don't want to be eaten. Walkingsticks are among the most amazingly cryptic insects; looking just like a stick, they are almost impossible to spot. They spend most of the day tightly pressed against a twig and if prodded, their movements are slow and swaying. • If a walkingstick loses a leg, it will soon grow another. **Where found:** brushy areas, edges and understory of deciduous forests; throughout, but scarcer northward.

Carolina Grasshopper

Dissosteira carolina

Length: 1¾ in; **Wingspan:** 3–4 in

One of North America's largest and most conspicuous grasshoppers, this big bug is easy enough to miss when motionless, but wait until it flushes. Large, black wings rimmed with pale gold flash boldly, and in flight the Carolina grasshopper suggests a mourning cloak butterfly (*Nymphalis antiopa*). Its wings make loud crackling sounds called crepitations when it is flushed from the ground. • Males engage in a courtship display in which they hover like tiny helicopters low over the ground. • Carolina grasshoppers can become so abundant locally that they can damage plants. **Where found:** nearly any open ground, often seen in weedy roadsides and lots; abundant throughout.

Common Katydid

Pterophylla camellifolia

Length: 1¾–2⅛ in

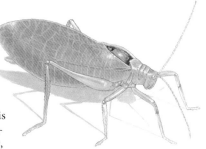

Come mid-summer, the onomatopoeic song of the katydid becomes a familiar melody wherever trees are found: a loud, raspy *Kay-tee-Did!* The insect produces this sound by rubbing its wing against a specialized plate on its body. • Females have long, sword-like ovipositors extending from their abdomen tip, which are used to inject eggs into plant tissue. • Katydids are excellent leaf mimics; if motionless among the foliage of a shrub or tree, they blend in with the leaves. Their slow, deliberate movements make them hard to spot even when in motion. **Where found:** treed sites; common in suburban shade trees; throughout southern Great Lakes region.

Common Water Strider

Gerris remigis

Length: ½–⅝ in

Gerris spp.

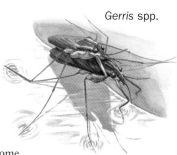

Sometimes called "skaters," water striders are one of the most familiar insects of quiet waters. Perfectly adapted to an aquatic lifestyle, they effortlessly zoom across the surface. Males and females communicate by sending ripples along the uppermost film of water. Voracious predators, they seek tiny insects and other animal life that stray into the top strata of the water column. There are numerous species, some winged, others not, and this species is probably the most commonly encountered. **Where found:** quiet, sheltered waters of ponds, lakes, streams; throughout.

Large Milkweed Bug

Oncopeltus fasciatus

Length: ⅜–⅝ in

When an insect is bold, brightly colored and active by day, chances are it is toxic. The splashy colors are, in effect, a loud sign that says "don't eat!" Milkweed bugs consume parts of milkweed plants (*Asclepias* spp.), taking in quantities of the toxic white sap, which in turn causes the showy beetles to become toxic. Check out milkweed plants and it won't be long before you discover some of these poisonous little gems. • Monarch butterfly larvae also eat milkweed and are similarly poisonous. **Where found:** open fields and woodland borders and openings; wherever milkweed occurs; common throughout.

Dog-day Cicada

Tibicen canicularis

Length: 1¼–1½ in

The loud, buzz-saw-like drone of the dog-day cicada lasts about 15 seconds and is loudest near the middle of the song. The singing begins in mid-summer and is a common, characteristic sound wherever large trees are found. • Although they look horrifying, cicadas are completely harmless and can be safely handled. Because they lurk high in the foliage of trees, their songs are far more conspicuous than the bugs themselves. • At least 9 other species occur in the region, including the well-known 17-year, or periodic, cicada. **Where found:** treed areas; nearly throughout.

Firefly

Photuris pennsylvanica

Length: ½ in

One of the most pleasing scenes of warm summer nights is the blinking lights of fireflies. This species is common, but there are at least 21 others in the genus *Photuris* and at least as many not yet described. • Most fireflies have bioluminescent pigments that create the flashes of light; the duration of this flashing often varies between species. Watch for different patterns of firefly illumination next time you encounter a field full of these beetles. Slug-like larvae live on the ground in leaf litter; called "glow worms," they also flash. **Where found:** open meadows, even suburbia; throughout.

Multicolored Asian Ladybug

Harmonia axyridris

Length: ⅜ in

Repeated, ill-advised introductions of this charming Asian invader were made throughout the 20th century by the U.S. Department of Agriculture as a biological control for crop-damaging aphids. They finally took, and now many households are plagued with swarms of the cute little pests as they enter houses to hibernate. Evidence suggests this invasive little beetle has out-competed native species in some areas; it is the most familiar species of ladybug in some places. • This species contains a chemical called isopropyl methoxy pyrazine that is secreted when threatened. It has a foul odor and can stain. **Where found:** nearly anywhere; often enters buildings; throughout.

Eastern Tiger Swallowtail

Papilio glaucus

Wingspan: 4–5½ in

Few butterflies are more striking than this
jumbo swallowtail. Tigers are fast, powerful
fliers and often course high in the treetops.
Fortunately, they often come down to our
level for flower nectar. They turn up in gardens
and are especially fond of butterflyweed (*Asclepias tuberosa*).
• The 2½-inch-long caterpillars feed on trees including cherry, tulip
tree, ash and birch. They produce sticky silk and roll a leaf into a tent-like shelter during
the day—a good bird-avoidance strategy. **Where found:** mature forests with appropriate
host plants; adults range widely; common throughout.

Cabbage White

Pieris rapae

Wingspan: 1⅛–2 in

Although a European introduction, this
species is probably our most widely seen
butterfly. Cabbage whites were accidentally
introduced near Montreal in the 1860s; since
then they have spread continent-wide. The larvae
feed on many types of mustards and can become localized
pests. The green caterpillars are nearly 1½ inches long and are
marked with 5 yellowish stripes; you probably encounter them on your cabbage plants.
• This adaptable butterfly is the most urban of our species; it can appear anywhere, even
in large cities. **Where found:** any open habitat; shuns large, dense forests; abundant
throughout.

Monarch

Danaus plexippus

Wingspan: 3½–4 in

This familiar butterfly stages the most
conspicuous and spectacular migration of
any North American insect. In late summer
and fall, millions of monarchs begin moving
southwestward toward Mexico. Ultimately,
they overwinter in masses in high-elevation fir forests. Sometimes huge swarms
rest in our region during migration. They lay eggs on milkweed, and their large
yellow, white and black-banded caterpillars are often easily found if you search
milkweed plants. **Where found:** can turn up in any open areas that support milk-
weeds; migrants abundant throughout.

Luna Moth

Actias luna

Wingspan: 3⅛–4½ in

These lime-green beauties are arguably the showiest moths in North America. Even a moth hater would admire them! Unfortunately, like many other species of large moths, lunas have declined, probably owing to habitat loss, increased use of pesticides and pollutants. Their caterpillars typically feed on hickory, walnut and birch, among other species. These tubular bags of protein can be over 3 inches long and are a striking emerald green with a pale yellow stripe down the side. **Where found:** most frequent in forested areas with suitable host trees; adults range into other habitats; uncommon to locally common throughout.

Carpenter Ant

Camponotus pennsylvanicus

Length: ½ in

Camponotus spp.

Woe to homeowners with a colony of these wood-borers in their homes. Carpenter ants damage the wooden infrastructure of a house. Their presence is characterized by small tunnels, or galleries, with occasional slit-like openings where they expel sawdust. Unlike termites, the ants don't actually eat the wood—they are making nests. Carpenter ants do best in wood with 15% or higher moisture content. • In the wild, they excavate trees and form extensive galleries. Pileated woodpeckers readily tune into these colonies and often rip apart large sections of bark to get at the ants. **Where found:** trees, logs; sometimes enters homes; throughout.

Eastern Yellowjacket

Vespula maculifrons

Length: ½ in

Vespula spp.

Big and boldly striped in black and yellow, these ill-tempered hornets are attracted to sweets, including soda—an unpleasant experience is accidentally swallowing an angry yellowjacket that entered your can of pop. • Yellowjackets nest in ground burrows, often those made by small mammals; people mowing lawns sometimes agitate a colony and are attacked. Females sting; males lack stingers. These predators kill a variety of other insects and sometimes nectar at flowers such as goldenrod. **Where found:** nearly ubiquitous in open areas; throughout.

Yellow Bumble Bee

Bombus fervidus

Length: 1 in

These large, fuzzy bees are intimidating but not aggressive, and they can be closely approached. Their dense, hairy coats help warm them, and "bumbles" can often fly in cooler weather than many other insects. Their hairy coats also make them extremely effective pollinators: as they visit flowers, the pollen adheres readily to their "fur" and is transferred to other plants. • Bumble bees usually build nests in underground burrows, and only young queens survive the winter to start new colonies the next spring. **Where found:** open habitats; frequent visitors to flowers and gardens; throughout.

Bombus spp.

Zebra Jumping Spider

Salticus scenicus

Length: ¼–⅜ in

Alert and highly mobile, these spiders are encountered around walls, cement porches and similar structures. Possessed of incredible vision, they have 4 pairs of eyes that enable them to quickly spot prey. Meals are secured with cat-like pounces, and victims may be as large as or larger than the spider itself. Next time you see one of these Lilliputians, slowly approach as close as possible. The spider will rear up, cock its head and seem to observe you closely. • Zebra jumping spiders occur throughout Europe as well. **Where found:** open sunny sites around homes, buildings, fences; common throughout.

Dark Fishing Spider

Dolomedes tenebrosus

Length: females over 3 in, if outstretched legs are included; males half this size

These terrifying-looking spiders occasionally wander into homes, causing horror and excitement. They are normally found near water and can even run over the water's surface in pursuit of prey. Fishing spiders usually feed on small insects, but they can capture small fish! While menacing in appearance, dark fishing spiders rarely bite people, and like most spiders are safe enough if not harassed. **Where found:** often around quiet waters of streams, ponds, wetlands, and will range considerable distances from water; throughout.

Banded Garden Spider

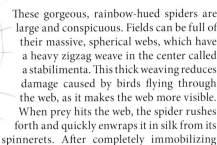

Argiope trifasciata

Length: 2 in (counting legs)

These gorgeous, rainbow-hued spiders are large and conspicuous. Fields can be full of their massive, spherical webs, which have a heavy zigzag weave in the center called a stabilimenta. This thick weaving reduces damage caused by birds flying through the web, as it makes the web more visible. When prey hits the web, the spider rushes forth and quickly enwraps it in silk from its spinnerets. After completely immobilizing the victim, they administer the *coup de grâce:* several venom-filled bites from sharp fangs. **Where found:** fields, meadows, sometimes gardens; throughout.

Harvestman

Order Opiliones

Body length: $\frac{1}{25}$–$\frac{5}{16}$ in (max ⅞ in)
Leg span: as much as 6 in+

Numerous species are in this poorly studied group of spider relatives called "daddy longlegs," but most are readily recognizable as harvestmen. They climb about in shrubs or on the forest floor hunting small insects and occasionally feeding on plant sap. An oft-repeated myth claims that harvestmen are poisonous but their fangs are too short to inject the venom. This myth is untrue; they have no venom glands, or fangs, and are utterly harmless. The total number of species in Order Opiliones worldwide may exceed 10,000 species, but much work remains to sort them out. **Where found:** nearly all habitats; common throughout.

PLANTS

Plants belong to the Kingdom Plantae. They are autotrophic, which means they produce their own food from inorganic materials through a process called photosynthesis. Plants are the basis of all food webs. They supply oxygen to the atmosphere, modify climate and create and hold soil in place. They disperse their seeds and pollen through carriers such as wind, water and animals. Fossil fuels come from ancient deposits of organic matter—largely that of plants. In this book, plants are separated into 3 categories: trees, shrubs (including vines) and forbs (herbaceous or non-woody plants).

TREES

Trees are long-lived, woody plants that are normally taller than 15 ft. There are two major types of trees: coniferous and broadleaf. Conifers, or cone-bearers, have needles or small, scale-like leaves. Most conifers are evergreens, but larches (*Larix* species), bald-cypress *(Taxodium distichum)* and dawn redwood *(Metasequoia glyptostroboides)* shed their leaves in winter. Most broadleaf trees lose their leaves in the fall and are often called deciduous trees (meaning "falling off" in Latin).

A single tree can provide a home or a food source for many different animals. Roots bind soil and play host to a multitude of beneficial fungi, and even support certain parasitic plants. Trunks provide a substrate for numerous species of moss and lichen, which in turn are used by many animals for shelter and nesting material. Tree cavities are used by everything from owls to squirrels to snakes. Leafy canopies support an amazing diversity of life, including butterflies, birds and insects. Oaks, hickories and beech produce fruit that is consumed by all manner of wildlife. Humans are grateful for sugar maples (*Acer saccharum*), the source of maple sugar.

Trees can provide windbreak, camouflage or shelter, and can hold down soil, thus preventing erosion. Streamside woodlands protect water quality. The types of trees within a forest control the other species of plants and animals that will be present. Old-growth forest is critical habitat for many species that use the fallen or hollowed-out trees as nesting or denning sites. Invertebrates live within or under the bark, providing food for birds. Fallen, decomposing logs provide habitat for snakes, salamanders, mosses, fungi and invertebrates. Logs degrade into nutrient-rich soil to perpetuate the growth of plant life and retain organic matter in the ecosystem. Large forests retain carbon dioxide, an important preventive factor of global warming. Responsibly managed forests provide wood products and jobs.

Tree heights in the accounts reflect the usual size and shape, but trees can reach greater heights in ideal conditions. Conifers have pollen cones (male) and seed cones (female); only mature seed cones are described. Cones are useful in identifying conifers because they are found year-round on the tree or on the ground nearby. Leaves, cone and fruit measurements and descriptions are given for mature plants only.

Pine
pp. 148–151

Cypress
pp. 151–152

Magnolia
p. 152

Pawpaw
p. 153

Laurel
p. 153

Plane-tree
p. 154

Witch-hazel
p. 154

Elm
p. 155

Mulberry
p. 156

Walnut
pp. 156–157

Beech
pp. 157–159

Birch
pp. 159–160

Linden
p. 160

Willow
pp. 161–162

Rose
pp. 162–164

Cassia
p. 165

Redbud & Locust
p. 165

Euonymus
p. 166

Maple
pp. 166–168

Quassia
p. 168

Olive
p. 169

Balsam Fir

Abies balsamea

Height: to 80 ft
Needles: 3/8–1 1/8 in long; flat, flexible
Seed cones: 1 1/2–4 in long; erect, grayish brown

Balsam fir needles have 2 white lines on the lower surface. Erect, barrel-shaped cones usually grow near the top of the tree's spire-like crown. • Cut trees do not immediately shed their needles, making this species a popular Christmas tree. The wood is used as pulp, and the resin, sold as "Canada balsam," is used as a mounting material for microscope slides, as glue and in candle- and soap-making. The oil-rich seeds are eaten by many species of birds, porcupines and squirrels. Spruce grouse forage on the leaves. **Where found:** low, swampy ground to well-drained hill-sides; requires moist soil; throughout all but southernmost Great Lakes region.

White Spruce

Picea glauca

Height: mature trees 80–140 ft
Needles: 1/2–7/8 in long; stiff, 4-sided
Seed cones: 2–2 3/8 in long; cylindrical, pale brown

Small white spruce often grow beneath old jack pines. This species can live for 200 years and eventually replaces pines in mature forests in a process called succession. It is a good choice for landscaping and is used in reforestation. • Spruce needles roll between your fingers, unlike the flat, 2-sided needles of fir. • Traditionally, Native peoples used the flexible roots to lace together birch-bark canoes. • White spruce is an important source of food and shelter for many forest animals, including grouse and seed-eating birds, porcupines and red squirrels. **Where found:** various soils and climates, but prefers moist, rich soil; throughout all but southernmost Great Lakes region.

Black Spruce

Picea mariana

Height: up to 50 ft (rarely to 100 ft)
Needles: ¼–¾ in long; stiff, 4-sided
Seed cones: ¾–1⅛ in long; dull grayish brown to purplish brown

This slow-growing wetland tree, which may live for 200 years, is an important source of lumber and pulp. • Northern explorers used black spruce to make spruce beer, a popular drink that prevented scurvy. Spruce gum was also chewed or boiled into cough syrup to relieve sore throats (spruce should be used in moderation). • Snowshoe hares love to eat young spruce seedlings and red squirrels harvest the cones, but in general black spruce is not favored as a wildlife food source. • Many black spruce have a club-shaped crown. **Where found:** well-drained, moist flatlands in the north to cool, damp, boggy sites in the south; throughout.

Eastern Hemlock

Tsuga canadensis

Height: 65–100 ft (occasionally to 150 ft)
Needles: ¼–½ in long; flat, flexible
Seed cones: ½–¾ in long; brown and dry

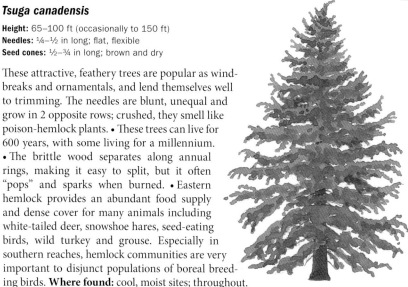

These attractive, feathery trees are popular as windbreaks and ornamentals, and lend themselves well to trimming. The needles are blunt, unequal and grow in 2 opposite rows; crushed, they smell like poison-hemlock plants. • These trees can live for 600 years, with some living for a millennium. • The brittle wood separates along annual rings, making it easy to split, but it often "pops" and sparks when burned. • Eastern hemlock provides an abundant food supply and dense cover for many animals including white-tailed deer, snowshoe hares, seed-eating birds, wild turkey and grouse. Especially in southern reaches, hemlock communities are very important to disjunct populations of boreal breeding birds. **Where found:** cool, moist sites; throughout.

Tamarack

Larix laricina

Height: up to 65 ft (rarely to 80 ft)
Needles: ¾–1 in long; soft, deciduous
Seed cones: ⅜–¾ in long; 20 or fewer scales; pale brown

The needles of this slender, exotic-looking tree are unusual among conifers: they turn golden yellow and drop in fall. They grow on stubby twigs in tightly spiraled tufts of 15 to 60. • Straight tamarack trunks are used as poles, piers and railroad ties. The tannin-rich bark was used for tanning leather. The sap contains a natural sugar gelatin that tastes like bitter honey. • European larch (*L. decidua*) is often used in landscaping. It has larger cones (up to 1³/₈ in long) with 40 to 60 scales and bright green needles in tufts of 30 to 55. **Where found:** moist, well-drained soils; also bogs, muskeg; throughout, although local in southern part of region.

Eastern White Pine

Pinus strobus

Height: 65–100 ft (can reach over 200 ft)
Needles: 2–6 in long; slender, flexible
Seed cones: 4–8 in long; brown and woody

Large forests of virgin white pine in eastern North America were once estimated to contain 900 billion board-feet of lumber. The trees were rapidly cut down to make everything from ship's masts to matchsticks. • The name strobus means a "gum-yielding" or "pitchy tree" in Latin or "cone" in Greek. White pine has an airy, graceful appearance and is easily recognized by its long, soft needles in bundles of 5. This valuable tree provides food and shelter for many bird and mammal species. • White pine is the state tree of Michigan. **Where found:** dry, rocky ridges to sphagnum bogs; humid sites with well-drained soil; throughout, although scattered and local in southern part of region.

Jack Pine

Pinus banksiana

Height: 35–50 ft (maximum 90 ft)
Needles: ¾–1½ in long; straight, slightly twisted
Seed cones: 1–3 in long; yellowish brown; closed, straight or curved inward

Jack pines are the first conifers to colonize areas burned by fire. The cones are held shut with a tight resin bond that melts when heated, allowing the seeds to disperse. • Cones usually occur in groups of 2 to 3 and point toward the tip of the branch. The needles grow in bundles of 2. • Animals and birds browse on young jack pine seedlings and eat the fallen seeds. The endangered Kirtland's warbler (*Dendroica kirtlandii*) depends on young, pure stands for nesting; jack pine stands must be between 5 and 15 years of age. Nearly the entire Kirtland warbler population occurs in northern Michigan. **Where found:** dry, infertile, acidic, often sandy or rocky soils; throughout northern half of region.

Arborvitae

Thuja occidentalis

Height: 35–50 ft (rarely to 80 ft)
Needles: ⅛ in long; scale-like, gland-dotted
Seed cones: ¼–½ in long; upright; green, becoming reddish brown with age

Arborvitae means "tree of life"—Native peoples and French settlers used parts of the tree to prevent scurvy. • Fragrant cedar lumber is known for resisting decay, but living trees are often hollow from heart-rot. The wood is used near water in cedar-strip canoes, shingles and dock posts. • Deer often browse lower branches of arborvitae, and pine siskins (*Carduelis pinus*) are fond of the seeds. • Sometimes known as white cedar, this species can live very long. A magnificent specimen on the Niagara Escarpment of Canada is at least 1050 years old. **Where found:** humid habitats with high snowfall and calcium-rich soils; throughout, although scattered and local in southern reaches of region. Also known as: eastern white cedar.

Eastern Red Cedar

Juniperus virginiana

Height: up to 35 ft tall (rarely to 60 ft)
Needles: ¹⁄₁₆–½ in long; flat, overlapping scales
Seed cones: male yellowish, ⅛ in long; female blue, berry-like, ¼ in long

This drought-resistant conifer can live for 350 years and is becoming increasingly common in sites disturbed by human activity. It prefers limestone soils, and under optimal conditions can form large stands. • Cedar storage chests are made from the beautiful, reddish wood—its aromatic oils deter insects. • Many birds use dense cedar foliage for cover or food. Quail, pheasant and wild turkey eat the "berries," and seed-eating cedar waxwings disperse the seeds. A gorgeous olive-colored butterfly, the juniper hairstreak (*Callophrys gryneus*) uses red cedar as its host plant. **Where found:** dry, open, rocky, disturbed sites, abandoned fields; throughout.

Tulip Tree

Liriodendron tulipifera

Height: up to 120 ft
Leaves: 2¾–6 in long; 2–3 lobes, square-notched tips
Flowers: 1½–2 in; showy, tulip-shaped; yellowish green with orange base
Fruits: green to straw-colored, dry nutlets in 2–3-in long, cone-like clusters

Tall and columnar, tulips are striking trees in the forest. Their gorgeous blooms are spectacular but high above the ground and not easily seen. This species is the only common native magnolia in the region; cucumber magnolia (*Magnolia acuminata*) also occurs but is rather rare and local. • The tulip tree is a valuable hardwood used in construction, furniture and cabinet making, and for musical instruments. The sturdy, straight trunks were carved into large canoes by Native peoples. Butterflies, including the eastern tiger swallowtail, use tulips as the larval host plant. • The tulip tree is Indiana's state tree. **Where found:** deep, rich, moist, well-drained soils; throughout, except MN, WI. **Also known as:** tulip-poplar, yellow-poplar, tulip-magnolia.

Pawpaw

Asimina triloba

Height: up to 30 ft
Leaves: 4–12 in long; elliptical, hang at branch tips
Flowers: 1⅛–1½ across; reddish purple
or maroon when ripe
Fruits: large, 1½–6 in long; dark brown
with yellowish pulp

This attractive shrub or small tree has unique, bell-shaped flowers that emit a foul scent and bloom before leaf emergence. Native peoples ate the juicy fruits—some reports liken the taste to that of apples, bananas or pineapples, while others say pawpaw tastes like turpentine or perfume! • Pawpaw is in the custard-apple family (Annonaceae), the only member to reach our region. Some 2000 species of this mostly tropical family occur in Central and South American jungles. It is the host plant for the beautiful zebra swallowtail (*Eurytides marcellus*). **Where found:** moist woods, wooded slopes and stream terraces; throughout, except MN.

Sassafras

Sassasafras albidum

Height: up to 60 ft
Leaves: 3–8 in long; ovate or broadly 2–3 lobed
Flowers: tiny; greenish-yellow in loose, stalked clusters
Fruits: dark blue, berry-like drupes sit in
red cup ⅜–½ in across

Sassafras is a common and often weedy pioneer. It has 3 types of distinctive leaves: one form is unlobed, one has 1 lobe like a mitten and the other is 2-lobed like a mitten with 2 thumbs. • The roots were used in root beer. Aromatic oils extracted from them have also been used in soaps and perfume. Iroquois nations used the twigs as chewing sticks, the leaves for seasoning meat or soups, and the bark or roots for spicing tea. **Caution:** sassafras is banned as a food flavoring in America because the essential oil contains safrole, a carcinogenic compound. **Where found:** dry to moderately moist, open, often disturbed sites; throughout, except MN.

Sycamore

Platanus occidentalis

Height: up to 115 ft
Leaves: 4–8 in long; 3–5 lobed, coarse toothed
Flowers: tiny; in dense clusters
Fruits: tiny; yellowish seed-like achenes borne in round, hairy, brown fruit

Sycamore trees have mottled, exfoliating, brown and white bark that forms as the trunk and limbs grow—irregular, jigsaw-shaped pieces of the parchment-like bark flake off to expose the lighter inner bark. • Historical accounts describe numerous men on horseback riding into hollowed sycamores, and even giant trees being used as blacksmith shops! The large trunks were hollowed out to make barges capable of carrying several tons. Such behemoths are seldom found today. • The yellow-throated warbler, formerly known as sycamore warbler, is closely associated with these trees. **Where found:** low, wet areas such as floodplains, lakeshores; moist, disturbed, upland sites; throughout, except MN.

Witch-hazel

Hamamelis virginiana

Height: up to 30 ft
Leaves: 6 in long; oval
Flowers: yellow to red, 4-petaled
Fruits: woody capsules ⅜ in across

Often more of a shrub or treelet, witch-hazel is a handsome multi-trunked plant. • Well known for its astringent properties and ability to stop bleeding, witch-hazel preparations are widely available commercially for topical use. The leaves and bark of witch-hazel are used in medicinal extracts, skin cosmetics, shaving lotions, mouthwashes, eye lotion, ointments and soaps. • Witch-hazel seeds are edible, oily and nutritious. • Forked witch-hazel branches were often used as divining rods to locate sources of underground water. **Where found:** moist, shaded areas; throughout, except westernmost areas of region.

American Elm

Ulmus americana

Height: up to 100 ft
Leaves: 4–6 in long; asymmetrical bases
Flowers: small; in tassel-like clusters
Fruits: winged nutlets ¼–½ in long

Large, graceful elm trees once lined our city streets and parks, but hundreds of thousands have been lost to Dutch elm disease since its arrival in the United States in 1930. This species is abundant in the wild, but seldom gets very large before being attacked and killed by the fungal infection. Occasional giants still occur as isolated specimens in the midst of agricultural fields, where the disease cannot readily reach them. • American elms are very important as hosts for many species of butterflies and moths, including question mark (*Polygonia interrogationis*), comma (*Polygonia* spp.), and mourning cloak (*Nymphalis antiopa*). **Where found:** generally bottomlands, stream terraces, sheltered slopes; throughout.

Hackberry

Celtis occidentalis

Height: up to 90 ft
Leaves: 1½–4¾ in long; asymmetrical bases, 15–40 coarse teeth per side
Flowers: small; greenish
Fruits: dark olive-purple, berry-like drupes ¼ in long

Hackberry has a broad crown and spreading branches, making it an ideal shade tree. It tolerates drought, transplants easily and lives up to 200 years. • Hackberries are "factory trees"; numerous species of wildlife use them and many butterflies and moths rely on them as host plants. The berries are a favorite of cedar waxwings and other songbirds and mammals, and the flowers are a source of pollen for honeybees. • The hackberry emperor butterfly (*Asterocampa celtis*) is always found around this tree. Hackberry often has "witch's broom," small bushy growths caused by fungi or mites. **Where found:** stream terraces, rich slopes, well-drained limestone soils; throughout.

Osage-orange

Maclura pomifera

Height: up to 50 ft
Leaves: 2⅜–4¾ in long; thick, shiny, smooth-edged
Flowers: tiny; in dense, round clusters 1–1½ in across
Fruits: green, dimpled, fleshy or pulpy aggregates of achenes 4–5½ in across

These thorny, shrub-like small trees are popular ornamentals, hedgerows or windbreaks in the eastern states, although not nearly as commonly planted today. • Because of its dense, gnarly growth, osage-orange makes excellent living fences—it was commonly planted for such purposes before barbed wire was invented. • The green, juicy fruits resemble dimpled oranges—or brains!—but they are pulpy and inedible, although cattle will eat them. The tannin-rich bark has been used for dying leather, baskets and cloth. • Osage-orange sap can irritate the skin of some people. **Where found:** rich lowland sites and disturbed sites; throughout, except northwestern MN.

Black Walnut

Juglans nigra

Height: up to 100 ft
Leaves: compound, 8–24 in long, pinnately divided into 13–23 leaflets; aromatic
Flowers: tiny, green; male in hanging catkins 2–4 ¾ in long; female in erect clusters
Fruits: round, aromatic, yellow-green to brown nuts 1½ –2⅜ in across

Black walnut is North America's most prized hardwood. The rich, dark brown wood has beautiful grain and is used in high-quality furniture. Standing trees have been auctioned for $5000. • The oily, edible kernels can be used like commercial walnuts, but the firm, slightly hairy husks can be tough to shell. • Walnut roots and decaying leaves exude a toxin known as juglone that prevents competing plants (including walnut seedlings) from taking root nearby. • Rich in toxins and tannins, ground walnut husks were used by Native Americans as a fish poison. The beautiful banded hairstreak butterfly (*Satyrium calanus*) uses black walnut as a host plant. **Where found:** rich, well-drained, fertile lowlands; throughout.

Shagbark Hickory

Carya ovata

Height: up to 100 ft
Leaves: pinnately compound, 6–12 in long, with
5 (occasionally 7) leaflets; aromatic
Flowers: tiny, green; male in catkins, hanging in 3s;
female in erect clusters of 2–5
Fruits: round, aromatic, greenish nuts ¾–1½ in long

Mature shagbark hickory trees have shaggy
exfoliating bark. This native pecan hickory is
an important source of edible nuts. The sweet
kernels can be eaten raw or used like walnuts
in recipes; they also provide an important food
for squirrels. The strong, shock-absorbing wood
is a favorite for tool handles, wooden wheels and
sporting goods. It is also used for smoking ham and
bacon. A yellow dye is made from the inner bark.
• The nuts of all hickories are split into 4, a feature that
distinguishes them from closely related walnuts, which
have a whole or smooth fruit husk. **Where found:** dry
to moderately moist sites; throughout.

American Beech

Fagus grandifolia

Height: up to 80 ft
Leaves: 2–6 in long; parallel veins end in coarse tooth
Flowers: tiny; male in dense, hanging clusters;
female in small erect clusters
Fruits: small, prickly, 3-angled burs ¾ in long

Mature beech trees produce edible nuts
enclosed in a bristly, greenish to reddish
brown triangular husk. They are said to
taste best after the first frost, but
should be eaten in moderation to
avoid an upset stomach. Traditionally, ground, roasted beech nuts
were used as a coffee substitute; the
oil was extracted and used as food
and lamp oil. Beech nuts have a high
fat content and are important food for
animals including squirrels and black
bears. • A tiny parasitic wildflower, beech-
drops (*Epifagus virginianus*) taps into beech
roots and will only be found nearby. **Where
found:** moist, well-drained slopes, bottomlands;
throughout, except westernmost parts of region.

White Oak

Quercus alba

Height: up to 100 ft
Leaves: 4–8 in long; deeply pinnate, rounded lobes
Flowers: tiny; male in hanging catkins 2–3 in long; female reddish and in clusters
Fruits: acorns ½–¾ in long; lower ¼ seated in cup

There are 2 major groups of oaks. Leaves in the white oak group have rounded lobes that lack bristle tips. Red oaks typically have sharper-angled lobes terminated by bristles. • This common species is valuable commercially. The strong, durable wood is widely used for flooring, cabinetry and furniture. The nutritious acorns can be eaten raw, but were traditionally ground or roasted and used as a flour substitute, soup thickener or caffeine-free coffee substitute. Many animals consume the acorns, and many species of moths and butterflies use white oak as a host plant. • White oak is the state tree of Illinois. **Where found:** deep, rich bottomlands, rocky uplands, well-drained forests, mixed with other trees or forming dominant stands; throughout.

Red Oak

Quercus rubra

Height: up to 100 ft
Leaves: 4–9 in long; 7–11 deeply pinnate, nearly triangular lobes
Flowers: tiny; male in hanging catkins 4–5 in long; female in clusters
Fruits: acorns ½–1⅛ in long; lower ¼ seated in cup

Members of the red or black oak group (including this common eastern tree, black oak and pin oak [*Q. palustris*]) have deep, pointed leaf lobes, bitter acorns that ripen in 2 years and non-scaly bark. • The wood's varying grain and durability make it a favorite for hardwood flooring, furniture and barrels. • The acorns contain tannins toxic to humans but are important food for squirrels, raccoons, black bears, white-tailed deer and birds. • The copious flowers of mature oaks attract masses of insects, which are consumed by birds traveling from the tropics to boreal nesting grounds. **Where found:** rich moist soil, often on lower and middle slopes of forests; throughout.

Black Oak

Quercus velutina

Height: up to 80 ft
Leaves: 4–8 in long; 5–7 often shallow to deeply pinnate, triangular lobes
Flowers: tiny; male in hanging catkins 4–5 in long; female in clusters
Fruits: acorns ½–¾ in long; lower ⅓–½ seated in cup

Black oak's tannin-rich inner bark contains a yellow pigment called quercitron, which was sold as a dye and used for tanning leather. • Black oak leaves have star-shaped (stellate) hairs on their undersides and are the largest of any of our oaks. Acorn cups are slightly fringed and have overlapping scales. • Identification can be challenging: this oak is highly variable and can hybridize with red oak and bur oak (*Q. macrocarpa*). Hybridization among oaks is very common, and crosses involving any species can be found. **Where found:** dry, well-drained sites, often on the highest ridges of forests or most elevated sand knolls in flatter regions; throughout most of region.

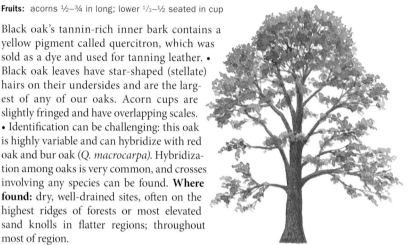

Yellow Birch

Betula alleghaniensis

Height: up to 100 ft
Leaves: 2½–4½ in long; toothed
Flowers: tiny; hanging pollen catkins 2–4 in long; erect seed catkins ½–¾ in long
Fruits: tiny; flat, 2-winged nutlets in hanging seed catkins

North American birches are divided into 2 groups: yellow birches (yellow and cherry birch [*B. lenta*]) and white birches (including paper and gray birches [*B. populifolia*]). Members of the yellow birch group have leaves with 8 to 12 straight veins per side, slender cone-like catkins and inner bark that smells and tastes like wintergreen (white birches have fewer veins and no distinct fragrance). • Yellow birch wood is used in tool handles, hardwood floors and furniture. The sap can be boiled into syrup or fermented into beer; the leaves and twigs can make a fragrant tea. **Where found:** rich, moist, often shady sites; throughout.

Paper Birch

Betula papyrifera

Height: up to 65 ft
Leaves: 2–3 in long; coarsely toothed
Flowers: tiny; hanging pollen catkins 2¾–4 in long; erect seed catkins ⅜ in long
Fruits: tiny; flat, 2-winged nutlets in hanging seed catkins

This small, showy tree has peeling, creamy white bark. The paper birch occurs across North America and was widely used by Native peoples for birch-bark canoes, baskets and message paper. To shield against snow blindness, they made "sunglasses" using bark strips with lenticels. • This species thrives in full sun and nutrient-rich habitats. In burned or cut areas, it can form near monocultures. • Birch bark is a winter staple for moose and white-tailed deer. Porcupines and snowshoe hares browse on the leaves, seedlings and bark, and common redpolls eat the catkins. **Where found:** open, often disturbed sites, forest edges on a variety of substrates; throughout, except southernmost areas.

American Basswood

Tilia americana

Height: up to 90 ft
Leaves: 3–7 in long; heart-shaped, sharply toothed, asymmetrical bases
Flowers: yellowish, in loose, hanging clusters ½ in across
Fruits: woolly, nut-like capsules ⅜ in long; fruits hang in long stalked cluster with bract

Large basswoods, with their fragrant flowers, large leaves and rounded crowns, are often planted in urban parks and gardens. It is among our handsomest native trees. Stump sprouts lend themselves well to transplanting. • The soft wood is ideal for carving and is also used for furniture, measuring sticks and pulp. The tough inner bark fibers were once woven into ropes, nets and clothing. Linden flower tea, sold in health food stores, provides a remedy for coughs, colds and bronchitis. • Bees attracted in droves to the hanging clusters of flowers produce strongly flavored honey. **Where found:** cool, moist, rich woods, often near water and mixed with other hardwoods; throughout. **Also known as:** American linden.

Quaking Aspen

Populus tremuloides

Height: up to 80 feet
Leaves: 1⅛–2¾ in long; finely toothed
Flowers: tiny; in slender, hanging catkins 1½–3 in long
Fruits: numerous hairless capsules in 4 in long
hanging, downy catkins

Suckers from the shallow, spreading roots of this deciduous tree can colonize many acres of land. Single trunks are short-lived, but a colony (clone) can survive for thousands of years. • Aspen are gorgeous in fall, when bright yellow foliage contrasts with silvery bark. • The greenish, photosynthetic bark produces a white powder to protect the trees from ultraviolet radiation in open areas. This powder can be used as sunscreen. • Pick a leaf and notice the long, slender, flattened petiole (stem) that allows the leaf to wobble or tremble in the breeze. • These trees are sometimes called "asbestos trees" because the trunk will not burn easily when a fast-moving fire passes through the forest. **Where found:** dry to moist sites; throughout.

Eastern Cottonwood

Populus deltoides

Height: up to 100 ft
Leaves: 2–4¾ in long; rounded triangular shape
Flowers: tiny, hanging catkins; male reddish, 2–4 in long;
female 6–8 in long
Fruits: tiny capsules in 6–10 in long loose,
hanging, downy catkins

Cottonwoods grow on floodplains or shorelines because the seeds require wet mud to germinate. The trees begin to "snow" in late May or early June, as rivers swollen from spring runoff begin to go down. These fast-growing trees can reach massive proportions—old cottonwoods are among the largest trees in many areas. Young trees can grow over 12 ft a year, and big ones can add 5 ft annually. • Ungulates browse on the young trees, and bees collect the sticky, aromatic resin from the buds to cement and waterproof their hives. Baltimore orioles and warbling vireos (*V. gilvus*) frequent eastern cottonwoods, building their nests in these trees. **Where found:** moist, warm, low-lying sites, floodplains, sand dunes near lakes; throughout.

Black Willow

Salix nigra

Height: up to 100 ft
Leaves: 2–6 in long; fine-toothed, tip tapered and curved
Flowers: tiny; yellow, hairy bracts
Fruits: hairless capsules in ¾ in silky-haired, hanging catkins ⅛ in long

There are over 400 willow species worldwide, and they have been cultivated since ancient Greece and Rome. The black willow is North America's largest native willow. Its distinctive leaves are uniformly green on both surfaces.
• Willows are used commercially in baskets, wicker furniture, paper pulp and rough wooden products. These fast-growing trees and shrubs are useful for reclamation and erosion control. During the American Revolution, willow was burnt down to charcoal for gunpowder. Traditionally, flexible willow branches were made into many common articles including walking sticks, fox traps, fish traps, cradle baskets, snowshoes and drums.
Where found: moist sites, riparian areas; throughout.

Black Cherry

Prunus serotina

Height: up to 80 ft
Leaves: 2–6 in long; fine, incurved teeth, 2 glands near blade
Flowers: tiny white cup flowers hang on 4–6 in long clusters
Fruits: reddish to blackish cherries (drupes) ⅜ in across

Black cherry has blackish, scaly flaking bark. The rich, mahogany red wood is used for furniture, engravings, etching and cabinet making. A large, well-formed tree can bring thousands of dollars.
• Edible, sour fruit of mature trees can be eaten raw or used in jellies, jams or wine. • Songbirds, game birds and small mammals feast on the berries and disperse the seeds. Many species of moths and butterflies, including the eastern tiger swallowtail, use black cherry as a host plant. **Caution:** the stones, bark, wood and leaves contain hydrocyanic acid and are toxic, so only the cherry flesh can be used. **Where found:** well-drained, disturbed sites; throughout. **Also known as:** black chokecherry, rum cherry, cabinet cherry, wine cherry.

American Plum

Prunus americana

Height: up to 30 ft
Leaves: 1½–4½ in long; elliptical, finely toothed
Flowers: white to pink, fragrant, 5 petals, ½–1 in across, in bundles of 2–4
Fruits: yellow or red drupes (plums) ¾–1⅛ in long

This small round tree is little more than a shrub. Fields and fencerows become misted with white in spring, when the plums bloom. At other seasons they are inconspicuous and over-looked. Wild plums are edible, but tougher and not so sweet as commercially culti-vated plums. They can be dried, or cooked, sweetened and made into preserves. • Sev-eral dyes can be made from plum: green from the leaves, grayish green from the fruits and red from the roots. • American plum is commonly used as a rootstock for commercially cultivated plums. **Caution:** the leaves, bark, wood and seeds (stones) contain hydrocyanic acid and can cause cyanide poisoning. The flesh is the only edible part. **Where found:** thickets, forest edges; throughout.

Showy Mountain-ash

Sorbus decora

Height: up to 35 ft
Leaves: compound, 4–6 in long, pinnately divided into 13–17 leaflets
Flowers: tiny; white, in dense 2⅜–6 in wide clusters
Fruits: shiny, red-orange berry-like pomes 5/16–½ in across

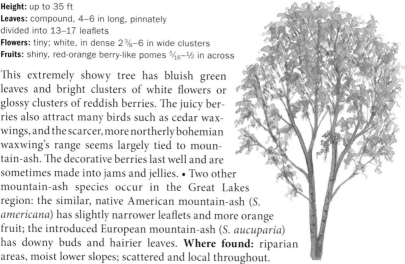

This extremely showy tree has bluish green leaves and bright clusters of white flowers or glossy clusters of reddish berries. The juicy ber-ries also attract many birds such as cedar wax-wings, and the scarcer, more northerly bohemian waxwing's range seems largely tied to moun-tain-ash. The decorative berries last well and are sometimes made into jams and jellies. • Two other mountain-ash species occur in the Great Lakes region: the similar, native American mountain-ash (*S. americana*) has slightly narrower leaflets and more orange fruit; the introduced European mountain-ash (*S. aucuparia*) has downy buds and hairier leaves. **Where found:** riparian areas, moist lower slopes; scattered and local throughout.

Cockspur Hawthorn

Crataegus crus-galli

Height: up to 25 ft
Leaves: 1⅛–2 in long; glossy, leathery, ovate, wedge-shaped base
Flowers: white, in loose, flat-topped clusters ⅜–½ in wide
Fruits: green to dull red egg-shaped haws (pomes) ⅜ in wide

Numerous hawthorn species grow abundantly here, and distinguishing among them can drive even accomplished botanists mad. Most of the easily recognized species have branched clusters of white, unpleasant-smelling flowers, reddish haws that remain on the plant throughout the winter, and are quite thorny. Look for thorny branches and larger leaves growing off the flowering shoots. • Cockspur hawthorn is a highly variable, fast-growing species that inhabits cleared land. It requires full sun, so it quickly becomes shaded out as larger trees grow around it. • Leaves, flowers and extracts of hawthorn may be used to treat a range of ailments, from coughs to back pain. **Where found:** open, disturbed sites such as old pastures; throughout.

Downy Serviceberry

Amelanchier arborea

Height: up to 40 ft
Leaves: 2–4 in long; sharply toothed, undersides hairy when young
Flowers: white; in showy clusters ¾ in across
Fruit: dark reddish purple dry, berry-like pomes ¼–½ in across

Serviceberry's beautiful snowy white blossoms provide one of the first splashes of color in leafless April woodlands. • Landscapers have picked up on the beauty of this species and it is now common in suburbia. • Many animals feast on the berries, including black bears, raccoons, skunks, chipmunks and birds. A mob of elegant cedar waxwings go crazy and will strip a tree in hours. • Serviceberry was originally called "sarvissberry," derived from "sarviss," a version of *Sorbus* (mountain ash). "Downy" refers to the woolly young leaves. The alternate name "shadbush" refers to the shad fish migration, which occurs about the same time this shrub blooms. **Where found:** dry, often sandy woods, rocky sites; throughout.

Redbud

Cercis canadensis

Height: up to 35 ft
Leaves: 2¾–4¾ in long; 5–9 prominent, radiating veins
Flowers: ⅜ in long; pale or deep pink, pea-like
Fruits: reddish brown, flat, thin pods 2–4 in long

This small, lovely tree is covered in showy pink flowers in spring and makes a wonderful garden tree in summer. The edible flowers may be added to salads or relishes and have a long history of herbal uses. Redbud is widely planted as an ornamental, but is only native from central Michigan south. • The leaves of redbud adapt to hot, dry conditions by curling and folding almost in half, thus exposing less of the leaf to sunlight, lowering temperatures and reducing water loss. • A beautiful little butterfly, the Henry's elfin (*Callophrys henrici*), uses redbud as a host plant. **Where found:** moist, fertile forests, especially in alkaline soils, typically along woodland margins; throughout southern part of region.

Black Locust

Robinia pseudoacacia

Height: up to 75 ft
Leaves: compound, 8–14 in long, divided into 7–21 leaflets
Flowers: ½–1 in long; white, pea-like with yellow dot
Fruits: reddish brown to black flattened pods, 2¾-4 in long

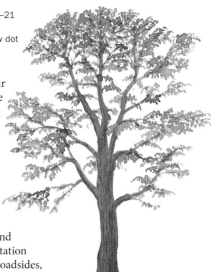

This species has been widely planted in our region and is now common well to the north of its original range. Black locust wood resists rot and has been used for railroad ties, shipbuilding and fence posts, but the wood is often weakened by borer beetles (*Megacyllene robiniae*). • The inner bark and leaves are toxic to humans and livestock, and Native peoples once carved the wood into poisonous arrows. • Black locust colonies have a suckering, nitrogen-fixing root system and are useful in erosion prevention, reforestation and supporting dikes. **Where found:** roadsides, pastures, open woods; throughout.

Eastern Wahoo

Euonymus atropurpureus

Height: up to 20 ft
Leaves: opposite; 1½–5 in long; elliptical, finely toothed, red in autumn
Flowers: purplish maroon, in clusters of 5–18¼ in across
Fruits: pink to purplish 4-lobed capsules $^3/_8$–½ in wide

This treelet is easy to overlook among snarls of more conspicuous foliage. But in fall, Wahoo explodes into attractive red foliage and strange reddish purple fruit. The odd name is derived from Native Americans, who used the bark in medicinal teas for a tonic, laxative, stimulant and expectorant. The branches were whittled into pipe stems and shoots were converted into a popular, easily erased artist's charcoal. This species was an extremely popular diuretic drug during the 19th century, especially in England. **Caution:** the seeds, fruit and bark of this tree are potentially poisonous and can cause nausea, diarrhea and cold sweats. Wahoo appears on the U.S. Food and Drug Administration's unsafe herb list. **Where found:** low, moist sites, woodland borders; throughout.

Sugar Maple

Acer saccharum

Height: up to 100 ft
Leaves: opposite; 3–8 in long; palmate, irregularly coarse toothed
Flowers: tiny; yellowish green, in clusters
Fruits: winged samaras ¾–1½ in long, in pairs

Sugar maples are famous worldwide for their sap, the main source of pure maple syrup and tasty maple sugar. Each spring, festivals celebrate the traditions of boiling sap and making maple syrup. About 40 quarts of sap yields 1 quart of maple syrup. Sugar maple, which is sometimes referred to as a "hard maple," is also prized for its wood. It is used in high-quality furniture, and the famous Longaberger baskets that are manufactured in Ohio. • Maples have winged seeds that "helicopter" downward. • The foliage turns an exceptionally showy orange-red in fall. • Sugar maple is the state tree of New York and Wisconsin. **Where found:** deep, rich soils in fairly dry woods, often with American beech; throughout.

Silver Maple

Acer saccharinum

Height: up to 80 ft
Leaves: opposite; 3–8 in long; 5 palmate lobes, irregular teeth
Flowers: small; greenish yellow, hanging in clusters on 1⅛–2¾ in long stalks
Fruits: winged samaras ¾–1½ in long, in pairs

Fast-growing, hardy silver maples are often planted as ornamentals, but have heavy leaf and seed production, brittle branches and aggressive root systems. The name comes from the silvery white undersides of the leaves, which are more deeply cleft than other maples. • The wood lacks strength and is used mainly for crates, veneer or pulp. Delicately flavored syrup is made from boiling the sap, but it is not as sweet as sugar maple sap. • The often hollow trunks provide nesting cavities for wood ducks and other birds, and dens for mammals. This species performs an important function in stabilizing stream banks. **Where found:** moist to wet sites near streams, swamps and lakes; throughout.

Red Maple

Acer rubrum

Height: up to 90 ft
Leaves: opposite; 2–6 in long; 3–5 lobed, irregularly double-toothed
Flowers: tiny; reddish clusters
Fruits: reddish or yellow winged samaras ½–1⅛ in long, in pairs

The red twigs, buds, flowers and fall leaves of this common maple add color to North America's eastern forests. The bright red, tassel-like flower clusters appear early in spring. • Red maple leaves have palmate lobes separated by shallow notches. The samara wings spread at a 50° to 60° angle. • The even, straight-grained wood is used in cabinets, furniture and flooring, and the bark can be boiled into a red ink or dark brown dye. The sap yields syrup that is semisweet. Canada has made this beautiful tree famous by stamping an image of its leaf on its flag. **Where found:** cool, moist sites near swamps, streams and springs, sometimes in drier upland sites; throughout.

Box-elder

Acer negundo

Height: up to 60 ft
Leaves: opposite, compound, 2–4¾ in long; irregularly coarse-toothed, divided into 3–5 leaflets
Flowers: tiny; pale yellowish green, male in hairy bundles, female in clusters
Fruits: winged samaras 1⅛–2 in long, in pairs, hanging in clusters

This species might not be recognized as a maple at first glance, because of its trifoliate leaves which suggest poison ivy. Box-elder is the only one of our maples to have compound leaves. Box-elder grows fast and is widely planted as a shade or shelterbelt tree. It can withstand drought and freezing temperatures, but snow, ice and wind can cause its weak branches to break. Samaras usually spread at less than a 45° angle, and the hanging clusters of fruit persist through winter. • The abundant samaras provide many seed-eating birds including evening grosbeaks, as well as rodents and squirrels, with an important winter food source. **Where found:** low, moist sites, disturbed ground, especially along streams; throughout.

Tree-of-heaven

Ailanthus altissima

Height: up to 80 ft
Leaves: compound, stalk 10–30 in long, pinnately divided into 11–41 leaflets
Flowers: small; yellowish green, in erect 4–12 in long clusters
Fruits: winged nutlets in dense, hanging clusters 1–2 in long

An arboreal cockroach, tree-of-heaven can grow nearly anywhere and is increasingly becoming a pest in natural areas. Native to Asia, it was introduced to England in 1751 and to North America in 1874. This rapidly growing ornamental is now a common sight in urban areas and does well in the most polluted urban areas—it even muscles its way up from sidewalk cracks. Female trees are favored because the male flowers have a disagreeable odor and can cause allergies. • Tree-of-heaven is the central subject in *A Tree Grows in Brooklyn*, a book by Betty Smith about an impoverished girl inspired by a tree's determination to survive. **Where found:** poor, dry soils; throughout, except northwestern MN.

White Ash

Fraxinus americana

Height: up to 80 ft
Leaves: opposite; compound, stalk 8–16 in, pinnately divided into 5–9 (usually 7) leaflets
Flowers: tiny; purplish to yellow, in compact clusters along twigs
Fruits: slender, winged samaras 1–2 in long

White ash is North America's main source of commercial ash. The strong, flexible wood is used in sporting goods (especially baseball bats), tool handles, boats and church pews. Historically, plow, airplane and automobile frames were made from ash. Native Americans made a yellow dye from the bark. • White ash leaves have smooth edges or a few rounded teeth, dark green above, dull and whitish beneath, and have tiny bumps called papillae. Ash leaves can be crushed to sooth mosquito and bee stings. • All species of ash in the Great Lakes states are under assault by the emerald ash borer (*Agrilus planipennis*). **Where found:** upland sites with rocky to deep, well-drained soils; throughout.

Green Ash

Fraxinus pennsylvanica

Height: up to 60 ft
Leaves: opposite; pinnately compound, stalk 10–12 in long, with 5–9 (usually 7) leaflets
Flowers: tiny; purplish to yellow, in compact clusters along twigs
Fruits: slender, winged samaras 1⅛–2⅜ in long

Green and white ash are very similar and often confused. Greens grow in wetter, more poorly drained sites. The best way to separate them are by samaras: in green ash samaras are very slender and elongate, and the actual seed below the wing is needle-like. In white ash, the seed is much plumper and cylindrical. Green ash is often marketed under the name "white ash" and is used in canoe paddles and other sporting goods, as well as tool handles and picture frames. The bark produces a red dye. • The long, tapered leaves of green ash leaves have short stalks and are shallow-toothed above the middle. **Where found:** moist to wet sites, floodplains, swamps; throughout.

SHRUBS & VINES

The difference between a tree and a shrub is sometimes rather gray, but in general shrubs are small woody plants less than 20 ft tall. They are typically bushy owing to multiple small trunks and branches that emerge from near the ground, and many species produce soft berries. Some shrubs occur in open sunny areas, and others are important dominant components of the understory in forests. They provide habitat and shelter for a variety of animals, and their berries, leaves and often bark are crucial sources of food. The tasty berries of some shrubs have been a staple of Native and traditional foods, and they are still enjoyed by people throughout the Great Lakes region. Some, like the highbush blueberry, are commercially valuable.

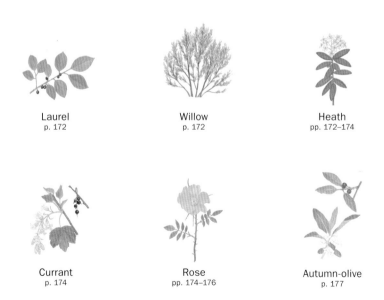

Laurel
p. 172

Willow
p. 172

Heath
pp. 172–174

Currant
p. 174

Rose
pp. 174–176

Autumn-olive
p. 177

Dogwood
p. 177

Mistletoe
p. 178

Holly
p. 178

Buckthorn
p. 178

Bladdernut
p. 179

Sumac
p. 179

Prickly-ash
p. 180

Buttonbush
p. 180

Honeysuckle
pp. 180–181

Gourd
p. 181

Pea
p. 182

Bittersweet
p. 182

Grape
pp. 182–183

Poison Ivy
p. 183

Morning-glory
p. 183

Spicebush

Lindera benzoin

Height: up to 15 ft
Leaves: 2–6 in long; elliptical, strongly aromatic
Flowers: small; yellow, in clusters
Fruits: shiny red berries ³⁄₈ in across

This common understory plant often forms dense, low "sub-jungles" in forests. It is named for the aromatic essential oil found in young leaves, twigs, and fruit. Crush a leaf and you'll detect a pleasant lemony odor. The fruit yields a spice-scented oil; dried and powdered, it can substitute for allspice. Twigs and bark produce a wintergreen-scented oil. • Native peoples used twigs and branches to make teas and season food. • The leaves contain small amounts of camphor and can be used as insect repellent and disinfectant. Spicebush is a host plant for spicebush swallowtails *(Papilio troilus)*. **Where found:** throughout, except westernmost areas; absent from MN, WI.

Pussy Willow

Salix discolor

Height: up to 20 ft (rarely taller)
Leaves: 1¹⁄₈–4 in long; somewhat variable, elliptical, wavy-edged
Flowers: tiny; on hairy catkins ³⁄₄–1½ in long
Fruits: hairy capsules ¼–½ in long

About 24 species of willows are in our range, and many are tough to identify. With its hairy felt-like catkins, pussy willow is common and distinctive. • Many butterfly species use willow as the larval host plant. Growing quickly with extensive root systems, willows are good for erosion control and re-vegetating burned areas. • The stems of some species are used for wickerwork or, traditionally, for dream-catcher charms. The wet inner bark fibers were twisted into fishing nets and ropes. The hollow stems were used as drinking straws or for making pipes. Green branches can be used to smoke meat. **Where found:** moist to wet open sites; throughout.

Labrador-tea

Ledum groenlandicum

Height: up to 3 ft
Leaves: ³⁄₈–2 in long; evergreen, leathery
Flowers: ¼ in across; white, in clusters
Fruits: drooping, dry, brown capsules <¼ in across

This small shrub keeps its leaves year-round. They are thick and leathery with rolled edges and distinctive reddish, woolly hairs on their undersides, all adaptations to help conserve moisture. • Native peoples and early settlers made the leaves and flowers into a tea, rich in vitamin C. **Caution:** consuming large amounts can be toxic; do not confuse this plant with other poisonous heaths such as bog laurel or bog rosemary *(Kalmia polifolia)*. **Where found:** moist, acidic, nutrient-poor soils, bogs; associated with black spruce; throughout, except southernmost parts of the region, absent in IN, IL.

Bog Laurel

Kalmia polifolia

Height: up to 3 ft
Leaves: opposite; ⅜–1½ in long; green, with flattened stems
Flowers: tiny; pink, saucer-shaped, in dense clusters
Fruits: round, 5-lobed capsules <¼ in with many seeds

Sometimes called bog rosemary, this species resembles the herb rosemary (*Rosmarinus officinalis*), but don't eat it. Bog laurel contains poisonous andromedotoxin compounds that can cause breathing problems, vomiting and even death if ingested in sufficient quantities. Symptoms may not develop until several hours after consumption. Poisoning and death of livestock have been reported, and even honey made from the nectar is said to be poisonous. • Nevertheless, this small shrub is a beautiful part of bog ecology. The leathery leaves curl under, and their undersides are covered with fine hairs to help prevent moisture loss. **Where found:** bogs; from central MN, WI, MI, NY north; absent in IN, IL, OH.

Leatherleaf

Chamaedaphne calyculata

Height: up to 3¼ ft
Leaves: 3/8–1¾ in; leathery, elliptical
Flowers: ¼ in across; white
Fruits: brownish capsules ¼ in across

Leatherleaf is a characteristic bog species that grows in nearly all of our sphagnum bogs. In May, bog mats come alive with the snowy flower racemes of leatherleaf, which often forms dense thickets or floating mats at the edges of open water swamps. The flowers give way to fruit capsules that contain abundant tiny seeds. • Leatherleaf is a member of the Heath family (Ericaceae), which includes blueberries, huckleberries and rhododendrons. Heaths are very important in the ecological makeup of bogs. **Where found:** wet sphagnum peat bogs; throughout.

Highbush Blueberry

Vaccinium corymbosum

Height: up to 9 ft (occasionally reaches 15 ft)
Leaves: 2–4 in long; elliptical
Flowers: ¼ in across; greenish white to pinkish, urn-shaped
Fruits: dull blue to black berries, ⅜ in across

Plentiful blueberries were the most important fruits for northern Native peoples, and blueberry picking remains a favorite tradition today. Historically, the berries were eaten fresh, dried or preserved in grease. The roots and stems were boiled into various medicinal teas, used for headaches, to regulate menstruation or even to prevent pregnancy (stems). **Where found:** variable in habitat; reaches peak abundance in bogs; sometimes dry sandy areas and open woods; throughout most of region, except MN and rare in IL and WI.

Large Cranberry

Vaccinium macrocarpon

Height: up to 8 in
Leaves: ¼–⅝ in long; oblong, round tip
Flowers: ⅜ in wide; pale pink, shooting-star-like
Fruits: red berries ¾ in across, remain on plant through winter

Tiny woody twiners, cranberries trail over wet peaty substrate of cool bogs. Their small white flowers resemble the head of a whooping crane; "craneberry" became cranberry. • Native peoples used dried cranberries in pemmican, soups, sauces and stews or whipped the cooked fruit with snow and fish oil to make an ice cream-like dessert. This species is the one cultivated commercially. • Cranberry juice has been used to treat bladder infections. The berries contain arbutin, which prevents infectious bacteria from adhering to the walls of the bladder and urinary tract. **Where found:** peaty bogs, fens; throughout but scarcer southward.

Wild Black Currant

Ribes americanum

Height: 3 ft
Leaves: 4 in wide; 3–5 pointed lobes, double-toothed edges
Flowers: small; creamy white to yellowish, bell-shaped, hanging in clusters
Fruits: black berries, ⅜ in across

Of the 10 native currants and gooseberries in our region, this species is perhaps the most common and wide-ranging. The edible if not delicious *Ribes* fruit were eaten by Native peoples, and some tribes nibbled the flowers or cooked the young leaves and ate them with raw fat. Currants are high in pectin and make excellent jams and jellies. Mixed with other berries, they are used to flavor liqueurs or make wines. Raw currants tend to be very tart, but these common shrubs provide a safe emergency food source. Small mammals and birds also consume currants. **Where found:** damp soil along streams, wooded slopes, open meadows, rocky ground; throughout.

Steeplebush

Spiraea tomentosa

Height: up to 3½ ft
Leaves: 1–2 in long; elliptical, tapered at both ends
Flowers: pink, 5 petals in steeple-shaped inflorescence less than ¼ in across
Fruits: small capsules with dense, woolly hairs

These small, woody shrublets often form dense, inconspicuous colonies when not in flower, but when they bloom—WOW! Steeplebush is one of the most striking plants in its habitats, bedecked in eye-catching, showy pink flower clusters. It is hardy and easily grown from cuttings, shoots or seeds, but once established, it spreads rapidly by rhizomes and can become difficult to control. Grouse eat the young leaves, and deer also browse on these shrubs. **Where found:** wet meadows, open sunny areas in damp soil; throughout.

Ninebark

Physocarpus opulifolius

Height: up to 10 ft
Leaves: 2–3 in long; 3 lobed, coarsely toothed
Flowers: white, 5 petals, in compact clusters ⅜ in wide
Fruits: reddish brown follicles, in dense, upright clusters ¼ in long

Ninebark is an attractive shrub of mostly limey soils, often in damp sites. Multiple stems emerging from the base create a dense, luxuriant appearance. The bark is flaky and exfoliating, giving the trunks a rough, papery look. • Although ninebark is slightly toxic, many Native groups used this plant medicinally following the adage that "what doesn't kill you, cures you." • This shrub is named for the supposedly 9 layers of bark that can be peeled away from the stem. • The leaves turn to intense reds and oranges in the fall. **Where found:** streambanks, moist thickets and rocky bluffs; throughout.

Shrubby Cinquefoil

Dasiphora fruticosa

Height: up to 3 ft
Leaves: pinnately compound, with 3–7 (usually 5) leaflets, each ¾ in long
Flowers: yellow, saucer-shaped, single in leaf axils or in small clusters at branch tips
Fruits: tiny; egg-shaped, hairy achenes

Frequently planted in parking lot islands, shrubby cinquefoil is a common garden ornamental with many cultivars. In the wild its presence often indicates high-quality habitats. Two attractive moths, large laceborder (*Scopula limboundata*) and chain-dotted geometer (*Cingilia catenaria*), use it as a host plant. • Traditionally, the leaves were used to spice meat and were boiled into a tea high in calcium. Medicinal teas, made of the leaves, stems and roots, were used to treat congestion, including tuberculosis and fevers. **Where found:** wet prairies and fens, rocky shores; throughout but becoming scarcer southward.

Black Raspberry

Rubus occidentalis

Height: 3–6 ft
Leaves: 2–5 in long; compound, with 3–5 toothed leaves
Flowers: 1 in wide; white, 5 petals
Fruits: black, seedy raspberries ½ in across

Delicious, plump raspberries can be eaten straight off the bush or made into jams, jellies or pies. Tender young shoots may be eaten raw once the prickly outer layer has been peeled off. Fresh or completely dried leaves make excellent tea, but wilted leaves can be toxic. • Traditionally, raspberry-leaf tea was given to women in childbirth or to treat painful menstruation, increase milk flow or aid in recovery. The numerous species of blackberries and raspberries in the genus *Rubus* can be difficult to separate. This distinctive species has strongly whitened, or glaucous, stems. **Where found:** thickets, clearings, open woods; throughout.

Multiflora Rose

Rosa multiflora

Height: up to 9 ft (sometimes scrambles up other objects)
Leaves: pinnately compound, with 7 elliptical leaflets, each ¾–1½ in long
Flowers: 1¼ in wide; white, 5 triangular petals
Fruits: red rose hips ⅓ in long, containing achenes

Starting in the 1930s, the U.S. Soil Conservation Service heavily promoted this aggressive Asian native for living fences and erosion control. It rapidly spread and is a nuisance in many areas. Dense growths exclude native plants—but anyone passing through a thicket will not doubt its utility as a living fence! A viral infection, rose rosette disease, is killing off some colonies. • Multiflora rose flowers are quite showy in early summer and sweetly aromatic. Most parts of rose shrubs are edible, but the hips are eaten most commonly. Avoid the seeds; their sliver-like hairs can irritate the digestive tract. **Where found:** dry to moist sites, roadsides, pastures; throughout.

Swamp Rose

Rosa palustris

Height: 2–7 ft tall
Leaves: pinnately compound, with 7 elliptical leaflets, each 1–2 in long
Flowers: up to 2 in wide, pink
Fruits: red rose hips, ½ in across, containing achenes

As its name implies, swamp rose commonly grows in swampy, wet areas and will even survive in standing water. It is distinguished from other roses by its large, pink flowers, seven leaflets and downcurved thorns. Roses, in general, are New York's state flowers. • Rose hips are rich in vitamins A, B, C, E and K; in fact, rose hips are one of the best sources of vitamin C. Three hips can contain as much vitamin C as an orange. Only the red flesh is edible, the hard seeds must be discarded. Rose hips are an important food source for deer. **Where found:** swamps and bottomlands; throughout.

Black Chokeberry

Photinia melanocarpa

Height: 2–6 ft
Leaves: 1–3 in long; elliptical, finely toothed
Flowers: white, 5 petals, in clusters ½ inch across
Fruits: shiny black pomes ¼ inch across

Black chokeberry has showy flower clusters and shiny dark green leaves that turn a beautiful orange-red in fall. It is less conspicuous when not in flower or fruit, but look closely for the elongate raised reddish glands in the leave's upper mid-ribs. A common trick used by naturalists is to turn your binoculars around and look through them backwards—they then become magnifying glasses. • This plant grows in conditions that vary from acidic tamarack bogs to dry prairies, and can tolerate pollution, salt and drought. **Where found:** variable, including acidic sites, bogs, lakeshores, dunes, thickets, dry prairies, old fields; throughout.

Autumn-olive

Elaeagnus umbellata

Height: 15–35 ft
Leaves: 1–3 in long; lance-shaped, pointed, with brown and green scales
Flowers: ⅜ in long; yellow, bell-shaped, 4 greenish sepals
Fruits: yellow to brownish, drupe-like berries up to ¾ in long

Introduced from Asia, autumn-olive is an invasive species in nutrient-poor waste sites. It and other species of autumn-olive are distinguished by scaly, brown and silvery leaves and twigs and long-stalked red berries. **Where found:** sandy soils, disturbed areas, waste sites; throughout, except MN so far. **Also known as:** umbellate oleaster, Japanese silverberry, Asiatic oleaster.

Bunchberry

Cornus canadensis

Height: 2–8 in
Leaves: ¾–3 in long; deeply veined, in whorls of 4–6
Flowers: tiny; in clusters of 5–15, surrounded by 4 white petal-like bracts
Fruits: round red, berry-like drupes ¼ in across

This tiny shrublet is more like a wildflower than a shrub. Small flowers are miniature clusters of tiny whitish blooms surrounded by showy, petal-like bracts (modified leaves). The gleaming white bracts attract insects and provide good landing platforms, thus aiding pollinators. • Bunchberry apparently cannot tolerate mean soil temperatures greater than 43° F, hence it barely extends to the southern part of the region. The drupes are edible, raw or cooked. They are not very flavorful, but the crunchy, poppy-like seeds are enjoyable. **Where found:** dry to moist sites; throughout but scarcer southward.

Red-osier Dogwood

Cornus sericea

Height: up to 10 ft (rarely 15 ft)
Leaves: opposite; ¾–4 in long; deeply veined
Flowers: tiny; white, in flat-topped clusters
Fruits: white, berry-like drupes ¼ in across

This attractive shrub has distinctive purple to red branches with white flowers in spring, red leaves in fall, and white, berry-like drupes in winter. It grows easily from cuttings, and because it is stoloniferous (spreads from roots), can form sizeable colonies. • Native peoples smoked the dried inner bark alone or with tobacco or bearberry (*Arctostaphylos uva-ursi*). The flexible branches were often woven into baskets, but also provide food for squirrels and birds. • The similar silky dogwood (*C. amomum*) has blue fruits, and the pith is brown, while in red-osier the pith is bright white. **Where found:** moist sites; throughout.

Dwarf Mistletoe

Arceuthobium pusillum

Height: less than 1 in long
Leaves: tiny and roundish
Flowers: tiny; yellowish brown, often not readily distinguishable from branches
Fruits: tiny; slender and ellipsoid-shaped

A tiny, semi-woody shrublet, this parasitic plant infests mostly black spruce but sometimes other conifers such as white spruce or tamarack. In dense concentrations they form "witch's-brooms," proiliferations of twigs produced in response to mistletoe attack. Mistletoe draws nutrients from the host tree and eventually kills it. • Male and female mistletoe flowers grow on separate plants. Fruits fill with fluid until they burst open, spraying seeds up to 50 mph and 20 ft in all directions. Seeds land directly on spruce trees or are carried there by birds. **Where found:** mostly on black spruce; from central MN, WI, MI, PA north.

Winterberry

Ilex verticillatus

Height: 10–15 ft
Leaves: 1⅛–4 in long; elliptical, thin, leathery
Flowers: tiny; 4–8 yellowish to greenish white petals
Fruits: bright red, berry-like drupes ¼ in thick

Winterberry is a member of the holly family, one of only two native species in our area. Other holly species in North America are southern in distribution. The most commonly used decorative species is American holly (*I. opaca*). The thick, green foliage and bright red berries make winterberry appear almost ornamental. • The leaves were traditionally browned and then steeped in boiling water as a tea substitute. **Caution:** the berries are toxic and can cause nausea, diarrhea and vomiting. **Where found:** wet areas, swampy woods; throughout.

Glossy Buckthorn

Frangula alnus

Height: up to 20 ft
Leaves: 1⅛–3 in long; elliptical, fine-toothed, 5–10 conspicuous parallel veins
Flowers: greenish yellow, on long stalks less than ¼ in
Fruits: green to red to blackish drupes ¼ in across

This ornamental shrub, introduced from the Mediterranean for the landscape trade, should never be planted. Having jumped the garden fence, like many non-native shrubs brought over from afar, this species is now a terrible pest in many high-quality natural areas and has displaced many native plants. • Glossy buckthorn is often an ingredient in laxatives. • Birds eat the glossy fruits and have rapidly spread this noxious shrub around. **Caution:** the berries are slightly **poisonous** to humans. **Where found:** moist, often disturbed sites, but also invades pristine bogs and fens; throughout.

Bladdernut

Staphylea trifolia

Height: 8–10 ft
Leaves: opposite; compound with 3 leaflets, 2–4 in long
Flowers: 2 in long; green-white, bell-shaped, in panicles
Fruits: papery capsules 1½ in long, 2–3 lobed

The bark on this delicate shrub is ornately striped with green, the foliage has attractive trifoliate leaves, and the beautiful, creamy white flowers are like bells. The unusual fruit, an inflated, papery capsule, holds up to 4 hard, brown seeds that mature in September and rattle when shaken. These airtight bladders float readily, an excellent adaptation for a plant that often grows near streams. • This heavily branched shrub suckers easily and readily forms thickets. **Where found:** rich, moist woodland soils, especially bottomlands and riparian areas; throughout.

Staghorn Sumac

Rhus typhina

Height: up to 20 ft (rarely taller)
Leaves: compound, 12–20 in long stalk with 11–31 leaflets
Flowers: tiny; greenish, in large, dense, erect clusters
Fruits: small; red, hairy drupes in large, dense, erect, cone-shaped clusters

Showy red fruit clusters and colorful fall leaves make staghorn sumac a favorite ornamental. In winter, the wide, woolly branches resemble velvet-covered deer antlers, inspiring the name "staghorn." Many birds, especially thrushes such as American robins and eastern bluebirds, depend on the fruit in winter. • A black ink was made from boiling the fruit and leaves, and dried fall leaves were rolled and smoked. Ripe fruits can be eaten raw or made into jelly. Delicious, pink "lemonade" is made by soaking crushed fruit in cold water (to remove hairs), then adding sugar. **Where found:** open, often disturbed sites, typically on dry, rocky or sandy soil; throughout.

Poison Sumac

Toxicodendron vernix

Height: up to 15 ft (occasionally taller)
Leaves: pinnately compound, 2–4 in long stalk with 7–13 leaflets
Flowers: tiny; yellowish green, 5 petals, in branched clusters
Fruits: white, pearl-like drupes, in clusters ⅛–¼ in long

Poison sumac is not as abundant as poison ivy, but it contains the same compound, urushiol, that causes a nasty skin reaction. Remove the resin by washing with a strong soap shortly after contact. Ointments and ammonia may relieve mild itching, but people with severe reactions should consult a doctor. Ill-effects aside, poison sumac is an extremely handsome treelet with large leaves contrasting with bright pink petioles, and in fall, showy clusters of white berries. Many birds and mammals consume the fruit and are unaffected by the toxins. **Where found:** primarily bogs, fens, seepage areas, sometimes swamps, wetlands; throughout.

179

Prickly-ash

Zanthoxylum americanum

Height: up to 20 ft (rarely tree-like)
Leaves: opposite; pinnately compound, 1–12 in long stalk
with 5–11 oval leaflets
Flowers: small; yellow, 4–5 petals
Fruits: red or reddish brown, tiny and pod-like berries in small clusters

All parts of this shrub or small tree impart a pleasant, orange-like perfume, but walking through a thicket is anything but pleasant—small thorns produce scratches aplenty. • Prickly-ash is said to have a generally stimulating effect upon the lymph system and mucous membranes, and has been prescribed as a massage lotion for rheumatism, arthritis and circulatory ailments. • This species is a host plant for the giant swallowtail *(Papilio cresphontes),* our largest butterfly. **Caution:** the leaves are phototoxic and will cause redness and blistering if crushed and applied to the skin in sunlight. **Where found:** rich woods, damp thickets; throughout.

Buttonbush

Cephalanthus occidentalis

Height: up to 14 ft (rarely 20 ft)
Leaves: 2–5 in long; opposite or rarely whorled in 3s; elliptical
Flowers: tiny, many, white, tubular with protruding styles, in spherical heads
Fruits: angular nutlets >¼ in long

This species often forms a distinctive wetland plant community known as a buttonbush swamp. Woodland pools can become choked, and the shrubs can grow in fairly deep water. In mid-summer, they are thickly festooned with showy white balls of flowers. Many species of butterflies, especially silver-spotted skippers *(Epargyreus clarus),* visit the blooms for nectar. • Traditionally, the bark was used for stomach ailments, toothaches, as an eyewash for inflamed or irritated eyes and as a quinine substitute to treat malaria. **Caution:** this plant can be toxic and has caused livestock poisoning. **Where found:** wooded wetlands, marsh borders, edges of ponds and lakes; throughout.

Twinflower

Linnaea borealis

Height: 1–4 in
Leaves: opposite; ¾ in long; rounded
Flowers: ¼–½ in long; in pairs, pink, bell-shaped
Fruits: tiny brown, egg-shaped nutlets

Named for Carolus Linnaeus (scientific epithet *Linnaea*), the Swedish scientist and father of binomial nomenclature, this species was said to have been his favorite plant. This trailing, semi-woody evergreen is an excellent native groundcover in partial shade. The small, delicate pairs of pink bells are inconspicuous on the forest floor, but their strong, sweet perfume may draw you to them in the evening. Hooked bristles on the nutlets catch on fur, feathers or clothing, which then carry them to new locations. **Where found:** northern woods with cool mean soil temperatures, and bogs; moist, open or shaded sites; throughout, but becoming scarce in southernmost areas.

Northern Arrowwood

Viburnum recognitum

Height: up to 12 ft tall
Leaves: opposite; 4–7 in long; coarsely toothed
Flowers: tiny; white, in flat-topped clusters
Fruits: blue-black, berry-like drupes ¼ in across

In spring, arrowwood puts out long shoots, and new leaves and flowers grow at the tips. The beautiful, showy white panicles of flowers bloom in early summer. The common name has its roots in a Native American use: the straight young shoots were used for arrow shafts. • Ruffed grouse and chipmunks eat the fruit, and deer browse on the stems and leaves. • Northern arrowwood has hairless twigs; the closely related southern arrowwood *(V. dentatum)*, which barely reaches our region, has downy twigs. Some authorities treat these species as one. **Where found:** low, moist woods; throughout region, except northernmost areas and MN.

Elderberry

Sambucus nigra ssp. *canadensis*

Height: up to 16 ft (normally much shorter)
Leaves: opposite; compound, 4–12 in long stalk with 5–11 leaflets (usually 7)
Flowers: tiny; white, in clusters 2–7 in across
Fruits: purplish black, berry-like drupes ¼ in across

Elderberry is conspicuous in early summer along county roadsides: the large, showy clusters of flowers command attention. Later, attractive purplish red panicles of berry-like drupes draw the eye to this strong-smelling, clumped, deciduous shrub. The berries can be made into jam, jelly, pies and wine, but raw berries are unpalatable and toxic (cooking destroys the toxins). Moose, deer and elk seem to enjoy them. You can make effective pea-shooters by removing the pith from large twigs. **Caution:** the leaves, bark and roots of this plant contain cyanide and are poisonous. Raw berries can cause vomiting. **Where found:** moist sunny sites; throughout.

Wild Cucumber

Echinocystis lobata

Height: to 25 ft; climbing vine
Leaves: to 5–6 in; 3–5 sharp, triangular lobes
Flowers: white, 6-parted, male flowers star-like, in clusters ⅓ in wide
Fruits: green, oval, beset with numerous long prickles 1 in long

This odd but showy vine can be quite common, especially in moist soils of alluvial thickets. The bizarre, densely prickly fruit are buoyant bladders, an excellent adaptation for water dispersal during floods. The pulverized roots of this plant were steeped into an aphrodisiac tea. • The scientific name comes from the Greek *echinos* for "hedgehog" and *cystis* for "bladder," referring to the fruit. **Where found:** wet to moist sites; streambanks, thickets, roadsides; throughout.

Hog-peanut

Amphicarpaea bracteata

Height: up to 5 ft; twining vine
Leaves: compound, 1–3 in long stalks with 3 oval leaflets
Flowers: ½ in wide; pea-like, pale lilac
Fruits: twisted pods 1½–2 in long

This delicate little vine in the pea family (Fabaceae) typically grows as a groundcover, sometimes clambering into low shrubs. The flowers appear in clusters in late summer, making this abundant vine more conspicuous. The edible legumes of this plant are a good source of carbohydrates, and the seeds are high in protein. The legumes must be well cooked for proper digestion. • A few species of skipper butterflies use hog-peanut as a host plant. **Where found:** roadsides, thickets, woodland borders; throughout.

Bittersweet

Celastrus scandens

Height: climbing to 15 ft, sometimes higher
Leaves: 2–3 in long; oval to lance-shaped, finely serrated leaves
Flowers: tiny; green, 4–5 petals, in terminal clusters
Fruits: yellowish capsule opens to expose scarlet berries, ¼ in across, in long, hanging clusters

Bittersweet often blends with other tangles of vegetation but becomes conspicuous when the bright orange and red fruit ripen. • Showy, berry-like bittersweet fruits provide winter food for species such as grouse, pheasant, quail, rabbit and squirrel. • In times of starvation, Native peoples reportedly boiled the palatable bark or inner bark to make a thick soup. **Caution:** all parts of the plant, including the berries, are potentially toxic and should not be consumed by humans, especially by pregnant and nursing women. **Where found:** thickets, fencerows, woodland edges, riverbanks; throughout.

Virginia Creeper

Parthenocissus quinquefolia

Height: to 50 ft or higher; climbing vine
Leaves: palmately compound with 5 leaflets, each 6 in long
Flowers: small; greenish white, in clusters
Fruits: clusters of purplish black berries, ¼ in wide

This common climber can scale the heights of the tallest trees, aided by tendrils tipped with adhesive suction cup-like disks. In fall, showy foliage provides a vibrant display of fiery red, purple and scarlet leaves. The purplish black berries and red stems remain on the plant after the leaves fall, providing winter interest. • Berries are poisonous to humans but are a popular food for winter songbirds. Deer and livestock browse the foliage. • The perennial root system makes this plant well suited for slope stabilization, and its groundcover habit provides cover for small mammals and birds. **Where found:** wooded habitats; throughout.

Riverbank Grape

Vitis riparia

Height: to 80 ft or higher; climbing vine
Leaves: 3–8 in long; 3-lobed (some unlobed), coarsely toothed
Flowers: tiny; greenish, in compact pyramidal clusters
Fruits: spherical, waxy, black with bluish cast, ½ in across, in hanging clusters

One of 5 species of wild grape in our area, riverbank grape is most frequently encountered. The small, tart fruit is juicy and flavorful, especially after the first frost. Eat them raw, made into jelly or fermented into a musky-flavored wine. • Riverbank grape is a key parent species in breeding modern grape varieties that are disease and cold-resistant. • Add a grape leaf to homemade pickle jars—a natural inhibitor in the leaf keeeps the pickles from going soft. **Where found:** moist thickets and woods; throughout.

Poison Ivy

Toxicodendron radicans

Height: to 3 ft; groundcover, shrublet or climbing vine
Leaves: compound, with 3 leaflets, each 2–6 in long
Flowers: tiny; greenish white
Fruits: white berries ¼ in across

This species is the one plant that anyone venturing outdoors should learn. Identification difficulties are compounded by its variable growth habit: trailing groundcover, small erect shrublet, or vine climbing high into trees or on other objects. A brush with this plant can cause a severe allergic reaction, obvious in an itchy rash and swelling. To hyper-responders, contact can even be life threatening. The rash can sometimes be alleviated by washing with plenty of soap, but if symptoms worsen, seek medical attention. • Poison ivy is actually rather showy, especially in fall when leaflets turn red and ripe berries become white. The fruit are eaten by many species of birds, and are a staple for wintering yellow-rumped warblers. **Where found:** opportunistic, various dry to moist upland sites; throughout.

Hedge Bindweed

Calystegia sepium

Height: up to 10 ft
Leaves: 2–4 in long; arrowhead-shaped
Flowers: 1½–3 in long; white to pink, funnel-shaped
Fruits: tiny capsules

This common twining vine climbs up shrubs and hedges throughout much of North America. It is quite showy, although some states consider it a noxious weed—reflected in names such as "devil's guts," "devil's vine" and "hellweed." There apparently is a native form, and introduced Eurasian ones. • The morning-glory family name, Convolvulaceae, comes from the Latin *convolvere,* meaning "to twine around." **Where found:** thickets, fencerows, overgrown fields, woodland borders, open weedy sites; throughout.

FORBS, FERNS & GRASSES

Forbs are non-woody, seed-bearing plants; essentially all broad-leaved plants that are not ferns, grasses, sedges, or trees or shrubs. They are often perennials that grow from a persistent rootstock, but many are short-lived annuals. Forbs include all of our spring wildflowers, prairie sunflowers, many flowering wetland plants, herbs used in gardening for food or medicine, and numerous weeds. Many herbs are used for adding flavor to foods and in herbal remedies, aromatherapy and dyes. Various forbs also flower into unique, delicate and beautiful colors and forms. Forbs are also vital to the ecology of the plant communities in which they occur, as food sources for pollinating insects and other animals, host plants for moths and butterflies, nest material for birds and cover for many species of animals.

The forbs illustrated here are but the most frequent and likely to be seen examples. The Great Lakes region hosts well over 2000 species of native forbs; far more than we could hope to include.

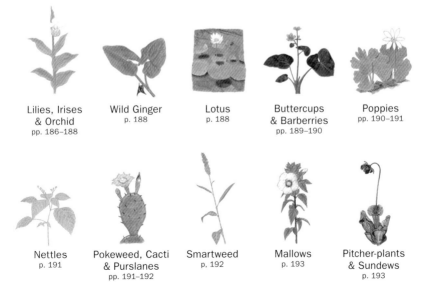

Lilies, Irises
& Orchid
pp. 186–188

Wild Ginger
p. 188

Lotus
p. 188

Buttercups
& Barberries
pp. 189–190

Poppies
pp. 190–191

Nettles
p. 191

Pokeweed, Cacti
& Purslanes
pp. 191–192

Smartweed
p. 192

Mallows
p. 193

Pitcher-plants
& Sundews
p. 193

Violets
p. 194

Mustards
pp. 194–195

Indian-pipes
p. 195

Loosestrife
p. 196

Saxifrages
& Roses
pp. 196–197

Peas
pp. 197–198

Water-milfoils
p. 198

Evening-primroses
pp. 199–200

Spurges
p. 200

Geraniums
& Balsam
pp. 200–201

Ginseng
p. 201

Carrots
pp. 201–203

Gentian
& Dogbane
pp. 203–204

Milkweed
p. 204

Nightshades
& Phloxes
pp. 204–205

Bluebells
& Vervain
p. 205

Mints, Figworts
& Acanthus
pp. 206–208

Bladderwort
p. 208

Bellflowers
pp. 208–209

Madders
pp. 209–210

Teasels
& Aster Family
p. 210–215

Aquatic plants
p. 216

Arums
p. 217

Grasses
p. 218

Cattails
& Pickerelweeds.
218–219

Ferns
p. 219

Michigan Lily

Lilium michiganense

Height: up to 5 ft
Leaves: 3–7 in long, to 1¼ in wide, whorls of 5–20, lance-shaped
Flowers: 2–3 in long, orange to red with many purple spots
Fruits: 3 parted capsule, 2 in long

The brilliant orange flowers of Michigan lily are especially striking in that their fawn-spotted tepals curve strongly back, almost touching at their tips. White-tailed deer apparently consider them succulent candy. • Native peoples ate the peppery bulbs, tiny tubers and flowers raw or cooked. The bulbs were used in poultices to heal wounds, heart problems and toothaches or were steeped into tea that was used to treat fevers or wash sores. • Dig these beauties visually; don't dig them out of the ground! Between deer and overzealous collectors, lilies have disappeared in places. **Where found:** moist woods, meadows; throughout, but rare in NY.

Large-flowered Trillium

Trillium grandiflorum

Height: up to 18 in
Leaves: 3–6 in, whorl of 3, prominently veined
Flowers: 1½–3 in long, 3 curving white petals fade to pink with age
Fruits: green berry-like capsule, ½ in long

The state wildflower of Ohio, large-flowered trilliums sometimes form incredible carpets of white in rich woodlands. They do not flower until they are several years old. • The ripe fruits split open to reveal many sticky seeds that contain special oily bodies called elaiosomes, which are as tasty as potato chips to ants. The ants carry the seeds to their nests and bite off the "ant snack," leaving the seed to grow far from the parent plant. • Older flowers become pinkish, and this change in color is thought to be triggered by successful pollination: the plant is indicating to pollinating insects not to waste their time. **Where found:** rich woods; throughout.

Yellow Trout-lily

Erythronium americanum

Height: up to 10 in
Leaves: 2 opposite, 4–6 in long, lance-shaped, brown or purple mottled
Flowers: ¾–1½ in long, yellow, often red-spotted, with anthers
Fruits: rounded, flat capsules

The early spring flowers of this species, one of our most common native lilies, are show-stoppers. Sizable colonies might have thousands of brown-mottled leaves but comparatively few blossoms, as young plants don't produce flowers. The bulbs of yellow trout-lily are edible and were traditionally cooked or dried for winter use—a good winter supply for a family was 200 lbs. • Trout-lily leaf tea can inhibit growth of a range of bacteria and can be used as an antiseptic wash for cuts, scrapes and sores. **Where found:** rich woods; throughout.

False Solomon's-seal

Maianthemum racemosum

Height: up to 36 in
Leaves: 3–6 in long, elliptical, prominent veins
Flowers: <¼ in long, white, in puffy, pyramidal clusters 2–6 in long
Fruits: red or green berries with red marks, ¼ in wide

In false Solomon's-seal the flowers form a plume at the terminus of the leaves, whereas in true Solomon's-seal (*Polygonatum* spp.) the flowers dangle in small clusters under the leaves. • The red or green berries of false Solomon's-seal are edible, but their taste is unremarkable. Beware, too many can cause diarrhea. • The leaves were crushed into a poultice and used by Native peoples to treat minor burns, sores, wounds and sore eyes. • Starry false Solomon's-seal (*M. stellatum*) occurs less commonly; it is smaller with much larger flowers and boldly striped fruit. **Where found:** moist woods; throughout.

Downy Solomon's-seal

Polygonatum pubescens

Height: up to 2½ ft
Leaves: 2–6 in long, elliptical, prominent veins, hairy beneath
Flowers: ½–1 in long, greenish to white, tubular
Fruits: blue-black berries, ⅜ in wide

The odd common name stems from the roots, which bear leaf scars said to resemble the seal of King Solomon. The small but beautiful flowers of this lily can easily be missed, dangling as they do under the foliage. Smooth Solomon's-seal (*P. biflorum*) also occurs here; it lacks hairs on the undersurfaces of the leaves. **Where found:** rich, moist woods; throughout, but becoming scarce in IL.

Southern Blue Flag

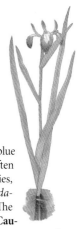

Iris virginica

Height: up to 30 in
Leaves: 15–30 in long, 1 in wide, basal, sword-shaped
Flowers: 3 purple-blue sepals 1½–2¾ in long; yellowish spot near base
Fruits: beaked, oblong capsules

This showy wetland plant rivals any cultivated garden iris. Northern blue flag (*I. versicolor*), lacks the basal yellow spot on the sepal blade and is often shorter in stature but more stiffly erect. • There are hundreds of iris species, named for the Greek goddess of the rainbow. The yellow-flowered *I. pseudacorus* occurs in our wetlands: it is an invasive Eurasian introduction. • The 3 parts of the flower are said to symbolize wisdom, faith and courage. **Caution:** highly poisonous roots and shoots can cause difficulty breathing, upset stomach and diarrhea if eaten. Handling this plant can cause severe skin rashes in some people. **Where found:** wet, sunny sites; throughout, except northernmost areas.

Showy Lady's-slipper

Cypripedium reginae

Height: 2–3 ft
Leaves: 4–10 in long, broad, pleated, hairy
Flowers: 2 petals (not twisted), 3 white sepals surround pink pouch
Fruits: oblong capsules

Finding any of our fewer than 60 native orchids is always a treat. Showy lady's-slipper, the state flower of Minnesota, has the largest flowers of any North American orchid: huge pink and white pouches adapted for pollination by large bumblebees. The plant depends on special mycorrhizal fungi for nutrient intake, water absorption and seed growth. **Do not transplant** these unusual orchids—they will likely not survive without the fungi. **Do not handle** as glandular hairs on the foliage can cause a blistering poison ivy-like dermatitis. **Where found:** cool, wet soil of bogs and fens; throughout, but scattered and local southward.

Wild Ginger

Asarum canadense

Height: 6–12 in
Leaves: 3–5 in wide; opposite, downy, heart-shaped
Flowers: 1 in long; maroon to greenish yellow, bell-shaped
Fruits: small, fleshy capsules

The heart-shaped leaves are obvious, but most people never notice the flowers. Fleshy and maroon, they arise from the base of the plant and nearly lay on the ground, probably to attract ground-dwelling beetles and ants for pollination purposes. • Wild ginger smells and tastes like culinary ginger, but the two plants are not related. The leaves of wild gingers are more strongly flavored than the rootstocks, and are milder than culinary ginger. • The rootstocks have been eaten fresh or dried as a ginger substitute, and the leaves may be steeped into a fragrant medicinal tea. **Where found:** moist, rich woods; throughout.

American Lotus

Nelumbo lutea

Height: to 3 ft above water surface
Leaves: 24 in across, round
Flowers: 10 in wide, showy, yellow
Fruits: acorn-like nuts, ½ in wide

This giant water-lily has the largest flowers of any native plant here. Carpets can form extensive colonies in shallow water. The large pods hold many seeds in cylindric chambers, and look just like shower heads. When changes in water levels induce germination of seeds, colonies can spring up where few or no plants had been. Seeds buried in mud may remain viable for decades or longer—seeds of a closely related Eurasian species have been successfully germinated after lying dormant for over 1200 years! **Where found:** shallow water of ponds, lakes; throughout, but scarcer northward, probably expanding.

Marsh-marigold

Caltha palustris

Height: up to 2 ft
Leaves: 6 in wide, basal, heart-shaped or kidney-shaped, toothed
Flowers: ½ in across, 5–9 yellow sepals surround numerous stamens
Fruits: follicle with red seeds, ½ in long

One of spring's great botanical spectacles is a mass blooming of these gorgeous buttercups in swampy woods. An early wildflower, marsh-marigold has come and gone by the time spring's procession of wildflowers reaches peak abundance. To humans, these flowers look evenly yellow, but insects can detect distinct ultraviolet light patterns along the petals that guide them to the center of the flower. • **Caution:** raw leaves contain a toxin that can irritate skin and is poisonous if eaten. **Where found:** swampy woods, sometimes wet meadows, bogs, fens; throughout.

Hepatica

Hepatica nobilis

Height: 6 in
Leaves: about 2½ in long, green with 3 rounded to pointed lobes
Flowers: 1 in wide, lavender, 5–12 petal-like sepals
Fruits: achenes

Hepatica flowers are exceptionally showy and among the first wildflowers to bloom in spring. Blossoms vary from deep china-blue to white. • Hepatica means "of the liver," and these plants have been used medicinally to treat liver ailments. The Greeks used this plant to treat cowardice and freckles, which were believed to be caused by an ailing liver. • Insects play an important role in hepatica reproduction. Bees and flies pollinate the flowers in spring, and ants disperse the seeds in fall. **Where found:** rich upland woods; throughout.

Hispid Buttercup

Ranunculus hispidus

Height: up to 2½ ft
Leaves: 2–4 in wide, divided into 3 toothed parts
Flowers: 1 in across, bright yellow, 5 petals
Fruits: smooth, round achenes

Some botanists believe there may be several species within this highly variable buttercup species complex. Forms growing in wet habitats are less hairy and weaker stemmed, while upland forms are hairier and stiffly upright. • Buttercups are named for the toxic ranunculin contained in their sap. It causes symptoms that include dermatitis, mouth blisters and intense burning pain of the digestive tract when ingested. Drying and cooking are said to degrade the poison, rendering plants or hay containing buttercups harmless. • Traditionally, the sap was applied to warts or plague sores, and the juice was used to irritate the skin to counteract arthritis and nerve pain. **Where found:** dry to wet woods; throughout.

Wild Columbine

Aquilegia canadensis

Height: up to 2 ft
Leaves: mostly basal, compound, 3 leaflets with 3 lobed, rounded tips
Flowers: 1½ in long, nodding, tubular, 5 yellow petals with 4 red spurs
Fruits: 5-parted pod-like follicle

A striking member of the buttercup family, columbine grows best on rocky outcrops. The colorful flowers entice hummingbirds and long-tongued butterflies, which pollinate the plants. The entire flower is edible and decorative in salads. • The common name means "dove" and the Latin name *Aquilegia* means "eagle." Both names refer to the yellow, talon-like spurs of the flowers. Occasionally the introduced European columbine (*A. vulgaris*), with blue to white flowers, jumps the garden wall and escapes to the wild. **Where found:** moist, rocky meadows, forest openings, clearings; throughout.

Mayapple

Podophyllum peltatum

Height: up to 18 in
Leaves: 8–15 in wide, umbrella-like, 5–9 segments
Flowers: 1½ in wide, nodding, white, waxy, 6–9 petals
Fruits: yellow, fleshy berries, about 2½ in long

This common woodland plant forms colonies, with leaves looking like little umbrellas. One of North America's more powerful and useful medicinal plants, may-apple has been used for a wide array of diseases, notably for liver and digestive disorders. • The fruit pulp is sweet, acidic and can be eaten raw or cooked into jelly, jams, and pies. **Caution:** remove the rind, and do not eat any other part of the plant, including the seeds, since they are strongly cathartic. Only fully ripe fruit should be eaten, because unripe fruit is strongly laxative. Box turtles seem unaffected by ill side-effects and gorge on mayapple fruit with impunity. **Where found:** moist woods; throughout.

Bloodroot

Sanguinaria canadensis

Height: up to 10 in
Leaves: up to 8 in wide, 3–9 lobes, embrace flower stalk
Flowers: 1–2 in across, 8–16 white petals, yellow center
Fruits: yellowish capsules

This very common wildflower blooms in early spring, the showy flowers lasting only a day or so. The common name stems from a brilliant red sap in the root that was traditionally used as a dye. • Bloodroot is well known for its anti-microbial, anti-inflammatory and anti-oxidant properties. The root's active compound sanguinarine is a potentially poisonous alkaloid at higher doses, but a good anti-microbial at lower doses. Sanguinarine was once added to tooth-paste and mouthwash to fight plaque and gingivitis, but was withdrawn owing to mouth sores in some patients. Research has shown that bloodroot may assist in treating cancer, cardiovascular diseases and arthritis. **Where found:** rich woods; throughout.

Dutchman's Breeches

Dicentra cucullaria

Height: up to 12 in
Leaves: 2–4 in long, basals, compound, divided
Flowers: 4 petals, each ¾ in long, with 2 outer divergent spurs
Fruits: capsules with black seeds

This easily identified spring wildflower provides a source of pollen for early emerging bumblebees. Bee species with proboscis too short to reach pollen deep in the flower chew holes through the side of the bloom. • Dutchman's breeches contains isoquinoline alkaloids, including aporphine and protopine (which is also found in the opium poppy, *Papaver somniferum*). Its underground tubers are considered the most toxic and the flowers and leaves less toxic. The most common symptom of poisoning is a staggering gait, giving rise to the other common name of "staggerweed." • The common name Dutchman's breeches refers to the flowers, which resemble a pair of breeches hung up to dry. **Where found:** rich woods; throughout.

Wood Nettle

Laportea canadensis

Height: up to 4 ft
Leaves: 2½–8 in, broadly oval, long stalked and alternate, serrated
Flowers: ¼ in long, greenish, petals absent, in cluster
Fruits: oblique achenes

This species is one of the main reasons nettles have a bad rap. Walking through a mature stand of it can leave you welted with stings even through jeans. It is our only stinging nettle species with alternate leaves, and woodland explorers would be wise to learn to recognize it. The stings fade within half an hour in most cases. None of these features bother beautiful red admiral butterflies, whose caterpillars use wood nettle as a host plant. • Some people use gloves to pick young, tender nettles to make soup or steam them as a delicious spring vegetable. **Where found:** damp, rich woods; throughout.

Pokeweed

Phytolacca americana

Height: 6–10 ft
Leaves: 3½–12 in long, lance-shaped
Flowers: ¼ in wide greenish-white, in racemes 2–8 in long
Fruits: dark purple berries, ⅜ in wide

Many gardeners are familiar with this coarse, robust weed. Although parts of it are toxic, birds can eat the colorful berries with impunity and thus spread it around. Pokeweed is a showy native plant when in fresh condition. It is an important medicinal plant, known for its immune-stimulating, antiviral, anti-inflammatory and anti-fungal properties. The plant was used as an emetic, purgative, laxative and expectorant; it was also used to treat chest colds and "bewitchment." • Pokeweed is being investigated as a potential treatment for AIDS. **Where found:** open, disturbed sites; throughout.

Prickly-pear

Opuntia humifusa

Height: prostrate; big pads might project 1 ft up
Leaves: pad (actually stems) 2–4 in by 4–6 in
Flowers: 1½–3½ in wide, large, brilliant yellow
Fruits: red-purple, fleshy, spiny, 1–2 in long

Prickly-pear, although native here, is scattered and local, inhabiting dry, sandy areas—relict habitats of a long ago hotter, drier time. • Prickly-pear were widely used for food by Native peoples. Raw cacti are said to taste like cucumber. Once the spines and seeds were removed, the flesh was eaten raw, used to thicken stews and soups or dried for later use. More recently, the sweet flesh has been added to fruit cakes or canned as fruit juice. Berries can also be boiled whole and strained to make jellies or syrups. **Where found:** rocky outcrops, gravelly soils, sand dunes; scattered sparingly throughout, mostly near shores of the Great Lakes.

Spring-beauty

Claytonia virginica

Height: 3–6 in
Leaves: 3 in long, narrow, lance-shaped (grass-like)
Flowers: 2 in long, showy, white or pink, 5-petals with pink veins
Fruits: oval capsules

The little potato-like corms (root structures) of this charming, abundant spring wildflower are persistent. It often comes up in lawns long after most other wildflowers have disappeared. The tiny white flowers are prominently striped with pink, which serve as nectar guides luring pollinating insects to the blossoms. • The nutritious corms of spring-beauty were valued food for Native peoples. The corms were rubbed clean then cooked in pits or steamed. Corms were also buried in underground caches for winter use. **Where found:** woodlands, often persisting in pastures, lawns, disturbed sites; throughout.

Water Smartweed

Polygonum amphibium

Height: terrestrial form up to 3 ft
Leaves: ¾–6 in long, lance-shaped, pointed, often reddish
Flowers: <¼ in wide, in dense, spike-like clusters
Fruits: dark achenes

This species is easily the showiest of our native smartweeds, sending forth large flaming pink spikes of flowers. There are 2 forms: variety *stipulaceum* grows in deep water and has floating leaves; variety *emersum* grows in moist soil and is stiffer and more upright. Smartweed achenes are important food and a winter staple for birds; rodents and deer eat the plants and fruit. The achenes can remain dormant in soil for decades, germinating when conditions become suitable. • The edible leaves have a hot, peppery taste and are very high in vitamins K and C. They can be used fresh in salads or eaten as steamed vegetable. **Where found:** shallow ponds, lakes, streams, wetlands; throughout.

Swamp Rose-mallow

Hibiscus moscheutos

Height: up to 5 ft
Leaves: 4–8 in long, oval to lanceolate, downy beneath
Flowers: 2–3 in long, white to pink, crimson center, 5 petals
Fruits: capsules, 1½ in long

When in flower, swamp rose-mallow can be the most conspicuous plant in the marsh. Huge blossoms bloom from June to September. They vary from brilliant pink to white, and nearly always have an attractive bull's-eye center of deep maroon. The genus *Hibiscus* contains about 200 species, but most are tropical. This species and one other are the only native *Hibiscus* that occur this far north. • It has very slimy inner leaves and roots (mucilaginous) that have traditionally been used medicinally to treat stomach, lung and urinary disorders. **Where found:** marshes, moist meadows; throughout, except westernmost part of region, especially Great Lakes shorelines.

Pitcher-plant

Sarracenia purpurea

Height: up to 16 in (flower stalks)
Leaves: to 12 in long, basal, often water-filled
Flowers: 2–2¾ in wide, purplish red, solitary, nodding
Fruits: capsules

Pitcher-plant's purple-streaked hollow leaves (pitchers) secrete chemicals that attract insects. Searching for snacks, the insect enters the tubular leaf. Stiff, downward-pointing hairs prevent its retreat should it realize something is amiss. It then reaches a zone of the inner leaf that is smooth and glassy, and plunges into the juice below, which is rainwater enriched with enzymes that reduce buoyancy and speed decomposition. The plant then absorbs the insect's proteins and nitrogen, which is how it gets sustenance in nutrient-poor bog soils. **Where found:** peaty bogs, fens; throughout, but rare and scattered southward.

Sundew

Drosera rotundifolia

Height: 2–4 in, occasionally taller
Leaves: tiny, round, basal, on round, hairy, flattened stalks 2½ in long
Flowers: <¼ in across, pink or white, 5 petals
Fruits: capsules, <¼ in long

Like something from a horror movie, this insect-eating plant has sticky, round leaves covered in gooey, reddish hairs that attract, trap and digest prey. The hairs are tipped with the botanical equivalent of glue, and investigating insects are caught and held fast. The hairs then slowly curl in a death-grip around the victim A secreted enzyme dissolves the prey within 48 hours, leaving only the exoskeleton. • Sundew has been used to treat respiratory problems and was made into love potions. **Where found:** peaty wetlands, primarily bogs, fens; throughout, but scattered and local.

Canada Violet

Viola canadensis

Height: up to 16 in
Leaves: 2–4 in long, broadly heart-shaped
Flowers: 1 in wide, white with yellow center and purple veins, 5 petals
Fruits: capsules with dark seeds

There are about 28 native violets in our region, and this species is perhaps the most stately and handsome of them all. Many species are difficult to identify, but Canada violet is easily recognized by its tall upright stems and bright white flowers with lemon-yellow centers. Seeds are often dispersed by ants that carry them to their nests then bite off the elaisome bodies (seed bases). • The flowers make a pretty garnish for salads, and the cooked or raw leaves are high in vitamins A and C. **Caution:** seeds and rhizomes are poisonous. **Where found:** damp woods; throughout, but endangered in IL.

Common Blue Violet

Viola sororia

Height: up to 8 in
Leaves: 2–4 in long, basal, heart-shaped
Flowers: 1¼ in wide, blue-violet to whitish, 5 petals
Fruits: capsules with dark seeds

Our many species of violets come in white, yellow and blue. Of the last, this species is by far the most abundant and wide-ranging. Violets have two growth habits: caulescent (having a leafy stem) and acaulescent (leaves growing directly off rhizomes). This plant is one of the acaulescent, or stemless species. In addition to the showy blue-purple petaliferous blossoms, this violet sometimes produces inconspicuous cleistogamous blooms that lack petals in fall. Fertilized flowers develop into capsules that burst open, explosively shooting out seeds. **Where found:** forests, thickets, disturbed sites, yards; throughout.

Cut-leaved Toothwort

Cardamine concatenata

Height: 8–16 in
Leaves: to 5 in, whorl of 3, each divided into 3 toothed segments
Flowers: ½–¾ in long, white, 4 petals
Fruits: 1½ in long, pod-like

One of our most common spring wildflowers often grows in profusion among the blooms of other showy wildflowers. It is a mustard, and like all members of this large family, the flowers have 4 petals. • Most species in the genus *Cardamine* can be eaten raw or cooked in soups, stews and casseroles. The delicate, slightly succulent plants add a refreshing, peppery flavor to sauces, salads and sandwiches. The pods of some species have been ground and mixed with vinegar to make a substitute for horseradish. **Where found:** moist, rich woods; throughout.

Dame's-rocket

Hesperis matronalis

Height: up to 3½ ft
Leaves: 2–6 in long, lance-shaped, sharply toothed, hairy
Flowers: ¾ in wide, purple to white, 4 petals
Fruits: pod-like, 4 in long

Widespread and abundant, Dame's-rocket is often mistaken for phlox, although it belongs to the Mustard family. It begins flowering in early summer and has conspicuous flowers that are most fragrant in the evening. These prolific self-seeders originate in the Old World and were introduced to North America as garden plants. • The edible leaves and flowers add a delicious twist to salads. **Where found:** open woods, roadsides, fencerows, weedy areas; throughout.

Garlic Mustard

Alliaria petiolata

Height: up to 3 ft
Leaves: 2½ in long, triangular, coarsely toothed
Flowers: ¼ in long, white, 4 petals
Fruits: 1–2 in long, narrowly cylindric, pod-like

A European introduction, garlic mustard was first detected in America in 1868 in New York. Since then, it has erupted throughout the East and is still spreading west. A botanical cockroach, this pest now ranks high among our most noxious non-native plants. A scourge of woodlands, it often forms solid stands, eliminating native flora. Conquering Garlic mustard "armies" are aided by allelopathic enzymes secreted from roots; these chemicals inhibit the growth of competing plants. We should declare war on this herbaceous invader and drive it from our shores. Eat all you can—the leaves are edible. Our native plants will be grateful. **Where found:** all manner of woods; throughout.

Indian-pipe

Monotropa uniflora

Height: 4–12 in
Leaves: scale-like, linear to oval, up to ⅜ in long
Flowers: ¾ in long, nodding, white, narrowly bell shaped, 5 petals
Fruits: capsule, erect when mature

Indian-pipe has no chlorophyll and looks like a white fungus. This odd plant is semi-parasitic; it grows with mycorrhizal fungi that provide it with all essential nutrients. In turn, the fungi depend on tree roots, thus the indirectly parasitic life cycle. The mycorrhizal fungi provide nutrients and water to the roots of photosynthesizing plants while receiving carbon-rich photosynthates from the host plant. Indian-pipe, through its connection with mycorrhiza, gets some of these photosynthates. Since it does not photosynthesize, Indian pipe can grow in darker environments than many other plants. **Where found:** rich, shady woods; throughout.

Fringed Loosestrife

Lysimachia ciliata

Height: up to 4 ft
Leaves: opposite, 2–5 in long, broad, hairy petioles
Flowers: ½–1 in wide, yellow, 5 pointed corolla lobes
Fruits: rounded capsule ¼ in long

An often abundant native summer wildflower of rich woods, fringed loosestrife is named for the prominent fringes of hairs along the leaf petioles. The common name "loosestrife" is applied to a number of plants, including the invasive non-native purple loosestrife. According to legend, the name loosestrife arose when King Lysimachus, a successor of Alexander the Great, was chased by an angry bull. When the quick-thinking king waved a loosetrife stem at the enraged animal, the bull suddenly relaxed, or was "loosened from strife." **Where found:** moist or wet sites, reaching peak abundance on wooded floodplains; throughout.

Grass-of-parnassus

Parnassia glauca

Height: up to 16 in
Leaves: roundish, to 2½ in; mostly basal, typically one smaller stem leaf
Flowers: about ¾ in wide, white with purple veins, 5 petals
Fruits: 4-valved capsules

Grass-of-parnassus does not look like a grass at all and is not even closely related to them. Dioscorides, a Greek botanist, apparently named these plants after a grass that grew on Mount Parnassus in Greece. Although the foliage is glossy and attractive, the flowers are the most striking aspect of this plant. White petals are boldly striped with green, and they almost glow. • Grass-of-parnassus requires the specialized wet alkaline soils of fens, a habitat that has largely been destroyed in many areas. **Where found:** wet, calcareous seep-fed meadows of fens; throughout, but becoming rare and local southward.

Common Strawberry

Fragaria virginiana

Height: up to 6 in
Leaves: 1–4 in long, divided into 3 coarsely toothed leaflets
Flowers: ¾ in wide, white, 5 petals
Fruits: red strawberry dotted with achenes

Few things beat running into a patch of fresh wild strawberries. The fruit is delicious, and many animals enjoy it. This plant is the ancestor of 90% of our cultivated strawberries. Each tiny red berry contains all the flavor of a large domestic strawberry. The rhizomes and runners produce tufts of bluish-tinged leaves with toothed leaflets. • Wood strawberry *(F. vesca)* has yellow-green leaflets with the end tooth projecting beyond adjacent teeth, whereas in wild strawberry the end tooth is shorter. Wood strawberry fruit are also dry and nowhere near as tasty. **Where found:** dry fields and open woods; throughout.

Common Agrimony

Agrimonia gryposepala

Height: 1½ ft
Leaves: to 8 in, compound, 5–9 leaflets, each 2–4 in, coarsely toothed
Flowers: ¼ in wide, yellow, 5-parted, in spike-like cluster
Fruits: dry seeds with hooked bristles

Outdoor enthusiasts know agrimony if not by name, by the sticky fruit that adhere to pant legs. Their stiff hooked hairs are adapted for dispersal by mammals, which now includes people. The generic name may stem from the Greek word *argema,* an eye disease, which this plant supposedly cures. *Gryposepala* comes from the Greek words "grypo" and "sepala," referring to the curved bristles on the fruit. This species is perhaps the most common of the 5 species of agrimony here. **Where found:** dry to moist woods; throughout.

Wild Lupine

Lupinus perennis

Height: up to 2 ft
Leaves: to 2 in long, with 7–11 leaflets in a palmately compound (hand-like) arrangement
Flowers: ½ in long, in dense elongate clusters to 6 in long
Fruits: flattened seedpods, turning blackish, to 1 in long

Few botanical sights are more fetching than a blanket of bright blue flowering lupine. They reach their peak after wildfires, carpeting the still blackened soils and enriching them with nitrogen. Fire removes competing plants and favors lupine, thus working to the advantage of Karner blue butterflies. These tiny beasts are federally endangered and require wild lupine as their host plant. The butterfly only occurs in small populations in Michigan and Ohio. **Where found:** dry, sandy soil of prairies, savannas; throughout, but scattered and local.

Crown Vetch

Securigera varia

Height: 1–2 ft
Leaves: compound, 11–21 oblong leaflets, each ½–¾ in long
Flowers: ½ in long, pink or purplish, pea-like, in clusters of 10–20
Fruits: linear pods to 2 in

Huge blankets of crown vetch sometimes grow along our roadways, where it helps stabilize soils and enriches the ground with nitrogen. This pea is indigenous to the Mediterranean, and is primarily used here as a groundcover. It essentially destroys all competing vegetation by clambering over it and smothering it. Fortunately, crown vetch remains largely in the disturbed zones where it was planted. An unexpected bonus to this species came when a butterfly, the wild indigo duskywing, which was declining in many areas, adopted it as a host plant. **Where found:** roadsides, open, disturbed sites; throughout.

Red Clover

Trifolium pratense

Height: up to 24 in
Leaves: divided into 3 leaflets, each ¾–2 in
Flowers: 1–1½ in long, pink to purple, in dense clusters
Fruits: 1-seeded pods

A ubiquitous weedy plant of open ground, red clover has round, pink to purple flower heads and large leaves. • Native to Europe, clover is widely used around the world as fodder. It depends on bumblebees for pollination, and is heavily used by native butterflies. Silver-spotted skippers are fond of nectaring at the blossoms, and both clouded and orange sulphurs probably use red clover as a host plant. • Medicinally, red clover has been used as a blood purifier, cough remedy and treatment for eczema. **Caution:** do not consume in fall, when the level of toxins increases. **Where found:** open, disturbed sites such as roadsides, fields, lawns; throughout.

Panicled Tick-trefoil

Desmodium paniculatum

Height: 2–3½ ft
Leaves: 3 in long, compound, 3 oblong leaflets
Flowers: many rose-purple flowers in panicles at top
Fruits: flattened triangular legumes (articles)

Nearly everyone who hikes knows tick-trefoils, if not by name. The small triangular fruits are beset with stiff hooked hairs that cause them to stick to pant legs. Getting them off isn't easy; they even survive a trip through the washer. The sticky fruit also adhere well to mammals, and that is how the plants spread themselves about. About 13 species are in our area, and telling them apart isn't easy. • The genus name comes from *desmos,* the Greek word for chain. **Where found:** dry woods, scruffy woodland borders; throughout.

Eurasian Water-milfoil

Myriophyllum spicatum

Height: submergent aquatic
Leaves: whorled, feather-like, 9–20 leaf segments per side
Flowers: tiny, in axils of flower bracts, emerging from the water in small spikes
Fruits: hard nutlets

Another aquatic invader introduced from Eurasia and possibly Africa, Eurasian water-milfoil appeared in North America in the mid 20th century and has since invaded water bodies throughout the eastern United States. Water-milfoil divides and spreads rapidly, forming dense canopies and blocking sunlight required by native plants, if it doesn't choke them out with its dense tangles. To stop the spread of this destructive plant, ensure all boats, motors, trailers and fishing equipment are cleaned of aquatic plants. **Where found:** lake waters to depths of 15 ft; throughout.

Purple Loosestrife

Lythrum salicaria

Height: 5 ft
Leaves: 3 in long, opposite or whorled, lance-shaped
Flowers: up to ½ in wide, red-purple, wrinkled petals, in showy spike
Fruits: many-seeded capsules

Note to gardeners: NEVER PLANT THIS SPECIES AGAIN! Since its introduction 200 years ago, purple loosestrife has spread across the continent, swallowing up and taking over many of our wetlands. This aggressive weed turns wetland communities into silent monocultures by smothering native plants. Birds, frogs, mammals and insects are forced out because they cannot use or eat purple loosestrife. This "silent killer" spreads rapidly through creeping rootstocks and prolific seeds (up to 2 million per plant), forming dense, brushy stands. Control methods include digging out and burning plants or removing and burning seed and flower heads. **Where found:** wet sites; throughout.

Fireweed

Chamerion angustifolium

Height: up to 6 ft (occasionally taller)
Leaves: ¾–8 in long, lance-shaped
Flowers: ¾–1⅝ in wide, pink to purple, in long, erect clusters
Fruits: narrow, pod-like capsules, 1⅝–3 in long

Aptly named, fireweed reaches peak abundance immediately after fires and can turn freshly scarred landscapes pink with its blooms. Fireweed serves an important ecological role by stabilizing barren ground, which eventually allows for other species of plants to recolonize. The erect, linear pods split lengthwise to release hundreds of tiny seeds tipped with fluffy, white hairs (comas). • Young shoots can be eaten like asparagus, and the flowers can be added to salads. **Where found:** open, often disturbed sites, burned areas; throughout, but increasingly scarce southward.

Common Evening-primrose

Oenothera biennis

Height: up to 5 ft
Leaves: 8 in long, lance-shaped, slightly toothed
Flowers: 1–2 in long, yellow, tube-shaped, open at dusk
Fruits: cylindrical capsules

The flowers of this well-named species open toward dusk, bloom throughout the night and generally close by mid-morning. Moths are the prime pollinators, so this strategy best accommodates them. Flowers open amazingly quickly, going from shrivelled wisps to robust blossoms in 15 to 20 minutes. • Evening-primrose is best known for its abundant, oil-rich seeds, which contain essential fatty acids. The seeds are processed into evening-primrose oil, used to treat eczema, high cholesterol, heart disease, PMS, asthma, arthritis and other ailments. **Where found:** dry, open sites; throughout.

Enchanter's-nightshade

Circaea lutetiana

Height: up to 2 ft (exceptionally motivated plants a bit taller)
Leaves: opposite, 2–4 in long, oval, shallowly toothed
Flowers: numerous, white or pinkish, with 2 deeply notched petals
Fruits: small nut-like pods

A charming, delicate little wildflower, enchanter's-nightshade is named after the mythological Greek enchantress Circe. Some sources say that she made a love potion from this plant. Others claim she was a powerful sorceress who used poisonous *Circaea* plants in her magic. To truly appreciate the miniscule flowers of this evening-primrose relative, you'll have to use a magnifying lens. An old naturalist trick for those wanting increased magnification is to just turn your binoculars around and look through the wrong end. **Where found:** moist, rich woods; throughout.

Flowering Spurge

Euphorbia corollata

Height: up to 3 ft
Leaves: 1½ in long, elliptic or linear, whorled
Flowers: tiny and greenish, dwarfed by 5 showy white bracts, in loose cyme
Fruits: 3-lobed capsule

A deceiver, the prominent white "petals" of this species are actually bracts. The true flowers are tiny and greenish, contained in the center of the bracts. **Caution:** contains a milkweed-like whitish latex that is extremely caustic and irritating to the skin, especially in contact with mucous membranes such as the eyes, nose and mouth. The compounds in the latex are 10,000 to 100,000 times more irritating than capsaicin, the main ingredient in pepper spray. Redness, swelling, blisters and photosensitivity occur after coming into contact with the plant. If ingested, it causes nausea, vomiting and diarrhea. **Where found:** peak abundance in prairies, fields, open woods; throughout.

Wild Geranium

Geranium maculatum

Height: up to 2 ft
Leaves: 4–5 in wide, 3–5 narrow lobes, hairy, deeply toothed
Flowers: 1½ in wide, showy, pink-purple, 5 petals
Fruits: long-beaked capsules, up to 1 in long

This species and others in the genus are often called crane's bill, from the fruit's resemblance to a crane's head. Wild geranium is an abundant and characteristic spring bloomer, often growing in profusion with other wildflowers. This native is an excellent landscaping plant. • Rubbing a fresh geranium plant, which has a strong smell, on exposed skin and clothes is said to repel mosquitoes. • Geraniums are considered astringent and are also used to stop bleeding. **Where found:** rich woods; throughout.

Spotted Touch-me-not

Impatiens capensis

Height: 3–5 ft
Leaves: 1–4 in long, oval, serrate margins
Flowers: 1 in long, orange-yellow, sac-like sepal
Fruits: green capsules, ¾ in long

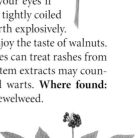

Exceptionally succulent, this plant practically wilts before your eyes if picked. The seeds are enclosed in fleshy capsules and held by tightly coiled elastic attachments. Press a ripe pod, and the seeds shoot forth explosively. Catch the seeds in your hand, pop 'em in your mouth and enjoy the taste of walnuts. The flowers are irresistible to hummingbirds. • Crushed leaves can treat rashes from poison ivy and stinging nettle. Poultices made from leaf or stem extracts may counteract skin ailments including dermatitis, insect bites and warts. **Where found:** moist, shaded woods, damp sites; throughout. **Also called:** jewelweed.

Ginseng

Panax quinquefolius

Height: 12–24 in
Leaves: 4¾–12 in long; whorl of 3, palmately divided into 5 leaflets
Flowers: tiny; whitish or yellow-green
Fruits: 2-seeded white berry, in clusters

This nondescript herb is the most coveted plant in the woods—prices run as high as $500 per pound. Ginseng root has a rich 5000-year history of herbal use. According to traditional Chinese medicine, it regulates the balance between yin and yang; promotes health, vigor and long life; and is considered an aphrodisiac. In the West, ginseng root promotes appetite and digestion. It is known for its ability to boost the immune system, increase mental efficiency, improve physical performance and aid in adapting to stress. • Excessive digging has greatly reduced or eliminated ginseng populations. Its sale is now regulated in some states. **Where found:** moist rich woods; throughout, but increasingly rare.

Clustered Snakeroot

Sanicula odorata (long known as *S. gregaria*)

Height: 1–2½ ft
Leaves: 5 in long; basal, opposite or alternate, compound, 3–5 leaflets
Flowers: tiny; yellow-greenish, in globular umbel ½ in across
Fruits: bur-like fruit with 2 seeds

This member of the Parsley family (Apiaceae) is abundant in woodlands and forms large colonies. Three other species of *Sanicula* are in our range; this one blooms earliest and is the only one with yellowish flowers. • Snakeroot is reported to have sedative properties for soothing nerves and relieving pain. Mashed roots were once applied to snakebites. Native peoples considered it a powerful medicine and used it to treat many disorders. **Caution:** roots contain irritating resins and volatile oils. **Where found:** moist, deciduous woods; throughout.

Smooth Sweet-cicely

Osmorhiza longistylis

Height: 3 ft
Leaves: to 12 in long, compound, fern-like, serrated leaflets
Flowers: tiny, white, 5 petals, in branched cluster
Fruits: capsules with flattened nutlets

Two species of sweet-cicely are abundant and wide-ranging here. The other is woolly sweet-cicely (*O. claytonii*), which is often hairier and lacks the strongly anise-scented aroma of this species. • Smooth sweet-cicely was widely used medicinally by Native peoples. Its leaves, stems and roots were pulverized and consumed as infusions for stomach discomforts and kidney troubles. Root infusions were also taken for absence of menses and for stomach problems. Root decoctions were consumed as an energizing drink, and poultices prepared with the root were applied to wounds and boils. **Where found:** moist to dry woods; throughout.

Queen Anne's Lace

Daucus carota

Height: up to 3½ ft
Leaves: 8–10 in long, compound, much divided
Flowers: tiny, in 3–5 in wide flat-topped clusters
Fruits: bristled nutlets (schizocarps)

Legend has it that these lace-like flowers are named for Queen Anne (1655–1714), who pricked her finger while embroidering lace. The drop of blood is represented by the central red flower (whose function is to attract insects). • The crushed seeds have been used as a form of contraceptive or "morning-after" pill, first described by Hippocrates in 4th century BC. • Beautiful black swallowtail butterfly caterpillars use Queen Anne's lace as a host plant. **Where found:** dry fields, disturbed areas, roadsides; throughout.

Poison-hemlock

Conium maculatum

Height: up to 9 ft
Leaves: up to 1 ft long, purple-spotted, triangular, 3–4 carrot-like leaflets
Flowers: tiny, white
Fruits: capsules

An increasingly common weed, this tall, coarse plant spreads rapidly along railroads and roadways. All parts are extremely **poisonous** (it is the poison reputedly taken by Socrates). The toxic alkaloid is most abundant in young plants, leaves and flowers. These toxins directly affect the nervous system, causing numbness and paralysis of the lower limbs, then paralysis of arms and chest. Symptoms include nervousness, confusion, weakness, vomiting, diarrhea, weak pulse, difficulty breathing and finally death from suffocation. If ingested, induce vomiting, administer a strong laxative and consult a physician. **Where found:** waste places, railroad tracks, roadsides; throughout.

Wild Parsnip

Pastinaca sativa

Height: up to 4½ ft
Leaves: to 12 in or more, pinnate, up to 15 leaflets, each to 4 in
Flowers: dull yellowish gold, tiny, in large compound umbels to 6 in across
Fruits: small, flattened, egg-shaped with small wings along the sides

Introduced from Eurasia long ago, wild parsnip is valued as a root vegetable. It is abundant and very weedy in many places and will form massive stands that are nearly monocultures. • Closely related to the carrot, it has been consumed since ancient times and is supposedly more vitamin-rich than carrots. An ill-effect of contact with parsnip is that it secretes an oil that causes phytophotodermatitis, a condition in which skin becomes excessively sensitive to ultraviolet light. Painful blistering can result if the affected person remains under the sun after exposure. **Where found:** open, disturbed sites such as roadsides, railroads; throughout.

Angelica

Angelica atropurpurea

Height: up to 6 ft (sometimes taller)
Leaves: 1–4 in long; compound, 3 major divisions, each divided 3–5 times again
Flowers: small; usually white, in large, flat-topped clusters
Fruits: >¼ in long; flat, winged and ribbed seed-like schizocarps

A blooming angelica inflorescence suggests a display of exploding fireworks with its large spherical clusters of whitish flowers. Angelica leaves smell like parsley and have a strong but pleasant taste, similar to that of garden lovage, and have been used as a spice in soups and stews or to flavor gin and liqueurs. The seeds taste like a cross between celery and cardamom. • Teas and extracts made from the roots and seeds have been used for centuries to aid digestion and relieve nausea and cramps. **Where found:** wet open sites; throughout.

Fringed Gentian

Gentianopsis virgata

Height: 6–20 in
Leaves: 1–2½ in long, ½–1 in long, narrow, lance-shaped
Flowers: 1–1½ long, 1 in wide, 4 fringed petals
Fruits: 2-valved capsule

This staggeringly beautiful plant inspired poet William Cullen Bryant to pen "To the Fringed Gentian." The silky blue flowers of this late bloomer stand up to the first frosts. Before the widespread introduction of hops, gentians were used in Europe for brewing beers. • Gentian roots have been used to treat various ailments. Present-day herbalists recommend gentian-root tea as one of the best vegetable bitters for stimulating appetite, aiding digestion, relieving bloating and preventing heartburn. This species was known as *Gentiana procera*. **Where found:** limey soil of wet seeps, prairies, slump bluffs; throughout, but scattered and local.

Indian-hemp

Apocynum cannabinum

Height: up to 4 ft
Leaves: 2–4 in long, opposite, oval, often hairy beneath
Flowers: >¼ in long; greenish white, bell-shaped, 5-petaled, in clusters
Fruits: paired, slender pods (follicles) 4 in long

This common, weedy native is tough, and can even push through asphalt. Long, strong fibers make a durable, fine thread. Traditionally, mature stems were soaked in water to remove the coarse outer fibers, then rolled against the leg into thread. Single strands or 3-plaited cords became fishing nets, net bags, bowstrings and rabbit hunting nets up to 1 mile long. • The tiny white blossoms attract butterflies. **Caution:** poisonous. The milky sap can cause skin blistering; ingestion has resulted in sickness and death. **Where found:** fields, roadsides, woodland edges, open sites; throughout. **Also called:** dogbane.

Common Milkweed

Asclepias syriaca

Height: 3–5 ft (occasionally taller)
Leaves: opposite, oblong, hairy beneath
Flowers: tiny, pinkish lavender, in rounded clusters
Fruits: spiny follicles, in erect clusters

By far our most common milkweed, these weedy plants contain glycosides that are toxic to animals and humans, so the insects adapted to feed on them are also toxic and tend to be brightly colored and conspicuous, indicating toxicity. Monarch butterfly larvae feed solely on milkweed leaves. They absorb the toxic glycosides into their bodies so both larvae and adult butterflies become poisonous to predators. Several species of milkweed beetles also thrive on milkweed; they are bright orange and black. **Where found:** open sites such as fields, meadows, roadsides; throughout.

Bittersweet Nightshade

Solanum dulcamara

Height: stems clamber to 8 ft
Leaves: 2–4 in long, oval, 2 basal lobes
Flowers: ¾ in wide, 5 back–curved, white to blue petals, yellow center
Fruits: oblong red berries

Although this plant belongs to the potato family, the immature (green) berries and leaves contain toxic alkaloids that can cause vomiting, dizziness, convulsions, paralysis and even death. However, a close relative, the tomato, is a ubiquitous food source. • Bittersweet has been used to treat skin diseases, sores and swellings. Extracts are reported to have antibiotic activity, which could be useful in salves and lotions for combating infection. The plant also contains beta-solanine, a tumor inhibitor that may prove useful for treating cancer. **Where found:** moist sites, open woods, disturbed sites; throughout.

Blue Phlox

Phlox divaricata

Height: up to 20 in
Leaves: 1¼–2 in long, oblong, widely spaced pairs
Flowers: ¾–1¼ in wide, purple to blue, tubular with 5 lobes
Fruits: 3-valved capsule, ¼ in long

A characteristic and abundant May-blooming wildflower of rich woods, this species is the most common of our half-dozen native phlox. Phlox have long corolla tubes, to which butterflies and moths with long tongues are perfectly adapted to pollinate. Each sweet-smelling blossom is a pinwheel-like fan of 5 petals fused at their bases into a tube ³/₈–⁵/₈ in long. **Where found:** rich, moist woods; throughout.

Virginia Bluebells

Mertensia virginica

Height: 12–24 in
Leaves: 2–6 in long, elliptic to oblanceolate
Flowers: 1 in long, pale blue, tubular
Fruits: 4 wrinkled nutlets

One of our most striking displays of early spring wildflowers occurs when masses of bluebells spring from still-cool soil. They explode into dazzling bursts of rich blue blooms, and even the most jaded botanist will pause to admire the show. Look quickly, Virginia bluebells are ephemeral, wilting quickly to ugly brown detritus and returning to the soil that spawned them. • The name *Mertensia* honors Franz Karl Mertens, a renowned German botanist. Mertens was primarily a collector of algae. **Where found:** moist or wet woods, bottomlands; throughout.

Blue Vervain

Verbena hastata

Height: up to 6 ft
Leaves: opposite, 2–4 in long, narrow, elliptical, coarse toothed
Flowers: ¼ in wide, violet-blue, in blunt-tipped spike
Fruits: 2-parted capsules

An abundant and conspicuous denizen of damp, open ground, blue vervain produces spikes of showy, small, deep blue blossoms. They develop in a ring, starting at the bottom of the flower spike, producing more buds at the top, and continuing to flower for weeks. This pretty wetland plant is important for insects, attracting numerous bees and butterflies. • The steamed leaves are palatable, and the flowers make a pretty garnish or addition to salads. Flowers and leaves can also be used as a tea substitute. Some European species were thought to be panaceas for all manner of illnesses. **Where found:** marshes, ditches, wet meadows, shores; throughout.

Heal-all

Prunella vulgaris

Height: 6–20 in
Leaves: 1–3 in long, opposite, lance-shaped, finely toothed
Flowers: ½ in long, purplish, hooded upper lip arches over 3-lobed lower lip
Fruits: dark, shiny, ribbed nutlets

An abundant and often weedy little mint, heal-all ranges throughout North America and Eurasia. This plant has been used to treat various conditions. Research indicates that the entire plant has antibacterial compounds and inhibits the growth of a number of disease-causing bacteria. Traditionally heal-all was steeped into tea and used to treat fevers, diarrhea, vomiting and soothe colicky babies. Externally, the leaves were used to treat boils, cuts, bruises and skin inflammations. **Where found:** open, weedy areas and lawns to rich undisturbed woods; throughout.

Wild Bergamot

Monarda fistulosa

Height: up to 4 ft
Leaves: opposite, 2–4 in long, lance-shaped
Flowers: 1 in long, lavender, 2-lipped, in round clusters 1½ in long
Fruits: tiny, shiny nutlets

Wild bergamot's long, tubular, rose to purplish flowers attract hummingbirds and hawk moths and a large number of butterfly species. • Wild bergamot provides a spice, potherb and tea (similar to Earl Grey). Native peoples used the tea to treat ailments ranging from colds and indigestion to pneumonia and kidney problems. Dried leaves were burned or sprinkled on items to repel insects and yet the living flowers are insect magnets. • This showy, aromatic perennial can easily be grown from seed in gardens, thus bringing a butterfly parade to your yard. **Where found:** moist to moderately dry, open sites; prairies, old fields, woodland edges; throughout.

Common Monkeyflower

Mimulus ringens

Height: 2–4 ft
Leaves: opposite, 2–4 in long, lance-shaped, clasp stem
Flowers: ¾–1¼ in long, lavender, long stalks, 2-lipped corolla
Fruits: oblong capsules with many yellow seeds

Looked at head on, the flower resembles a monkey, hence the common name. *Mimulus,* the diminutive form of the Latin *mimus,* means a buffoon, an apparent reference to the small, grinning, ape-like faces of the blossoms. This relative of garden snapdragons brightens moist open habitats with pale purple blooms. • A similar species, winged monkeyflower *(M. alatus),* with long-petioled leaves and short-stalked flowers, occurs along streams. **Where found:** marshes, wetlands, damp open sites; throughout.

Common Mullein

Verbascum thapsus

Height: up to 7 ft
Leaves: to 12 in, broadly oblong, thick, densely hairy
Flowers: to ¾ in wide, yellow, in thick terminal spike
Fruits: 2-parted capsules

Towering mullein spikes are conspicuous and persistent. It was introduced to North America from Europe in the 18th century as a medicinal herb and quickly became an abundant, naturalized weed. In a pinch, the fuzzy leaves can be used to line shoes and ward off cold, as early settlers once did. • In Europe, dried stems were used for lamp wicks or dipped in suet to make torches, which were believed to drive away witches and evil spirits. This important medicinal plant was used to remedy many conditions, including spasmatic coughs, fevers and diarrhea. **Where found:** open, disturbed sites; throughout.

Foxglove Beardtongue

Penstemon digitalis

Height: up to 3 ft
Leaves: 2–4 in long, basal or opposite, lance-shaped or oblanceoloate, smooth
Flowers: 1 in long, white, sometimes suffused faintly with purple, 2-lipped corolla
Fruits: ½ in long capsules

This species often grows in old fields and dry weedy areas, the gleaming clusters of showy white flowers adding a jolt of color to barren areas. Its tubular flowers attract hummingbirds and bees. It is sometimes a host plant for the gorgeous buckeye butterfly (*Junonia coenia*). A related European species, *Digitalis purpurea*, is the original source of the heart drug digitalis. **Where found:** dry woods, barren sites; throughout, but increasingly scarce westward.

Wood-betony

Pedicularis canadensis

Height: 6–16 in
Leaves: 2–6 in long, elliptical, deeply divided, fern-like
Flowers: ¾ in long, pale yellow to maroon or bicolored, hooded, in spike
Fruits: dry capsules ¼ in long

Odd-looking with fern-like leaves, wood-betony flowers can be maroon and white or creamy yellow. This plant depends on a special root fungi for nutrient intake and should not be transplanted or disturbed because it will not survive. • The genus name derives from *pediculus*, meaning "louse," and an alternate common name is lousewort. It was once thought that if cattle consumed wood-betony, they would become louse-ridden. **Where found:** moist to dry forested habitats; throughout.

Water-willow

Justicia americana

Height: 18–30 in
Leaves: 3–6 in long; opposite, lance-shaped
Flowers: bluish-white with purple markings; dense, spike-like clusters ½ in long
Fruits: brown capsules containing 4 rough seeds

The flowers of this abundant aquatic plant resemble orchid blossoms, with pale lavender flowers ornately marked with rich purple. Dense colonies of water-willow are important to stream ecology: they harbor fish fry, and animals take shelter in the beds. The American rubyspot damselfly is most often found around water-willow. • Water-willow is not a true willow (*Salix* spp.), but both plants have lance-shaped leaves and grow in wet, riparian habitats. **Where found:** shallow water and gravel bars of streams, lakes; throughout, but becoming rarer north and westward; absent in MN.

Common Bladderwort

Utricularia macrorhiza

Height: 4–10 in
Leaves: minute, usually underground, linear with tiny bladder
Flowers: ½ in long, yellow, 2-lipped corolla
Fruits: tiny capsules

Most carnivorous plants trap and eat insects, but aquatic bladderworts digest everything from tiny worms to small crustaceans. Like other carnivorous plants, bladderworts are typically found in cold, acidic, nitrogen-poor environments. They get their nitrogen from the invertebrates they digest, so they are able to grow where others cannot survive. • About 9 other bladderworts are found here, but common bladderwort is the most frequent species. They float in water or creep along muddy shores, their tiny bladders festooning roots and providing the "traps" to capture prey. **Where found:** shallow to deep water of ponds, lakes, marshes; throughout.

Tall Bellflower

Campanulastrum americanum

Height: 2–5 ft (giants can reach 6 ft)
Leaves: 3–6 in long, lance-shaped, toothed
Flowers: 1 in wide, blue, star-shaped
Fruits: capsules

Tall bellflower is one of mid-to-late summer's characteristic woodland wildflowers. Some related species truly have bell-shaped flowers, but the face of these flowers is flat. The 5-lobed corolla forms a star, with a curved style protruding outward. • The small openings at the base of the capsules close quickly in damp weather, protecting the seeds from excess moisture. On dry, windy days, the capsules swing widely in the breeze, scattering the seeds. **Where found:** moist woods, shaded streambanks; throughout.

Cardinal-flower

Lobelia cardinalis

Height: 2–4 ft (occasional giants can reach 7 ft)
Leaves: 2–6 in long, lance-shaped, toothed
Flowers: ¾–1½ in long, intense red or scarlet, in showy spike
Fruits: spherical capsules

A real showstopper, cardinal-flower is the same color as the robes of cardinals in the Roman Catholic Church. This is a gorgeous landscape plant for moist areas, and like many brilliant red flowers with long corolla tubes, is well adapted to attract its primary pollinator, hummingbirds. • Some *Lobelia*, including this species, have medicinal properties. They are said to induce feelings of mental clarity, happiness and well-being. The plants contain lobeline, an alkaloid similar to, but weaker than, nicotine. Lobeline allegedly stimulates peripheral and central nerves, followed by respiratory depression. **Caution:** excess doses can cause nausea, vomiting, drowsiness, respiratory failure and potentially death. **Where found:** wet woods, meadows, damp areas; throughout.

Bluets

Houstonia caerulea

Height: up to 6 in
Leaves: up to ½ in long, mostly basal or opposite, spatulate
Flowers: ½ in wide, whitish blue with yellow center, tubular, 4-lobed
Fruits: capsules, <¼ in long

Bluets grow en masse and often mist the ground with carpets of blue in spring. The tiny flowers' bright yellow center acts like a runway for insects, guiding tiny bees to the pollen found inside the tubular flower. The pale yellow eye of the flower seemingly glows from within. The flowers also attract the bumblebee-like beefly *(Bombylius major),* a small hovering insect. Bluets cannot withstand much competition from other plants, and typically grow in barren soil. **Where found:** dry, barren soil of deciduous forests, clearings; throughout, but increasingly scarce northward.

Partridgeberry

Mitchella repens

Height: prostrate, trailing along the ground
Leaves: opposite, ¼ –¾ in long, oval to round, leathery
Flowers: ½ in long, white, trumpet-shaped
Fruits: scarlet berries ¼ in wide

This showy, diminutive creeping plant is often used in terraria. The reddish berries are edible, though not very tasty. The Micmac, Iroquois, Montagnais and Malecite Indians ate them fresh or cooked into a jam. • The trailing stems and berries make good Christmas decorations, though we discourage taking plants from the wild. Wildlife such as ruffed grouse (sometimes called partridge) and wild turkey eat the bud, leaf, flower and fruit of this plant. **Where found:** rich deciduous forests in acidic soils, especially under conifers; throughout.

Cleavers

Galium aparine

Height: weakly clambering to 3 ft
Leaves: 1–3 in long, narrow, in whorls of 8
Flowers: tiny, white, 4 lobed, in 3-flowered cluster
Fruits: dry carpels with bristles

Cleavers are so named because their bristled fruit cleave (adhere) to animals and clothing, aiding in seed dipersal; their nickname is "Velcro-weed." Species in the genus *Galium* are also called bedstraw because early Americans used dried stems to stuff mattresses. • Cleavers are related to coffee; their tiny paired, short-hairy nutlets can be dried, roasted and ground as a coffee substitute. Cleaver juice or tea was applied to many skin problems. The tea may speed weight loss, but continual use irritates the mouth and people with poor circulation or diabetes should not use it. • About 17 other bedstraws occur here. **Where found:** open woods, fields, roadsides, often weedy; throughout.

Common Teasel

Dipsacus fullonum

Height: 2–6 ft
Leaves: opposite, 4–12 in long, lance-shaped
Flowers: tiny lavendar lobes on cylindrical heads 1¼–4 in long
Fruits: tiny nutlets

Introduced from Africa and Eurasia, teasels have an interesting sequence of blooms. The first flowers begin in a central belt around the prickly head, then expand up and down, dying in the middle. The egg-shaped flower clusters have long, pricky bracts protruding from the base. • The names "teasel" and *fullonum* refer to the hooked bracts of a related cultivar once used in cloth making to "tease" or "full out" wool fibers. Unfortunately, these prickles sometimes snare and kill small birds like kinglets. **Where found:** open, disturbed sites, roadsides; throughout.

Green-headed Coneflower

Rudbeckia laciniata

Height: 3–9 ft
Leaves: to 8 in long, pinnately divided into 3–7 pointed lobes
Flowers: ray flowers yellow, 2½ in long; disk greenish, ¾ in wide
Fruits: brown achenes, >¼ in

A whopper of a sunflower, green-headed coneflower reaches peak abundance on rich, wooded stream terraces. Stands often tower well above head-high. A cultivated double-flowered form is known as "Golden Glow." Insects are attracted to the gorgeous lemon-yellow blossoms, and when the seeds ripen, American goldfinches and other birds feast on them. • Medicinally, the plant was taken internally to increase urination or expel worms. It was also used in a wash to soothe snakebites and wounds. **Where found:** primarily moist soil of floodplains, occasionally other low-lying areas; throughout.

Sneezeweed

Helenium autumnale

Height: 2–5 ft
Leaves: 1½–6 in long, toothed, narrowly lance-shaped
Flowers: 13–21 white ray flowers, up to 1 in long; bulbous yellow disk ¾ in wide
Fruits: achenes

Sneezeweed's sunny, yellow, flowers are among the showiest on the floodplain. • Sneezeweed leaves were once crushed into a snuff used to promote sneezing. Why? To expel evil spirits from the body. Modern medicine has abandoned this treatment, apparently. • Sneezeweed is beneficial to many species of bees, wasps, butterflies and beetles that collect nectar or pollen from the flowers. **Caution:** toxic to mammals and has caused poisoning and death in cattle and horses. If ingested by humans, it will irritate the eyes, nose and stomach. **Where found:** low, moist sites, especially floodplains; throughout.

Nodding Beggar's-ticks

Bidens cernua

Height: up to 36 in (often only a few inches tall)
Leaves: 2–8 in long; opposite, lance-shaped; sessile or bases fused together around the stem
Flowers: ¾ in long; 6–8 yellow ray flowers
Fruits: achenes, with 2 barbed horns

The flattened, 2-barbed fruit of nodding beggar's-ticks easily attach to clothing and animals but are difficult to brush off. This strategy for mammalian seed dispersal is annoying, particularly on hikers' pants. • "Nodding" refers to the large, marigold-like drooping flower heads. This plant is extremely variable in stature, depending on where it grows. On sun-baked mudflats, it might be but a few inches tall; in lusher situations it may reach a few feet in height. **Where found:** damp soils along streams, lakes, bogs, marshes; throughout.

Giant Ragweed

Ambrosia trifida

Height: 3–12 ft
Leaves: 2–4 in long; opposite, 3–5 lobes
Flowers: tiny, greenish, in terminal spikes
Fruits: brown, beaked achenes

Huge stands of this abundant plant sometimes cover old fields, and its airborne pollen causes much hay-fever suffering. • Ragweed seeds 4–5 times larger than today's wild species were found in archaeological digs in North America, suggesting that this plant was selectively bred, perhaps for its seed oil. The seed contains up to 20% oil, a small percentage of which is the essential fatty acid, linolenic acid.
• Ragweed was a salve for skin problems among several Native groups. The astringent leaves were crushed and smeared on insect bites, minor skin eruptions and hives to speed healing. **Where found:** moist soils, disturbed sites; throughout.

Common Yarrow

Achillea millefolium

Height: 1–3 ft
Leaves: 2–6 in long, feathery appearance
Flowers: <¼ in long; white, in flat-topped cluster
Fruits: compressed achenes

The fern-like leaves of this member of the sunflower family (Asteraceae) are distinctive. • This hardy, aromatic perennial has served for thousands of years as a fumigant, insecticide and medicine. The Greek hero Achilles, for whom the genus was named, used it to help heal his soldiers' wounds. • The flower heads are white (sometimes pinkish) and the seed-like fruits are hairless and flattened. • Yarrow is an attractive ornamental, but beware—its extensive underground stems (rhizomes) soon invade your garden. **Where found:** dry to moist open sites; throughout.

Oxeye Sunflower

Heliopsis helianthoides

Height: 2–5 ft
Leaves: 2–6 in long, lance-shaped with serrate margins
Flowers: to 3 in wide, cone-shaped central disk with up to 16 showy yellow rays
Fruit: small smooth papery achenes

This species is often called "false sunflower," but it is a true sunflower in the family Asteraceae with the other sunflowers, daisies, asters and the like. In the field, look for a conical disk of central flowers, unlike the flattened disk of most similar allies. • Oxeye sunflower is quite showy and easy to grow along shaded garden margins. American goldfinches will thank you as they feast upon the seeds. **Where found:** semi-shaded woodland borders; throughout.

Lake Huron Tansy

Tanacetum bipinnatum ssp. *huronense*

Height: up to 3 ft
Leaves: 4–8 in long, fern-like, hairy, gland-dotted
Flowers: disk flowers yellow, in dense, button-like heads
Fruits: tiny seed-like achenes

This rare, beautiful plant has declined significantly along the Great Lakes, and is now confined to a limited region. Although well adapted to natural disturbance such as wave or wind action, it is defenseless against erosion caused by all-terrain vehicles or foot traffic. Human disturbance has eliminated it from many areas. • This plant is closely related to common tansy *(T. vulgare),* a rapidly spreading weed introduced from Europe. • Tansy contains toxic volatile oils that are potentially fatal; plants have been strewn on floors to repel insects and boiled into an insecticide or a wash for lice or scabies. **Where found:** calcareous dunes and beaches of Lake Huron, Lake Michigan, south shore Lake Superior; threatened in MI, probably extirpated in WI.

Golden Ragwort

Packera aurea

Height: 12–30 in
Leaves: 5 in long, heart-shaped basal leaves, purplish beneath
Flowers: 10–12 yellow ray flowers, ¼–½ in long, yellow disk ¼–½ in wide
Fruits: brownish, cylindrical achenes in tufted white pappus

In early spring, colonies of golden ragwort mist shady roadsides and low-lying meadows. Basal leaves are dark purple below, possibly allowing the plant to absorb additional heat to aid growth during cool spring weather. Golden ragwort grows rapidly and is a good choice for moist, shady areas of the garden. The showy flowers attract pollinating bees and other insects. • Historically, medicinal ragwort tea was used to relieve heart and lung problems, prevent pregnancy, aid in childbirth and treat urinary disorders. **Caution:** contains toxic alkaloids and should not be consumed. **Where found:** moist woods, fields; throughout.

Canada Goldenrod

Solidago canadensis

Height: 2–5 ft (sometimes taller)
Leaves: 3–6 in long, lance-shaped, downy, toothed
Flowers: 10–17 yellow ray flowers, 6–12 yellow disk flowers in plume-like cluster
Fruits: hairy achenes in tufted white pappus

Canada goldenrod is a classic pioneer forb of old fields. Growth-inhibiting enzymes released from its roots discourage other plants, sometimes allowing near monocultures to form. Many people think goldenrod flower clusters cause hay fever, but the real culprit is probably ragweed, which shares the same habitat. • Masses of blooming goldenrod attract hordes of nectar-seeking insects. The goldenrod gall fly (*Eurosta solidaginis*) lays its egg in the stem, which causes the plant to form a hardened, perfectly round mass of tissue that looks like it swallowed a golf ball. **Where found:** moist to dry fields, open sites; throughout.

Awl Aster

Symphyotrichum pilosum

Height: 2–5 ft
Leaves: 1–4 in long, mainly basal, oblanceolate
Flowers: 15–30 white ray flowers, ¼–⅜ in long; yellow to reddish disk, up to ⅜ in wide
Fruits: hairy achenes in tufted, bristly pappus

Although native, awl aster is one of our most common and weediest species. It grows with Canada goldenrod in old fields, but also in the weediest urban lots. It even pokes through asphalt. The yellow disk flowers in the center of the inflorescence are surrounded by white ray flowers, a combination that is only showy up close. • In this species, tiny green bracts form a cup under the flower. The tips are tightly rolled, just like the business end of an awl. **Where found:** old fields, dry, open waste sites; throughout.

New England Aster

Symphyotrichum novae-angliae

Height: 2–5 ft (sometimes taller)
Leaves: 1–4 in long, lance-shaped, clasp stem at base
Flowers: showy; violet, rose or magenta, >50 ray, ¾ in long; yellow disk ¾ in wide
Fruits: hairy achenes in tufted, bristly pappus

Of the dozens of aster species in our region, this one is the showiest. Enthusiasts have no problem finding this aster, abundant in old fields with Canada goldenrod. The flowers are typically rich purplish-magenta but can vary to lilac and nearly white, and the blooms persist after the first fall frosts. • New England aster is a host plant for the beautiful pearl crescent butterfly. • Traditionally, the roots of this plant were boiled to treat pink eye or crushed and applied as a poultice to stop bleeding. **Where found:** moist to dry meadows, open sites; throughout.

Common Boneset

Eupatorium perfoliatum

Height: 2–4 ft
Leaves: 3–8 in long; opposite, lance-shaped, fused at base
Flowers: 9–23 white disk flowers in flat-topped inflorescence
Fruits: resinous achenes in tufted white pappus (hairs that subtend seeds)

The leaves of this common wetland plant are fused at the base. Very rarely a ternate form occurs, with whorls of 3 rather than 2 opposite leaves. Researchers in Germany have isolated active compounds from *Eupatorium* species that are able to boost the immune system, providing support for traditional medicinal uses. Early herbalists believed that the perforated leaves of boneset indicated that the herb was useful in setting bones, and so the leaves were wrapped with bandages around splints. • **Where found:** wet meadows, low, moist sites; throughout.

Common Burdock

Arctium minus

Height: up to 5 ft
Leaves: to 18 in; heart-shaped, white-woolly beneath
Flowers: ½–¾ in wide, stalkless, bur-like flowers
Fruits: 3–5-sided, hairless seed-like achenes

Large, vitamin- and iron-rich, burdocks are edible plants indigenous to Eurasia brought to North America as food plants. Young leaves may be used in salads, soups or stews, although leaf fibers can be tough. Peeled, sliced roots of first-year plants can be used in stir-fries and soups or served as a hot vegetable. • Some Native peoples dried burdock roots for winter supplies or roasted and ground them for use as a coffee substitute. • Burdocks were widely used in tonics for "purifying the blood," and they are still recommended as a safe but powerful liver tonic. **Where found:** waste sites, roadsides; throughout.

Canada Thistle

Cirsium arvense

Height: 2–5 ft (occasionally taller)
Leaves: 2–6 in
Flowers: purple or pink disk flowers, flower head less than ¾ in long
Fruits: seed-like achenes

Much expense and effort is spent on eradication of this botanical invader. Introduced to Canada from Europe in the 17th century, it then spread here and acquired its common name. Today colonies of this aggressive, ubiquitous weed choke out other plants and reduce crop yields. They grow from deep underground runners that contain a substance that inhibits the growth of nearby plants. Each year, one plant can send out up to 20 ft of runners, and female plants can release up to 40,000 seeds. • Fortunately a bacteria, *Pseudomonas syringae,* attacks Canada thistle and can kill them. A sign of infection are whitish-yellow leaves. **Where found:** disturbed sites; throughout.

Common Dandelion

Taraxacum officinale

Height: 2–20 in
Leaves: 2–16 in long, basal, oblanceolate
Flowers: 1–2 in wide, numerous yellow rays, disk flowers absent
Fruits: tiny achenes in white, fluffy pappus

Emerald green lawns sprinkled with yellow dandelion blossoms create a rather showy palette, but rankle fastidious lawn-keepers. • Brought to North America from Eurasia, dandelions were cultivated for food and medicine. Young dandelion leaves and flower heads are full of vitamins and minerals and make nutritious additions to salads. They can be cooked like vegetables or added to pancakes, muffins or fritters, or even made into wine. The roots can be ground into a caffeine-free coffee substitute or boiled to make a red dye. **Where found:** disturbed sites; throughout.

Chicory

Cichorium intybus

Height: 1–4 ft (occasionally taller)
Leaves: 3–10 in long; oblong, toothed
Flowers: 1 in long; blue ray flowers (sometimes white)
Fruits: seed-like achenes

Introduced to North America from Europe, chicory is now a ubiquitous roadside weed. The bluish flowers are quite showy, but the rest of the plant is coarse and unattractive. The plant has a prolonged blooming period: each flower lasts but a day, but few open simultaneously. Its long taproot is ground and used as a coffee substitute or coffee additive. The young green leaves and edible blue flowers can be added to salads. • Cultivated chicory, known as Belgian endive or radicchio, and true endive (*C. endivia*) are grown under special, dark conditions to keep the leaves tender. **Where found:** disturbed sites, dry roadsides; throughout.

Broad-leaved Arrowhead

Sagittaria latifolia

Height: up to 40 in
Leaves: 6–16 in long; arrowhead-shaped
Flowers: to ¾ in long; white, showy, 3 petals
Fruits: beaked achenes in clustered heads

This characteristic marsh plant can be extremely variable in leaf shape, although they always have long basal lobes. Arrowhead flowers are some of the showiest in a marsh: small whorls of snow-white, 3-part blossoms. • The entire rootstock is edible, but the corms (short, vertical underground stems) are preferred. Cooked corms taste like potatoes or chestnuts but are unpleasant raw. Native peoples often camped near arrowhead sites for weeks, harvesting the crop or seeking out muskrat caches for the corms. **Where found:** shallow water or mud of sunny marshes, ditches, other wetlands; throughout. **Also called:** duck potato.

Eel-grass

Vallisneria americana

Height: submerged aquatic growing to depths of 7 ft
Leaves: up to 6½ ft long, ⅓ in wide, ribbon-like, finely serrated,
light green stripe down center
Flowers: 3 petals, 3 sepals in tubular (female) or oval (male) spathe
Fruits: cylindrical pod with dark seeds

By the mid-1980s, eel-grass had become rare in many areas, especially Lake Erie. Excessive siltation had clouded waters and reduced the plant's ability to photosynthesize. With water clarity now greatly improved, in part owing to filtering by non-native zebra mussels, eel-grass is once more locally abundant. It forms dense underwater beds, called "seaweed" by the botanically uninformed. Eel-grass is an important food source for waterfowl, especially canvasbacks. Extensive wracks of this plant sometimes wash onto beaches in late summer and fall. **Where found:** shallow waters of lakes and streams; throughout.

Long-leaved Pondweed

Potamogeton nodosus

Height: underwater stems up to 6 ft
Leaves: elliptical; floating leaves 11–19 veined;
submerged leaves 1–3½ in long, stalked
Flowers: small, whorled clusters up to 1 in long
Fruits: green, nut-like achenes

Pondweeds can grow in deep water and are very important in aquatic ecosystems. Waterfowl feed on pondweed tubers; tangled underwater stems and leaves are excellent habitat for fish fry and aquatic invertebrates that fish feed on. Many species are vulnerable to water pollution; as a result many native pondweeds have declined alarmingly in many areas. Long-leaved pondweed remains abundant and is one of the first aquatic plants to colonize new ponds. **Where found:** shallow, stagnant waters of ponds, lakes, rivers; throughout.

Skunk-cabbage

Symplocarpus foetidus

Height: up to 2 ft
Leaves: 15–22 in long; heart-shaped, cabbage-like
Flowers: tiny; clustered on a ball-like spadix inside a purple hooded spathe 4–6 in high
Fruits: brown-black berries in rounded cluster 4 in wide

This odd-looking plant is our first wildflower to bloom each year. As early as late February, the spathes push from the boggy ground, aided by heat produced through cellular respiration that melts nearby snow and ice. The giant cabbage-like leaves emerge after flowering and persist through summer. • This foul-smelling, wetland plant emits a mild odor when left alone but reeks when damaged. The smell attracts carrion-feeding and other pollinating insects, but repels animals that may eat or otherwise damage the plant. **Where found:** spring-fed boggy wetlands; throughout.

Jack-in-the-pulpit

Arisaema triphyllum

Height: up to 2 ft (occasional whoppers to 3 ft)
Leaves: 3–6 in long; 1–2 leaves, each divided into 3 leaflets
Flowers: tiny; in clusters on a spadix 3 in long
Fruits: smooth, shiny, green berries (red at maturity)

Jack-in-the-pulpit's odd flowers are composed of a spadix (jack) covered with tiny male and female flowers and surrounded by a spathe (hood, or pulpit). Spathe color varies, from bright green to boldly striped with purple. One or two basal leaves, each divided into 3 leaflets, overshadow the flower. This species is a botanical hermaphrodite: in young plants, most flowers are male, becoming female as the plant ages. • The entire plant and the bright red berries are **poisonous** if eaten fresh. Native peoples pounded the dried roots into flour and used jack-in-the-pulpit in cough and cold remedies. **Where found:** moist hardwood forests; throughout.

Lesser Duckweed

Lemna minor

Height: floats on water surface
Leaves: up to ¼ in, oval
Flowers: minute, 2 stamens, 1 style
Fruits: minute, dry pericarp

Lesser duckweed is the most common of a number of tiny, floating aquatic plants that are often mistakenly called algae. Some authorities describe 8 species, all of which occur here. Sometimes regarded as a nuisance, duckweed filters unwanted phosphorus and nitrogen from the water, acting as a natural filter and improving water quality. Many insects use duckweed for perches, shelter and sites to deposit eggs. • The tiny flowers are seldom seen as flowering is rare. Most reproduction is vegetative, with leaves dividing into new ones. **Where found:** surface of ponds, lakes, rivers; throughout.

Beach Grass

Ammophila breviligulata

Height: up to 3 ft
Leaves: ¼–½ in wide, up to 15 in long
Fruits: spike-like seed cluster

Beach grass is a very important pioneer plant of loose sand in open dunes. The stems continue to grow higher as blowing sand builds up around them. The buried stems eventually turn into roots that reach deep under the sand • Beach grass provides cover for various animals and nesting birds, including the piping plover *(Charadrius melodus)*. This beautiful grass has become rare in some states such as Ohio, because it doesn't tolerate heavy trampling associated with recreational beaches. **Where found:** dry, sandy dunes and beaches along Great Lakes; throughout.

Common Reed

Phragmites australis

Height: 3–10 ft
Leaves: 8–15 in long, 1 in wide
Flowers: tiny, purple-brown, in plume-like panicle 4–16 in long
Fruits: seed-like grains

This giant non-native grass is one of the most conspicuous plants along the Great Lakes. It forms massive stands that tower to 15 ft high, displacing native flora and fauna. Most are a Eurasian form, although a native type occurs as well. • The grass stem contains a sugary substance with many uses. Some Native peoples converted the dried, ground stalks into a sugary flour that would bubble and brown like marshmallows when heated. Others shook the sugar crystals from dried stems or collected the sweet, gummy substance that bleeds from cut stems and ate it like candy. • Reeds are used for weaving mats and thatching roofs. **Where found:** marshes, ditches, wetlands, shores; throughout.

Broad-leaved Cattail

Typha latifolia

Height: 3–10 ft
Leaves: linear, up to 10 ft long, ½–1 in wide
Flowers: tiny, yellowish green, in dense spikes 4–6 in long
Fruits: tiny achenes in fuzzy brown spike (cattail)

Cattails rim wetlands and line lakeshores and ditches across North America, providing cover for many animals. They are critical for supporting marsh birds. They grow from long rhizomes that were traditionally eaten fresh in spring. Later in the season, when the rhizomes became bitter with maturity, they were peeled and roasted or dried and ground into flour. • Fresh, dried seed heads were used to bandage burns and promote healing. • Narrow-leaved cattail (*T. angustifolia*) has narrower leaves and a gap between the male and female flower spike. It is also darker green overall, while broad-leaved cattail is bluish-green. **Where found:** marshes, ponds, ditches, damp ground; throughout.

Pickerelweed

Pontederia cordata

Height: up to 2½ ft
Leaves: 3–7 in long, mostly basal, variable heart, arrow or lance-shaped
Flowers: ⅜ in long, lavender to white, funnel-shaped in 2–6 in long spike
Fruits: achenes

This beautiful wetland plant is one of the showiest species in the marsh. Once common in many areas, it has not fared well in competition with recent non-native invading plants. • Young leaves may be eaten as a salad green or potherb, cooked like spinach or added to soups. The starchy seeds have a nutty flavor and can be eaten fresh, dried or roasted and ground into a powder. • Pickerelweed has beautiful flowers, each lasting for a day, and is an attractive addition to water gardens. **Where found:** shallow water of marshes, lakes, streams, ponds; throughout.

Bracken Fern

Pteridium aquilinum

Height: fronds up to 3 ft
Leaves: blades triangular, 10 or more leaflets

Pioneers of recently disturbed open sites, bracken ferns can form sizeable colonies from creeping root systems. They flourish in dry sandy soil. Their success is aided by allelopathic chemicals exuded through the roots, which inhibit the growth of competing plants. This fern occurs on nearly every continent. • Bracken fern's 2- to 3-times divided pinnate leaves form a triangle. Like many other ferns, lines of brown spore cases dot the undersides of the leaves. • **Caution:** Native peoples ate the fiddleheads and rhizomes, but bracken ferns are carcinogenic to humans and animals. Cattle can be poisoned by eating the plants. **Where found:** well-drained, open woods, forest margins, fields; throughout.

Cinnamon Fern

Osmunda cinnamomea

Height: up to 3½ ft
Leaves: oval to lance-shaped, with oblong, deeply lobed pinnae, each 2–4 in long

Cinnamon ferns reach peak abundance in swampy woods, where they can form profuse, luxuriant clumps. Like many ferns, they have 2 types of leaves. The sterile leaves are large, green and evident throughout the growing season; the short-lived fertile leaves look like cinnamon sticks and are loaded with spores. Airborne and nearly microscopic, spores are the seeds of ferns. A giant cinnamon fern might produce thousands of spores. • The genus name is from the Saxon god Osmunder the Waterman (equivalent to the Norse god Thor) who, according to legend, hid his family from danger in a clump of these ferns. • The edible fiddleheads (young unfurling leaves) taste similar to asparagus once cooked. **Where found:** wet woods, bogs, wetlands; throughout.

219

REFERENCES

Annin, Peter. *The Great Lakes Water Wars*. 2006. Island Press.

Black, Charles and Gregory Kennedy. *Birds of Michigan*. 2003. Lone Pine Publishing.

Budliger, Bob and Gregory Kennedy. *Birds of New York State*. 2005. Lone Pine Publishing.

Conant, Roger and Joseph T. Collins. *Reptiles and Amphibians: Eastern/Central North America*. 1998. Peterson Field Guides, Houghton Mifflin Company.

Douglas, Matthew and Jonathan Douglas. *The Butterflies of the Great Lakes*. 2005. University of Michigan Press.

Fisher, Chris and David Johnson. *Birds of Chicago*. 1997. Lone Pine Publishing.

Foster, Steven and James A. Duke. *Medicinal Plants and Herbs, Eastern/Central*. 2000. Peterson Field Guides, Houghton Mifflin Publishing.

Grady, Wayne. *The Great Lakes: The Natural History of a Changing Region*. 2007. Greystone Books.

Haas, Franklin and Roger Burrows. *Birds of Pennsylvania*. 2005. Lone Pine Publishing.

Janssen, Bob, Daryl Tessen, and Gregory Kennedy. *Birds of Minnesota and Wisconsin*. 2003. Lone Pine Publishing.

Kaufman, Kenn and Eric Eaton. *Kaufman Guide to Insects of North America*. 2007. Houghton Mifflin Company.

Kershaw, Linda. *Trees of Michigan*. 2006. Lone Pine Publishing.

McCormac, James S and Gregory Kennedy. *Birds of Ohio*. 2004. Lone Pine Publishing.

National Audubon Society. *National Audubon Society Field Guide to North American Mammals*. 1996. Alfred A. Knopf.

Page, Lawrence and Brooks M. Burr. *Freshwater Fishes*. 1991. Peterson Field Guides, Houghton Mifflin Company.

Spring, Barbara. *The Dynamic Great Lakes*. 2002. Independence Books.

Weatherbee, Ellen Elliot. *Guide to Great Lakes Coastal Plants*. 2006. University of Michigan Press.

GLOSSARY

A

achene: a seed-like fruit (e.g., sunflower seed)

altricial: animals who are helpless at birth or hatching

alvar: a natural formation created when glaciers scrape away overburden and leave exposed limestone. This limestone plain has little or no soil and very sparse vegetation.

annual: plants that live for only one year or growing season

anther: the enlarged upper part of the stamen that produces pollen

aquatic: water frequenting

arboreal: tree frequenting

B

basal: forming part of the bottom or base (compare distal)

benthic: bottom feeding

bract: a leaf-like structure arising at the base of a flower or inflorescence

bracteole: a small bract borne on a leaf stalk

brood parasite: a bird that parasitizes other bird's nests by laying its eggs and abandoning them for the parasitized birds to raise (e.g., brown-headed cowbird)

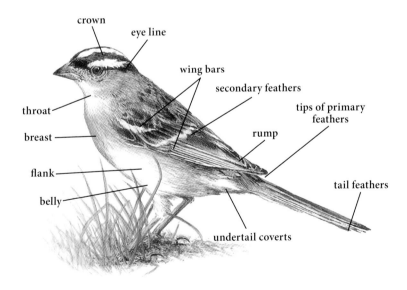

C

calyx: the collective of sepals

cambium: inner layers of tissue that transport nutrients up and down the plant stalk or trunk

capsules: a dry splitting fruit

carnivorous: feeding primarily on meat

carrion: decomposing animal matter or carcass

catkin: a spike of small flowers

compound leaf: a leaf separated into two or more divisions called leaflets

coniferous: cone-bearing. Seed (female) and pollen (male) cones are borne on the same tree in different locations.

crepuscular: active primarily at dusk and dawn

cryptic coloration: a type of camouflage designed to conceal by resembling the background

D

deciduous: a tree whose leaves turn color and shed annually

defoliating: dropping of the leaves

distal: located away from the center or from the point of attachment (compare basal)

diurnal: active primarily during the day

dorsal: the top or back

drupe: a fleshy fruit with a stony pit (e.g., peach, cherry)

E

echidna: an insectivorous, egg-laying mammal of Australia and New Guinea, also called spiny anteater

echolocation: navigation by rebounding sound waves off of objects to target or avoid them

ecological niche: an ecological role filled by a species

ecoregion: distinction between regions based upon geology, climate, biodiversity, elevation and soil composition

ectoparasites: skin parasites

ectotherm: an animal that regulates its body temperature behaviorally from external sources of heat, i.e., from the sun

endotherm: an animal that regulates its body temperature internally

estivate: a state of inactivity and a slowing of the metabolism to permit survival in extended periods of high temperatures and inadequate water supply

evergreen: having green leaves through winter; not deciduous

exoskeleton: a hard outer encasement that provides protection and points of attachment for muscles

F

food web: the elaborate, interconnected feeding relationships of living organisms in an ecosystem

H

habitat: the physical area in which an organism lives

hawking: feeding behavior where a bird leaves a perch, snatches its prey in mid-air, and returns to its previous perch

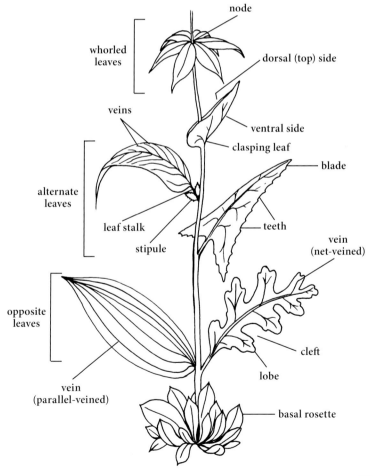

herbaceous: a plant, such as most perennials and annuals, with little or no woody tissues.

herbivorous: feeding primarily on vegetation

hibernate: a state of decreased metabolism and body temperature and slowed heart and respiratory rates to permit survival during long periods of cold temperature and diminished food supply

hind: female elk

hips: a berry-like structure

hybrid: the offspring from a cross between two species

I

incubate: keeping eggs at relatively constant temperature until they hatch

inflorescence: the flowering structure of a plant, including stems, stalks, bracts and flowers

insectivorous: feeding primarily on insects

invertebrate: animals lacking backbones (e.g., worms, slugs, crayfish, shrimps)

K

keys: winged fruits

L

larva: immature forms of an animal that differ from the adult

leaflet: a division of a compound leaf

lenticel: lens-shaped pit of loose cells on bark that allows air to pass to the trunk

lobate: having each toe individually webbed

lobe: a projecting part of a leaf or flower, usually rounded

M

metabolic rate: the rate of chemical processes in an organism

metamorphosis: the developmental transformation of an animal from larval to sexually mature adult stage

mycorrhizal fungi: a fungi that has a mutually beneficial relationship with the roots of some seed plants

N

neo-tropical migrant: a bird that nests in North America, but overwinters in the New World tropics

nocturnal: active primarily at night

node: a slightly enlarged section of a stem where leaves or branches originate

nutlet: a small, hard, one-seeded fruit that remains closed

O

omnivorous: feeding on both plants and animals

ovoid: egg-shaped

P

pappus: a cluster of hairs or bristles on the achenes, or seeds, of plants (e.g., dandelion, daisy, sunflower)

parasite: a relationship between two species where one benefits at the expense of the other

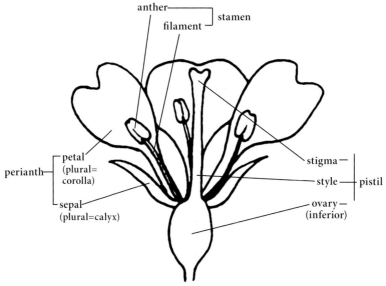

patagium: skin forming a flight membrane

pelage: fur or hair of mammals

perennial: a plant that lives for several years

photosynthesis: conversion of CO_2 and water into sugars via energy of the sun

pinnate: a compound leaf with leaflets arranged in pairs opposite each other on either side of the stem

pollen: the tiny grains produced in the anthers which contain the male reproductive cells

pollen cone: male cone that produces pollen

pome: a fruit with a core (e.g., apple)

precocial: animals who are active at birth or hatching

proboscis: elongated tubular and flexible mouthpart of many insects

R

redd: a shallow depression in riverbed gravel used by female salmon or trout to deposit her eggs

resinous: bearing resin, usually causing stickiness

rhizome: a horizontal underground stem

riparian: adjacent to or relating to the banks of rivers or streams

riprap: loose pieces of large rock or rubble piled on slopes or embankments to prevent erosion from flowing water or waves

rookery: a colony of nests

runner: a slender stolon or prostrate stem rooting at the nodes or the tip

S

seed cone: female cone that produces seeds

sepal: the outer, usually green, leaf-like structures that protect the flower bud and are located at the base of an open flower

spadix: a spike of small flowers surrounded by a spathe

spathe: a large bract in the shape of a sheath that surrounds the flower cluster in some plants

spur: a pointed projection

stamen: the pollen-bearing organ of a flower

stigma: a receptive tip in a flower that receives pollen

stolon: a long branch or stem that runs along the ground and often propagates more plants

subnivean: below the surface of the snow

suckering: a method of tree and shrub reproduction in which shoots arise from an underground stem

T

taproot: a main large root of a plant from which smaller roots arise (e.g., carrot)

terrestrial: land frequenting

toothed leaf: a leaf with small lobes

torpor: a state of physical inactivity

tragus: the prominent cartilage structure of the outer ear directly in front of the ear canal; found in bats and others

tundra: a high altitude (alpine) or high latitude (arctic) ecological zone at the limits of plant growth, where plants are reduced to shrubby or matlike growth

U

ungulate: an animal that has hooves

V

ventrally: of or on the abdomen (belly)

vermiculations: wavy, patterned markings

vertebrate: an animal possessing a backbone

vibrisae: bristle-like feathers growing about the beak of birds to aid in catching insects

W

whorl: a circle of leaves or flowers about a stem

woolly: bearing long or matted hairs

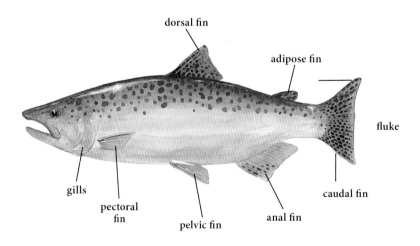

dorsal fin

adipose fin

fluke

gills

pectoral fin

pelvic fin

anal fin

caudal fin

INDEX

Names in **boldface** type indicate primary species.

INDEX

ABOUT THE AUTHORS

Jim McCormac is a lifelong Ohioan who became passionate about natural history at a very early age and began actively pursuing birds before he was 10 years old. Some 35 years later, his Ohio list stands at 356 species, one of the largest Ohio lists. He has birded in nearly every state and most Canadian provinces, as well as far-flung places like the Australian Outback, Costa Rica, and Guatemala. Jim is keenly interested in rarities and bird distribution, and served as secretary of the Ohio Bird Records Committee for seven years.

Jim is also an enthusiastic educator and writer, giving as many as 50 talks and lectures yearly on a range of natural history topics. In 2004, his book *Birds of Ohio* was released, published by Lone Pine. This 360-page guide is copiously illustrated, and includes all birds recorded in Ohio to date. His new book, *Wild Ohio: The Best of our Natural Heritage* was released in March 2009 and profiles the best remaining lands in the Buckeye State. It is richly illustrated with several hundred photos taken by renowned nature photographer Gary Meszaros.

You can follow some of Jim's adventures via his blog:
http://jimmccormac.blogspot.com/

Krista Kagume is a passionate writer of natural history and a born adventurer. She began birding at her family's cabin at the age of five. At age 17, she began a long solo voyage across the country. En route she worked as a helicopter mechanic, a reporter for a weekly newspaper, a deckhand on a commercial fishing boat and a cycling tour guide. Eventually Krista earned a BSc in conservation biology and began writing articles on natural history for magazines and newspapers. She remains an avid cyclist and frequently heads off the beaten track in search of wildlife and plants.